European Socialism Since World War I

European Socialism Since World War I

Edited with an Introduction by

Nathanael Greene

A NEW YORK TIMES BOOK

Quadrangle Books
CHICAGO

 For information, address: Quadrangle Books, Inc., 12 East Delaware Place, Chicago 60611. Manufactured in the United States of America. Published simultaneously in Canada by Burns and MacEachern Ltd., Toronto.

Library of Congress Catalog Card Number: 70-130385
SBN Cloth 8129-0168-1
SBN Paper 8129-6141-2

The publishers are grateful to the contributors herein for permission to reprint their articles.

Contents

European Socialism Since World War I

Introduction

Arise ye wretched of the earth. . . .
This is the final battle,
Let us unite and tomorrow
The International
Will be all mankind.

—*L'Internationale*

THE STRAINS of the *Internationale* have been sung by, and presumably have provided inspiration and confidence for, several generations of Socialists since 1888. Adopted as their revolutionary hymn by the Second (Socialist) and Third (Communist) Internationals and by diverse revolutionaries to the present day, the *Internationale* has conveyed both certainty about the future and instructions for the present: tomorrow will be ours if only we can unite our forces, work for the revolution, and pledge ourselves to internationalism. The formula is beautifully simple, but the realization of its goals has proved to be extraordinarily difficult. The final battle has turned out to be one of indefinite duration, its numerous skirmishes so varied as to make the outcome uncertain at best. Socialists have found the attainment of unity habitually elusive, and, amusing as it is to the imagination, in fact persons as ideologically different as Harold Wilson, Golda Meir, Aleksei Kosygin, and Daniel Cohn-Bendit may each rightly lay claim to the *Internationale* as his very own inspiration. Indeed, from its beginnings as a serious political and social movement in the nineteenth century, "socialism" has as often as not denoted a family whose members have scorned and denounced each other as the real enemy: Karl Marx's famous struggle against the anarchist Bakunin for control of the First International is echoed almost a hundred years later in the bitter polemics between France's Communist party and the leaders of the French student revolutionaries in 1968. Socialism, then, can be defined only in its varieties—especially during the half-century that separates the Armistice of 1918 from the "events of May" that nearly toppled the proud regime of Charles de Gaulle.

This anthology, composed of twenty-five articles from the *New York Times* over a span of fifty years, does not pretend to provide complete coverage of the several strands of socialist thought and action that have arisen over the past half-century. (A subsequent volume in this series will be devoted to European communism, thus excluding it from this collection.) The choice of articles has been further limited by the nature of the source: newspapers, by their very function, are more concerned with the discussion and analysis of political parties and movements rather than with individual thinkers or marginal groups within a particular movement. Anarchism, for example, was rarely mentioned in the *New York Times* until its adherents played a key role in the Spanish turmoil of the 1930's (I have included a splendid article on the subject by Herbert L. Matthews of the *Times* staff.) The *Times*'s coverage of the major Socialist parties has been fairly rich, although much more attention has been given to the British Labor party than to its distant cousins in Europe. In short, this collection deals basically with reformist socialism and Socialist political parties generally identified with that branch of the socialist family known as democratic socialism. The history of "European socialism," then, is here interpreted as the record of the vicissitudes of democratic socialism in Great Britain, Germany, and France, with secondary attention to Italy, Spain, and Sweden. Finally, most of these articles were written by able and perceptive members of the *Times* staff, although several were written by sympathizers with, as well as critics and observers of, the various European Socialist parties.

Defining reformist or democratic socialism is not as simple a task as one might suppose. As a body of doctrine, democratic socialism has been marked by variety and often plagued by ambiguity. In his classic defense of the "old house" in 1920, the French Socialist Léon Blum argued that socialism was indeed a doctrine of revolution, but that the road to revolution could be traveled in different ways. Blum's own confidence in the legal, parliamentary approach to revolution was not, to be sure, shared by a majority of his comrades at a time when a violent seizure of power in the Bolshevik fashion was thought to be a realistic possibility, and the ranks of the "old house" were thinned by massive defections to the Third (Communist) International. Perhaps unwittingly, Blum pointed to the ambiguity at the very heart of international socialism before 1914: socialism's lingering affection for revolutionary rhetoric more often frightened away would-be friends than terrorized capitalist opponents, even though Socialist parties had committed themselves to observe the rules of parliamentary democracy. While Socialists were pledged to employ *all* means to promote revolution, in fact their activities were geared to, and circumscribed by, conditions within their various nations. In France this meant that Socialists expected the liberal, democratic Republic someday to mature into a social republic, presumably by majority vote. German Socialists increasingly sought to influence their nation by the weight of their parliamentary legislation, serving in effect as a lobby in the interests of the working class. Most of the European Socialist parties aspired to create social equality by means of progressive legislation. Yet they never abandoned their insistence upon socializing the means of production once they had captured political power—either by the ballot box or by violence. The building of socialism would not be just for the benefit of the proletariat but for all mankind. The preference for a peaceful rather than violent victory was clear and became even more evident with the passage of time, much to the chagrin of the many Socialists impatient for deliverance from capitalism.

Socialists before World War I actually gave little attention to what ought to be done in the post-revolutionary period, and for good reason: the vexing problem was how to promote revolution in the first place. Would the revolution be international at its outset, or would it be triggered by a national uprising or a peaceful capture of power within a single nation? Would the international revolution be a peaceful one, or should Socialist energies be devoted to preparation for inevitable violence? Should Socialists seek only to instruct, to inculcate a consciousness of class and class action among the workers, or should they aspire to lead the working class, even in directions not of its choosing? Should Socialists gear their activities mainly to preparing for revolution, or instead to bettering the workers' conditions? Is socialism itself likely to come about as the result of piecemeal accumulation of reforms, or is it to be realized only *after* the seizure of power? What should be socialism's attitude toward the existing state? Could Socialists cooperate with democratic parties without compromising their own revolutionary vocation, and should such cooperation include participation in power under direction of parties well to the right of socialism? What should be socialism's attitude toward labor unions? In Germany, liaison with the unions dictated that the Socialist party give priority to day-to-day action for the improvement of workers' conditions, while in France anarcho-syndicalist unions steadfastly rejected any common action with Socialists. Should Socialists give primacy to international action, or should their first priority be to their own nations to the exclusion of internationalism? Should Socialists help precipitate an international general strike to prevent war, or should they in time of war rally to the defense of their nation? In essence, all these problems and issues could be reduced to one basic question: If Socialists did not reject the existing system totally, then to what degree ought they to cooperate with those who were supposed to be their class enemies?

Beneath the façade of unity presented at gatherings of the International, and within their respective national parties, Socialists were divided and deeply troubled by these questions. Few Socialists went so far as to deny that existing institutions offered opportunities that should be utilized: even Lenin and Rosa Luxemburg realized that parliaments offered a splendid stage for propaganda, although they warned against placing any confidence in them. As Lenin put it: "To decide once every few years which member of the ruling class is to repress and oppress the people through parliament—this is the real essence of bourgeois parliamentarism." Yet in the decade preceding 1914, Socialists increasingly showed a willingness to participate seriously in parliamentary politics—whether in Britain's House of Commons, France's Chamber of Deputies, or Imperial Germany's Reichstag. Yet in so doing, Socialists were to make themselves vulnerable to the charge of abandoning their revolutionary commitment, although this charge did not exact a significant toll until after World War I.

Once Socialists had determined that benefit could be derived from the parliamentary course, they were compelled to reckon with its disadvantages. Chief among these was the fact that they dared not alienate democratic liberals on their right, which deprived them of the use of a threat of force. Other and only slightly less important problems followed from this decision. The lure of participation in power seduced many able men away from Socialist ranks. Once reforms were enacted, the revolutionary appetite of the working class was alleged to be diminished, even when Socialists had nothing to do with the reforming legislation. Some theorists, delighted with the reforms of the capitalist system, advanced the view that a sudden revolution was not only undesirable but unnecessary, thereby widening ideological divergences between Socialists. By giving priority to parliamentary activity, Socialists in effect emphasized national, as opposed to international, action, with, as some argued, a consequent weakening of whatever leverage the threat of international proletarian action had given to them.

As Socialists increased their share of the popular vote, becoming the largest party in France and Germany by 1914, the parliamentary path doubtless must have seemed the correct one. Socialists could expect to share in power, shape legislation, and feel confident that a Socialist majority was just over the horizon. But what they failed to recognize was their own increasing confidence in the liberal promise of progress, rationality, and the ultimate perfection of political and social systems; rather than revolutionaries, they had become partners in the liberal dream. By wagering on the parliamentary process, by holding revolution in abeyance, Socialists had mortgaged their very *raison d'être* to the good will of the beneficiaries of the existing system. Even so, the Socialist choice might have returned even greater rewards had it not been for the First World War, a holocaust that called all values into question, especially those cherished by liberalism and its new allies.

Although Europe's Socialist parties had been fervent in their denunciation of war before 1914, and had discussed interminably what they would do to prevent it, at the moment of truth in the summer of 1914 few among their ranks raised their voices in opposition to the war. French Socialists, shorn of their leader Jean Jaurès, who was felled by an assassin on the eve of war, rallied to national defense. German Socialists, fearful for their own existence as a party and certain that German workers were willing to enter the hostilities, voted the Kaiser's war credits. Among Italian Socialists, a minority led by a then leftist Benito Mussolini actively pushed for Italy's participation in the war in 1915. In Britain, Labor's pacifism gave way to support of their government's decision to enter the conflict. French Socialists went so far as to join the government and to participate in a "sacred union," while German Socialists vowed not to disturb political tranquility by their criticism. Why did Socialists support the war at its outset, evidently in betrayal, if not of their ideals, certainly of their rhetoric? Many of them claimed that the worker wanted to fight for his country, many sincerely believed that their country was waging a defensive war, and many feared that their party would be suppressed if they did not acquiesce in the war effort. Nonetheless, the choice was the fruit of the Socialist decision to share in the political system in each nation; it was a confession of solidarity with their own nation and a denial of the internationalism that they had championed so loudly and so often.

As the war developed into a bloody stalemate, at the absurd cost of millions of lives, many Socialists came to doubt the wisdom of its continuance. Some began to speak quietly of a peace without annexations and indemnities, and urged a renewal of contact among Socialist parties as a first step toward the cessation of hostilities. Within the German and French parties such strong and articulate opponents of the war as Karl Liebknecht, Jean Longuet, and Paul Fauré emerged. By 1916 Socialists were dividing sharply and openly over the war, and sizable pacifist minorities moved to challenge the majorities by seizing the initiative in party debates. Then, in 1917, Socialists were faced with the reality of revolution in Russia, and the Bolshevik capture of power in October, followed by Allied assistance to Lenin's right-wing opponents in 1918–1919, moved many Socialists away from the doctrinal and tactical stance they had taken before 1914. War and revolution simply called everything into question. Could one continue to believe that the legal, parliamentary path was the correct one when liberal regimes seemed to be just as chauvinistic and repressive as the authoritarian monarchies, and when the Bolsheviks apparently had demonstrated that revolution *now* was possible? The advance of a brief, if unsuccessful, revolutionary wave across Europe profoundly shook the old Socialist parties and the beliefs upon which they had rested, and its recession by 1920 left a legacy of bitterness and division. Socialists by then were in desperate need of reorganization, revitalization, indeed of reorientation of their Socialist timetable. Many, in some cases a majority, of their comrades went over to communism, and the "old house" began to appear as discredited as the liberal regimes that it had sought to emulate. A rebuilding, with careful attention to protecting both flanks, was now in order. With the rise of the Communists, Socialists were no longer the only party committed to workers and to revolution. At the same time, they were also confronted with a resurgence of conservatism.

Faced with defections to a Communist International which called for a vigorous struggle against existing regimes of whatever political stripe, supported an internationalism that denied that workers should participate in national defense, and demanded the most rigorous obedience to Soviet leadership—to the virtual exclusion of the autonomy of national parties—the remnant Socialist parties took up the task of rebuilding. Socialists in the 1920's sought to reassert the validity of their prewar ideology by emphasizing the democratic nature of their parties and their intentions, by attempting to participate once again in the political systems of their separate nations, and by insisting that they were citizens who were willing to share in national defense. Indeed, the activity of the Socialist International constituted little more than a partial resurrection, formal and unconvincing. The Socialist effort was, at least superficially, rewarding: electorally, Socialists easily outdistanced Communists—who had withdrawn into sullen intransigence—and established themselves as responsible politicians who shared a taste of power in Britain, France, and Germany. The rebuilding, then, was along the old lines, and its shortcomings were equally familiar. Socialists were nowhere close to winning complete power, and the ascendancy of moderate conservatism all over Europe appeared to postpone the possibility of their doing so indefinitely. Political tactics took precedence over long-range Socialist objectives, and political compromises often led to intra-party squabbles over the alleged sacrifice of principles. The rewards of cooperation, in terms of progressive social legislation, were meager. In the 1920's the price of admission for Socialists to liberal political systems was high. Often it meant a loss of vitality, even a loss of will to fight to save themselves. Italian Socialists crumbled before Mussolini's fascism in 1922; among the major nations in the terrible 1930's, only French Socialists and the British Labor party escaped the scourge of fascism in their own countries.

The dilemma of the Socialist position was demonstrated, in differing ways, by the fate of the German Social Democratic party and the British Labor party. Each participated actively in its national government and each held power briefly, but by 1932 both were on the outside—the former destined for annihilation at the hands of Hitler, the latter condemned to the role of anemic opposition to the Tories.

In November 1918 the German Socialists had what many regarded as a splendid opportunity to carry out a socialist revolution. The Imperial Army had been defeated on the battlefields, the old ruling groups were discredited, the Kaiser in flight, the country seemingly moving toward chaos with workers, soldiers, and sailors spontaneously creating soviets, or representative councils, after the fashion of the Russian Revolution. Power simply fell into the hands of Social Democratic leaders. Yet these same leaders chose not to run the risk of social revolution, and instead proclaimed a democratic republic, agreed to cooperate with the army to maintain order, and won concessions from employers that fell far short of undermining capitalism. In January 1919 the Socialist-led government crushed an uprising inspired by a Socialist faction called the Spartacists, their former comrades, and acquiesced in the murder of Liebknecht and Rosa Luxemburg by paramilitary organizations.

German Social Democratic leaders balked at revolution for several possible reasons. They may have feared their own overthrow and the consequent loss of democracy at the hands of the Spartacists, or by the right and the army, or by the victorious Allies; this being the case, a policy of prudence and caution offered tangible advantages. But these very same Socialists were also the product of years of effort to participate in the German political system, and were representative of a working class that had benefited, through social legislation dating from Bismarck's time, from the wealth of German society—a fact that took the edge off their revolutionary aspirations. Better to take the reins of power, thought the Socialists, cooperate with progressive elements and even with the army, and strike a bargain with the industrialists; this would insure the victory of German democracy and make the transition to socialism that much easier in the long run.

German Socialists collaborated in the construction and in the politics of the Weimar Republic (1919–1933), and in the process slid from the commanding heights that they had held in 1918. Unable to win a parliamentary majority in their own right, Social Democrats at first shared power with other parties, and ultimately found themselves powerless against the advance of Nazism. In their attempt to become a peoples' party and to draw votes from several sectors of German society, the Socialists further diminished their revolutionary purpose, only to discover too late that their appeal was limited primarily to relatively prosperous skilled workers. Socialist ideology still alarmed wide sections of the middle class, and the Socialists' lack of revolutionary zeal in a time of crisis dismayed thousands of workers and young people, many of whom turned to communism and even to Nazism. In the 1920's the Social Democratic party fell victim to the infirmities of old age—including, as recent scholarship has shown, the ossification of its party structure, the timidity of its leaders in political affairs, and a bureaucratization that deadened its will to action. In short, the party became a hierarchal society of its own, one increasingly remote from the mainstream of German political life and more concerned with protecting its members than with initiating change.

When the need to protect took on the urgency of survival, German Socialists were intellectually and psychologically disarmed. No profound and sustained challenge to Nazism came from the Socialist ranks, although Socialists figured prominently among Hitler's first official victims. This was so not only because of the formidable nature of the Nazi phenomenon, given the multiple crises of German society and the truculent refusal of Communists to cooperate with Socialists, but also because German Social Democracy had divested itself of the means to fight. Too concerned with their own limited success, too patient with Weimar democracy, Socialists were incapable of resisting the unprecedented challenge posed by Adolf Hitler.

The case of the British Labor party in the 1920's is somewhat similar to that of German Social Democracy, although neither the challenge nor the result was nearly so sinister. Nonetheless, Labor participated substantially in its own undoing. The Labor party had been born in the first decade of this century, the product of the union of Fabian socialism (which stressed the gradual accumulation of reforms as the proper prescription for socialism) with the trade unions, which needed protection against Conservative politicians and offensive employers. Very much outdistanced by the Conservative and Liberal parties before 1914, Laborites could act only as a parliamentary lobby in the service of British workers. As for socialism, the party had great difficulty in deciding just what its real intentions were, and consequently participated in the affairs of the International with distinct unease. Labor espoused a nonviolent approach to socialism, emphasizing its reforming mission and democratic intent, and in the 1920's the party replaced the Liberals as the major opponent of the Tories. Painted with a careless Red brush by its enemies, from Lloyd George in 1918 to Winston Churchill in the 1940's—the latter generally implied that Labor's modest Socialist aspirations were somehow akin to Bolshevism—Labor engaged in a relentless drive to make itself respectable (an affliction from which it still seems to suffer). Although dependent on the sufferance of the small Liberal contingent in the House of Commons, Labor won a narrow victory in 1923 and Ramsay MacDonald became Britain's first Labor Prime Minister. (There have been but three Labor Prime Ministers since World War I, as opposed to eight for the Conservatives.)

Seeking to rebut the opposition's oft-repeated assertion that "Labor cannot govern," MacDonald gave every indication that Labor would do nothing to disturb the social status quo and considered socialism as at best a very distant goal. The task was to govern, but MacDonald created an impression of aimlessness and drift rather than of responsibility. His most energetic act, a decision to open commercial relations with the Soviet Union, provoked a political storm, and in a hastily called election in 1924 the tactic of the "Red scare" employed by the Conservatives led to a smashing defeat for Labor. Still, under MacDonald's leadership Labor returned to power in 1929, once again as a minority government dependent upon Liberal support, once again unable to carry out a Socialist program "even," as A. J. P. Taylor put it, "if the leaders had believed in socialism or had known what it meant." This time Labor fell afoul of the Great Depression, and in 1931, unable to agree upon measures to heal the economic illness, the cabinet split into warring camps.

Refusing even to hint at ruthlessness or illegality, or even at the possibility of an unbalanced budget, MacDonald bowed to pressure from financial circles to cut the relief doles as a means of reestablishing the cherished balanced budget. He resigned, and returned to office in an almost indecent haste at the head of a so-called "National" government—a shabby euphemism for a government heavily weighted toward the Conservatives. Accusing MacDonald of preferring power to principle, the majority of the Labor party expelled the Prime Minister from its fold and retired into the opposition. Such were the experiences of government by Labor. Whatever else they might have been, surely they were not experiences in socialism. Socialism in Britain would have to wait until 1945.

The outlines of the dismal decade of the 1930's are too familiar to require retelling in any detail here. It was a time of depression and repression, with economic hardship and authoritarianism setting the rules of the game. The beleaguered outposts of liberal democracy, France and Britain, seemed powerless or unwilling to combat the dynamic appeal and the sheer force of the fascist regimes. The strategy of appeasement of Hitler and Mussolini, once employed, acquired a rationale and a drive of its own, and the decade ended in the misery of another European war. With the exceptions of the splendid failures of the Popular Fronts in France and Spain, it was equally a somber period for socialism: the Italian and German parties were shattered, their leaders driven into barren exile, while British Labor became very much a minority party.

Yet these Popular Fronts, despite their immediate failure, are today remembered, even admired, for their determined efforts to halt the spread of fascism; in many circles—on the French left, for example—the Popular Front era is still recalled with profound nostalgia. Popular Fronts were comprised of many different elements put together for various purposes: democratic alliances of liberal, Socialist, and Communist forces against internal and external threats of fascism, alliances which were inherently fragile and destined to be of brutally short duration; efforts at profound social reform, "New Deals" within the existing socio-economic structures; and mass movements generated by a fear and a hatred of fascism. For some on the extreme left, Popular Fronts were viewed as opportunities for opening short-cuts to revolution, opportunities which were lost because of pusillanimous Socialists and scheming Communists whose main loyalty was to the Soviet Union. On the right, Popular Fronts were greeted as sinister forerunners of revolution, and provoked counterrevolution in Spain and emotional hostility in France. For most Socialists, especially in France, the Popular Front was intended to be a simple defense against fascism as well as an opportunity to secure social reform, but they could not escape the spontaneous mass enthusiasm that the Popular Front aroused.

The French Popular Front took shape slowly from 1934 to 1936. It won the legislative election of 1936, and, under the premiership of Socialist Léon Blum, directed the affairs of the nation through mid-1937, leaving a record of frustration as well as accomplishment, but also a promise for the future. The *Front Populaire* was born of fear: on the night of February 6, 1934, a little more than a year after Hitler's accession to power, rightist mobs swirled around the French Chamber of Deputies demanding the fall of the government. Although the rightists were dispersed by the Republic's forces of order, many people were convinced that a fascist *coup d'état* was near. In the summer of the same year, Socialists timidly joined hands with Communists in defense of Republican institutions, despite fourteen years of bitter polemic between the two parties; and early in 1936 they were joined by the Radicals, the powerful liberal party, in a Popular Front formally resolved to defend the Republic, undertake social reforms, and maintain peace in Europe against the threat of fascist aggression. The formation of this political alliance was both accompanied and encouraged by generous enthusiasm from several sectors of French society—while it exacerbated latent hatreds in others. Hundreds of thousands adhered to the parties of the left, labor unions, clubs, and organizations in a great popular movement against fascism and for a "New Deal" for France.

None of the three partners—Socialists, Communists, or Radicals—were willing to be propelled by this popular wave, and all sought to canalize it into their own interests. The Communists were now pleased to accept the duty of national defense and to save democracy, if only to provide the Soviet Union with a viable ally against Hitler, and the Communist leadership sought to dissipate any signs of revolutionary activity. Radicals joined because of the imperative of Republican defense, and also because the Popular Front would pay them handsome dividends at the ballot box. The Socialists, briefly smothering all their hesitations and suspicions (particularly of the Soviets and their servants, the French Communists), believed that they had no choice but to participate. Yet Blum's own conception of the Popular Front, not wholly shared by his Socialist comrades, was not simply defensive or negative, for he believed it to be a new phenomenon in French history when popular forces could be harnessed to state power for the benefit of all. To defend democratic liberties, thus reviving Europe's confidence in the democratic ideal, and to lift France from the depression, would be to set an example to the world. In essence, Blum believed that the Popular Front should create a government of the public good, not a revolutionary government nor a simple defense mechanism against fascism. For Blum the Popular Front's task was immense; he was to discover that it could not be achieved in his time.

Blum's experiment, led by Socialists but practically exclusive of socialism, lasted little more than a year. As leader of the party with the largest bloc of seats, Blum was chosen as Premier of a coalition government. A wave of sit-down strikes greeted the installation of his government. This pressure insured agreement between labor and management, which was followed up by legislation that guaranteed vacations, social insurance, higher wages, and the right of collective bargaining. These were hardly Socialist measures but rather were long overdue reforms, the likes of which had been enacted long before by conservative governments elsewhere. Applying socialism to the economy only in a peripheral way, such as by nationalizing the armaments industry, Blum endeavored to persuade capitalists to trust his government and to invest in French business. His wager on the patriotism of the financial interests proved a poor one, for they increasingly applied a financial squeeze on the government which resulted in Blum's defeat by the Senate, France's upper house of parliament. In foreign affairs, Blum refused to heed the demands of his Communist partners and others on the left to help the Spanish Republic in its struggle against Franco's army. To fight the battle for democracy at home was one thing, Blum felt, to export it quite another. Faced with serious dissension within the Popular Front alliance, marked by Communist sniping at his foreign policy and Radical uneasiness over the political situation they had helped to create, and dismayed by his inability to secure further reforms within the framework of capitalism and of the Republic, Blum chose to resign in June 1937 without making any effort to employ mass support in his behalf against the Senate. Resolute in his conviction that this was not the time for political illegality, let alone for revolution, Blum departed office in the correct parliamentary way.

The achievements of the Popular Front were undone from 1938–1944, but were restored after the Liberation. Blum failed to revive confidence in democracy and his experiment may have divided the nation, but the enthusiasm that moved the Popular Front was reborn in the Resistance during World War II. Blum may have made no contribution to Socialist theory, but he demonstrated that Socialists could use the existing state to improve the quality of life for the unfortunate. Finally, despite their apparent failure in power, French Socialists did do something to fight fascism at home—a task that both Italian and German Socialists had found to be overwhelming.

Socialism has not been a major force in Spanish politics in this century, although the Spanish Socialist party has marked its own status as the second oldest Marxian Socialist party in Europe. It played a minor role in the establishment of the Republic in 1931, and had long worked for the benefit of labor, although much of Spanish labor gave its allegiance to other contending groups, such as anarchists or liberals, or was indifferent to the appeals of politicians and other would-be liberators. Until 1931 Spanish socialism had been essentially reformist in nature, though its opportunities to secure reform were limited and its success almost nonexistent. By 1936 the infant Spanish Republic, whose history had been marred by turmoil from the beginning, fell victim to an eruption of social hatreds that has had few equals in modern history. Not all Socialists were innocent of responsibility in helping to precipitate Spain's terrible civil war.

Not long after the birth of the Republic Socialists began to divide sharply over questions of tactics. Personal rivalries had unsettled the party for some time. One wing, identified with Indalecio Prieto, followed reformist lines and expected much from the Republic; the other wing, led by Largo Caballero, with powerful support from the Socialist trade union, moved with astonishing speed from a reformist to a revolutionary position. Largo had few illusions, but those he did cherish were catastrophic. He began to advertise himself as the "Spanish Lenin," employing all the threats and promises befitting such a title. The party voted to participate in a Popular Front with Communist and progressive forces for the election of 1936, and the Front's victory opened a period of uninterrupted violence that flourished into civil war in July with the uprising of the army against the Republic. During the months between the election and the civil war, Largo Caballero's Socialists did little to assist the Republic and nothing to calm social tensions; indeed, they seemed to welcome the uprising as the outbreak of the final struggle for socialism. The revolution, sparked by opposition to the uprising in many sections of the country in the summer of 1936, may have given fleeting justification to these expectations, although Socialists quickly found that it had escaped their control. Largo himself, serving as Premier from the fall of 1936 through the spring of 1937, discovered that his authority was increasingly circumscribed by Communist influence as a result of the Soviet Union's role as the major supplier of arms to the Republic.

It turned out, as is now well known, that the Communists were actually counterrevolutionary in their determination to maintain the Republic's "bourgeois respectability" as part of the Soviet Union's effort to win an alliance with Britain and France—powers unlikely to welcome the prospect of a revolutionary Spain. Largo himself, who was ousted by Communist machinations, began to argue that the Communists had betrayed the Spanish revolution (articles to this effect by one of Largo's lieutenants figure in this collection). Indalecio Prieto served in the subsequent government, hoping to make the best of what he came to regard by 1938 as a hopeless situation. He recognized that the civil war had set back socialism in Spain for at least a generation. Divided and misled Socialists, who pushed their zeal beyond the boundaries of common sense, helped to bring about a catastrophe, although the burden of fault certainly lies not with them but with the Spanish right. The Popular Front's failure in Spain was of greater consequence than its failure in France. Spain still awaits her Liberation.

Powerless to prevent war or even to help shape decisions that led to its outbreak in 1939, many Socialists nonetheless welcomed it as a necessity, and the experience of the war years fostered a new confidence in the validity of Socialist ideals. The shock of the Nazi sway over Europe and of the impotence of socialism persuaded many Socialists to rethink both doctrine and tactics, and to dwell upon the lessons of the dreary past. Socialists contributed to the struggle against Hitler in several ways, the most striking of which was active participation in Resistance movements, notably in France and Italy. In Britain, Labor joined the Churchill cabinet for the duration of the war. While French Socialists like Blum, who was incarcerated by the collaborationist French regime at Vichy and then by the Germans, reaffirmed their confidence in the future of democratic socialism, they were overshadowed by those Socialists who were caught up in the spirit of the Resistance. Indeed, the Resistance produced its own ideology, one assumption of which was that liberated Europe would swing sharply leftward after the war, realizing much of the old Socialist program. The Resistance movements were composed of men of differing ideological persuasion, even though most were of the left, and their cooperation generated much comradeship and brave optimism. At the Liberation in 1944–1945, Socialists assumed leading positions in France and Italy. At the end of General de Gaulle's provisional rule in 1946, French Socialists emerged as likely candidates to reshape politics and society in collaboration with liberals, Communists, and Christian Democrats. In Italy the collapse of Mussolini's regime, followed by a plebiscite against the old monarchy and for a republic, seemed to indicate a major role for Socialists in Italy's future. Yet by 1948 the euphoria of the Resistance had been eclipsed by the harsh realities of postwar Europe—the eviction of the French Communists from the government in 1947, the Communist *coup* in Czechoslovakia in 1948, and the Berlin blockade of the same year. In a Europe increasingly polarized by suspicion and military power—Stalin and the Marshall Plan left no doubt as to which powers dominated Europe—Socialists, perplexed and disappointed, were hemmed in by these realities. They were compelled to abandon the confident expectations of 1944–1946 and to become either part of conservative and liberal governments against the menace of communism or to sit idly by on the sidelines.

The dilemmas of postwar socialism were amply demonstrated by the French and Italian parties. In the aftermath of Liberation, French Socialists reaffirmed their doctrinal allegiance to Marxism, indeed to a more rigid confidence in the inevitability of the class struggle than Blum, with his commitment to a broadly based socialist transformation of society, would have liked. Yet by 1948 the disparity between Socialist doctrine and tactics was quite wide: the threat of communism to the Socialist left and the Gaullist movement to its right, both in the Socialist view enemies of the Republic, demanded a soft-pedaling of ideology and a suppleness in tactics which insured that Socialists could be only minority partners in political alliances that were increasingly conservative. The Cold War, political fragmentation under the Fourth Republic (1946–1958), and France's colonial problems spelled the end of the Liberation dream. A coalition government headed by Socialist

Guy Mollet in 1956–1957 found itself stymied by the immobility built into the political system by the endless need for compromise and the appeasement of special interests (even the Socialists represented special interests—teachers, civil servants, and skilled workers). Mollet was also undermined by the intractability of the Algerian problem: fearing that he could not begin serious negotiations with the Algerian National Liberation Front, which had launched its rebellion in 1954, Mollet pursued a dead-end policy of no concessions, which was essentially a colonial policy of the right. But rightist leaders refused to sanction higher taxes to pay the costs of their own policy, thereby setting in motion the parliamentary machinery that finally toppled Mollet. A year later, in May 1958, the Republic itself was toppled by the threat of civil war or military rule, or both, owing to the refusal of the European settlers in Algeria and key figures in the army to envisage any change in the status of French Algeria. Mollet found himself in the curious position of urging General de Gaulle to take power in order to prevent a catastrophe. Thus Socialists appealed to the very man who had announced his intention to alter profoundly the political institutions which they themselves had helped to create only twelve years before. Under de Gaulle's Fifth Republic the Socialist decline continued, and the party dwindled in size and influence—in the presidential election of 1969, the Socialist candidate polled less than 5 per cent of the vote cast. The party of Jaurès and Blum seems to have died, a victim not of disease but of old age.

Italian Socialists also saw the promise of the Liberation elude their grasp. Confronted with the political dominance of Christian Democracy under exceptional leadership on the one hand, and the strength of communism among voters and within the unions on the other, Italian Socialists split into two camps—one following the veteran leader Pietro Nenni, the other under Giuseppe Saragat. Refusing to emulate what he regarded as the dismal choice of the French Socialists, Nenni called for working relationships with the Communists and refused to consider participation in the political system without them. Saragat defended the traditional aims of democratic socialism, although his party played little or no part in the making of government policy. As a consequence of their division, as well as of factors over which they had no control, Italian Socialists accomplished neither real social reforms nor advance toward the goal of a Socialist society.

Curiously, it was only in Britain that the promise of the Liberation came close to being fulfilled. The wartime leadership of Winston Churchill had been generally regarded as inspiring, and with the death of President Roosevelt the British Prime Minister became the leading statesman of the western world. The Labor party, scarred by its experiences in the 1930's and lacking the charismatic leadership of a Churchill, thus astonished the world in the election of 1945: not only did Labor win its first outright majority in parliamentary history, but the margin of its victory was so great as to imply a solid rejection of Churchill as well as the Conservatives. Those who were incredulous at the prospect of Clement Attlee as Prime Minister, a man who appeared fully as humdrum as Churchill did dynamic, underestimated the sweeping demand for social reform that accompanied the triumph over fascism. Labor came to office promising to carry out a program of democratic socialism by nationalizing key industries, by providing for a national health service, and by bettering appreciably the condition of all workers. Surprisingly, Labor accomplished much of what it set out to do, despite very unfavorable economic conditions and the exigencies of the Cold War. Labor's reforms brought with them high taxes, a host of petty inconveniences, and a slow pace of economic development. These difficulties served to loosen Labor's hold on the electorate, and after Labor won a slim victory in the election of 1950, the Conservatives were swept back into office in 1951, not to be dislodged until 1964. Out of power, Labor slipped back into its old vice of quarreling within its own house, this time over the development of nuclear weapons. Steadily losing strength at the polls, its unity called into question by the intensity of its internal divisions, at the end of the 1950's Labor seemed to have slipped back into its former place as parliamentary lobby for the working class. It had achieved much between 1945 and 1950, but the task of defending those achievements seemed to be the full extent of its role in British political life.

Thus at the end of the conservative 1950's European socialism seemed to have been cast aside by history, its aspirations only partially achieved, its past more attractive than its present, its likely future dim indeed. The expectations of the Liberation had been shown to be illusory; conservative regimes identified with private capitalism were firmly in the saddle, tolerating but not dismantling the state enterprises that had been created in the immediate postwar period. Only in the Scandinavian states did democratic socialism flourish, and it was denounced as immoral by the American President Dwight D. Eisenhower. In an era of rapidly developing prosperity, in which there was much talk about the end of ideology, the rise of technocracy, and a Europe moving toward unity, the old Socialist message seemed to have little appeal.

The early 1960's appeared to bear out predictions of Socialist decline. Chancellor Konrad Adenauer's Christian Democrats won another solid victory over the Social Democrats in 1961. France's Socialists were undergoing what has been described as prolonged "tribulations" while de Gaulle, fresh from winning peace in Algeria in 1962, had a virtual free rein that was to last until 1968. Italy's Socialist parties began the decade frozen in rivalry, engaged in the same tired quarrels. With the sudden death of Labor's attractive leader Hugh Gaitskell in 1963 and his replacement by Harold Wilson, who was distinguished mainly by his opportunism, the British Labor party's prospects were less than outstanding. Socialist parties rarely got beyond day-to-day political concerns, and questions of updating doctrine were regarded as so much waste of time. Those who did think seriously about Socialist doctrine were encouraged to do so outside the mainstream of political parties, as in France where the growth of political clubs was symptomatic of a distaste for the aging official party, whose leaders were deaf to appeals for change. Young people found little that was intellectually or politically exciting in the old Socialist parties.

By the mid-sixties, however, Socialist parties began an uncertain revival that may continue into the seventies, although Labor's stunning defeat in the British election of 1970 may indicate that the revival has already run its course. Italy's feuding Socialists reunited to participate in an "opening to the left" with the progressive leadership of the Christian Democrats; discarding old ideological fetishes, Nenni himself joined the government. But by

1969 disappointment with the meager accomplishments of the "opening" sent some Socialists off to seek collaboration with the Communists and once again put the future of participation with the Christian Democrats in doubt. In Britain, Labor won victories in the elections of 1964 and 1966, profiting from lackluster and discredited Conservative leadership. Yet the Wilson government did almost everything to exclude socialism from its official vocabulary, and its efforts from 1964 to 1970 mainly constituted a political holding operation that attempted to tide Britain over a severe economic crisis. Wilson made haste toward socialism very slowly, if indeed he could be said to have had any direction whatever; his government provoked as much indifference as hostility. Labor's defeat in 1970 appeared to stem from a housewives' revolt against inflation, although Wilson's fall may well have been due to a new surge of conservatism in the Western world—as evidenced by Richard Nixon's victory in 1968 and Georges Pompidou's easy triumph in 1969 in France.

The only major exception appears to be the elevation of Socialist Willy Brandt to the West German chancellorship in 1969, which came about because of a peculiar parliamentary alliance of Socialists with a right-wing party. Brandt, former mayor of West Berlin, was chosen leader of the German Socialists in 1961 and presided over the liquidation of his party's cumbersome Marxist baggage. Since that time he appears to have been successful in his drive to make the party a "respectable" one pledged to democratic reform. Brandt's predecessors as Socialist leaders, Kurt Schumacher and Erich Ollenhauer, had sought to integrate the Social Democrats into the political life of the nation, particularly by emphasizing that it was a German party, not just a branch of an international movement. But they never desired a wholesale purge of the party's Socialist aspirations. Chancellor Brandt devoted his first months in office to launching diplomatic initiatives with East Germany and the Soviet Union, and these may have caused Socialist setbacks in local German elections in the spring of 1970. Certainly Brandt's government made few moves toward social innovation, being wary of interfering in West Germany's powerful capitalist-controlled economy. As in other countries, Socialists in power mean Socialists without the will or the power to take large strides toward socialism.

The half-century of Socialist history chronicled here has emphasized continuity rather than change in Socialist aims and tactics. Shortly after World War I those Socialists who maintained fidelity to the "old house" reaffirmed their intent to work within existing political systems wherever possible, to employ their political leverage to secure social reform, and vowed to combat communism as a dangerous heresy. Revolution remained inscribed on the Socialist program, but its realization was not thought to be over the immediate horizon. The risk this involved—namely, the loss of any profound revolutionary thrust—was clear and understood, but despite the "unexpected" problems of fascism and the Cold War, the risk seems overall to have been rewarding in terms of social legislation, a rising standard of living for workers in Western Europe, and Socialist participation in representative institutions. The irony of Socialist history may well be that as Socialist parties have become accepted and integrated into the political systems of many countries as broadly based democratic parties of reform, they have had less and less appeal to the young, many of whom seek direction along the lines of ideologies that Socialists themselves discarded long ago as irrelevant.

Part 1

AGAINST BOLSHEVISM AND CONSERVATISM, 1918–1929

PROBLEMS OF war and peace, revolution and bolshevism, dominated Europe as World War I drew to a close in 1918. The political and social turbulence of the years 1919 and 1920 demonstrated that these problems, generated by four years of European civil war, could not be settled or otherwise easily liquidated, and Socialists were profoundly affected by them. The first article in this section is by a well-known American banker, Paul M. Warburg, and while it may seem exaggerated in its pessimism about the political and economic health of Europe, it does succeed in capturing the fears and confusion of the period. Warburg was persuaded that he was witnessing the disintegration of European civilization, a fatal consequence of the disastrous impact of a great war that had left the contesting nations exhausted and vulnerable to social upheaval. Warburg was especially alarmed by the European-wide appeal of bolshevism, but he was antagonistic to extreme nationalists and revolutionaries alike. His own prescription for social health called for the collaboration of capital with "constructive labor," by which Warburg meant unions and Socialist parties, and he insisted that workers must be given a voice in management. His article is instructive not only because it conveys something of the emotional quality of the time to us, but also because it outlines the response of Socialists to the multiple problems of that era.

The next three articles are concerned with the postwar fate of socialism in Germany, France, and Italy, and were written by regular contributors of the *Times*. Writing from outside of Germany, George Renwick pieced together dispatches into an account of the German revolution of November 1918, in which he emphasized the speed of revolution and the ease that characterized the establishment of a republic. He points out the role of Social Democratic leaders and the enthusiasm shown in the streets, but as early as November 13, 1918, two days after the Armistice, Renwick indicates that the Socialist leaders had no intention of pushing a political revolution into a full-fledged social revolution. Walter Duranty, observing the Socialist Congress held at Tours in December 1920, describes the forces that split the old party into rival factions, Communist and Socialist, noting that the "French Socialist Party is like a worm that has been cut in half." The failure of Socialists to help extinguish the violence that was leading Italy to disaster is colorfully analyzed by Anne O'Hare McCormick. She demonstrates what everyone should now realize—that violence on the left breeds violence on the right and a popular demand to be done with turmoil, regardless of the cost to freedom. Although we are certain to question her belief that there was nothing healthier than Italy's "rebellion against rebellion," since the final cure for Italy's ill-health was Mussolini, we can learn how moderate Socialists were caught between pincers of violence and were helpless to escape their grasp.

The final articles in this section by *Times* reporter P. W. Wilson deal with the British Labor party's disappointing history in the 1920's. The first article traces Labor's efforts to become "respectable" despite a flood of working-class discontent after 1918, while the second demonstrates why Labor, though it might be in office, was not in power. Both argue that Labor, despite a lingering desire for nationalization of industry, actually represented a party of remodeled liberalism that had shelved socialism "for the time being."

Europe Near to the Brink

by Paul M. Warburg

BETWEEN AGRA and Delhi, surrounded by the wild woods and jungle of India, lies the deserted city of Fatipur Sikri. It is twenty-eight years ago that I entered its deep silence in the middle of the night, the moon throwing her mysterious light upon the sleeping walls and towers, which seemed to dream of the splendors and glories of centuries gone by.

The memory of that picture remains deeply engraved upon my mind. In brown granite that the rough hand of time had not been able to touch, there stood before me, practically intact, the residency of mighty King Akbar. There were his palaces, his treasury and the building of the heads of his departments, the house of worship and the strange little hall, shaped like a lantern, where, in the middle on a high pillar, presided the King, while in each of the four corners, from which narrow stone bridges led to the column in the centre, sat a representative of one of the four leading religions—a Hindu, a Mohammedan, a Christian and a Jew. It was King Akbar's ambitious plan to take the best out of all creeds and to blend them into one great religion. He had wives of all these denominations (and probably more), whose individual houses still stand with all their grace and charm.

Whoever visits this remarkable spot, with a mind not entirely barren of imagination and not completely devoid of reverence for the eternal growth and struggle of the human race, cannot but visualize a great leader, powerful and chivalrous, bold and refined, who sought to find a way of removing the causes for bloody strife and misery resulting from narrow intolerance, hatreds and jealousies between nations, creeds and races. It would seem that in his own way he tried the experiment of a league of nations, and today there is nothing left but deserted houses of brown granite standing silently in the wide wilderness. And what occurred 500 years ago had happened over and over again a thousand, and several thousand years ago. Then, as today, nations rose to their full glory and then tottered and fell into pitiful unimportance and decay.

Who can think of Egypt, Babylonia, Greece, Rome, Carthage or Byzantium and believe that modern Europe has a charmed life as a leader in progress and civilization? We are prone to believe that the world has grown old and that certain conditions have reached their final forms in which they are to stay. But the world is as much in a state of flux as it ever was. The migration of the people is as active in our generation as 2,000 years ago. Our large steamers transport in a week more people than Hengist and Horsa or William the Conqueror carried into England. Civilization, starting in Central Asia, kept on marching west—to Asia Minor, the Mediterranean and Eastern Europe. A few generations hence will the historian find that it crossed the Atlantic and made America the standard bearer? Who knows? It will depend upon Europe's ability to arrest the present process of disintegration before it is too late. Let us hope that the well-springs of European civilization will not be laid dry. We cannot spare the inspiration and the contributions of the Old World. The decay of one country does not mean the corresponding rise of another. Quite to the contrary, closely interrelated as all peoples are today, retrogression in one involves the lowering of the general level of living and progress of all.

When men of science, clad in rags like beggars, are cleaning the streets, because in following their literary pursuits they can no more earn the pittance paid to the women that used to tidy up their rooms, when scientific books can no longer be printed on account of the expense involved, do we not see before our mind's eye the phantom of hundreds of Fatipur Sikris arising in Europe?

A great war, like a severe illness, always leaves the participants in a condition of exhaustion which can be overcome only after a long period of recuperation. The speed of the recovery depends upon the extent of the ravages, not only of the war, but also of the peace. The wiser the peace the sooner the return to normal economic conditions and the quicker the accomplishment of the healing process.

Violent social evolutions, like the transformation of slave-driven pagan Rome into a Christian world of free men, or like the establishment of the "tiers état" as the result of the French Revolution, have left countries in a similar protracted state of intense suffering and confusion.

Few people realize clearly enough that the world at present is suffering not only from the aftermath of four years of one of the fiercest wars ever conducted, and of two years of continued extermination after the cessation of open warfare, with actual peace still unaccomplished, but also from the consequence of a social evolution as far-reaching as those connected with the liquidation of the Roman Empire and the French Revolution. It is this combination of circumstances that renders the problem so complex and so desperately grave and should make us apprehend a long period of recuperation.

Europe at present is like a big steamer sunk by a torpedo. It is idle to discuss today what kind of a Ritz restaurant or social hall she should have when she is afloat again. The first question is: "Can we raise her at all?" The second is, "After we raise her, can we repair her engines and make her go?" It is evident that we cannot raise her without first stopping the leak—the breach, still wide open, between France and Germany. We cannot make her go without straightening out her machinery; that is, without settling the labor question. When these two tasks are disposed of, I am confident the good old ship Europe will gradually right herself. It is to these two outstanding problems that we must devote ourselves, body and soul, if we want to save her from fatal disintegration.

It will probably prove the greatest tangible result of the war that, all the world over, labor has ceased to be considered as simply a dead item in the cost sheet of production. Labor, instead of being a means, has become an end in itself, as (in the language of Immanuel Kant) is the unalienable right of every human being.

At present the world is divided into four camps. On the far right and left we see the extreme and destructive wings of capital and labor, respectively. We find the Bolshevik and his like as unmindful of the human rights of others as the ultra-capitalist and nationalist. Wedged in between these two there are progressive capital and constructive organized labor. It is the union of these two constructive factions that may be hoped to save what will prove worth preserving of our old society. Of these two, however, conservative organized labor in Europe has shown itself quicker to recognize its duties and opportunities. Constructive organized labor has found ways to get together across national lines, and it has shown the courage and vision to think and act, both nationally and internationally at the same time. It is conservative organized labor in its various forms—let us make no mistake about it—that so far has stemmed the tide of Bolshevism in Europe. It is on the sanity and sagacity of the leaders of conservative labor more than on any other factor that Europe's hopes must rest today.

Unlike the Bolshevik, conservative organized labor does not wish blindly to confiscate and destroy, but to preserve and construct. For that reason it does not approve of imposing on its former enemies contributions in excess of any endurable or practicable means of taxation, which would send the debtor nation on the certain road to complete depreciation of its currencies, with resultant bankruptcy and violent social upheavals, such as have annihilated Russia.

At the British Trades Union Congress held at Portsmouth during the Summer, we find the Joint Committee on the Cost of Living submitting a report on money and prices, in which occur the following passages: "As regards the international aspect of the problem of high prices we think that: (a) the reestablishment of peace throughout the world is a prime essential; (b) war indemnities should be defined and reasonable in amount."

Other paragraphs from the report run as follows: "We look to the development of productive capacity all over the world to bring about ultimately a substantial fall in prices"; "the Government should cease entirely to resort to bank credits to meet expenditure," and "the floating debt should be wholly or largely repaid, the remainder, if any, being funded." Time prevents my mentioning other passages worth quoting and others worth contradicting;

but the above abstracts are highly significant of the admirable progress of thought made in these circles.

This progress is not confined to English labor, for we find the "Second International" at Geneva committing itself in the most unqualified fashion against Bolshevism and, at the same time, against the extreme clauses or interpretations of the Versailles Treaty.

It is interesting and most encouraging to find progressive capital in Entente and neutral countries in practically complete accord with conservative organized labor on these points. In talking to enlightened leaders in London, Paris, Brussels and Amsterdam, or to Swiss and Scandinavian bankers, I did not find any divergence of opinion on the proposition that the determination of the maximum measure of indemnity that Germany would be able to bear and survive was the one and outstanding question to be satisfactorily disposed of before any headway could be made toward starting Europe on a course away from the social and economic collapse for which she is now headed.

British financiers were most outspoken in this respect. They are keenly alive to the fact that every day the solution of this problem is postponed means that Germany is sliding nearer the precipice. It is realized that today she is dangerously close to the brink, and that her plunge would without doubt involve others. British leaders complain bitterly about the powerful coterie in the English and French press that keeps peoples in ignorance about the true state of conditions in other countries, fans hatred and suspicion and blocks the way to a fair settlement.

But, somehow or other, leaders of business and finance have not been able, as effectively as labor, to get across the national border lines, cutting loose, if necessary, from the apron strings and embargoes of party governments. They have not been able to get together as independently upon a broad international program. Their efforts have remained unorganized, sporadic and timid, while the Governments that hold them in leash have not been able to emancipate themselves from the sway and influence of the chauvinists. Capitalistic society, as represented by the various Governments, has not been able to shake off its extremists as rapidly and as energetically as has conservative labor. It is largely because of this and because these Governments are too slow in retracing certain steps—taken inadvisedly, but finding their explanation in the temper, time and stress in which they occurred—that labor had lost its confidence in their efficiency and their moral strength. Labor, therefore, defies their authority by taking recourse to so-called "direct action."

It is unnecessary for me to say that I am not an advocate of "direct action," nor am I blind to the grave blunders that labor leaders have made. They have overreached themselves at times, like all other leaders. But no Government can rest its success and authority upon the mere exploitation of the wrongs done by its opponents. If it wishes to survive it is most essential that it clear its own skirts from mistaken acts or policies. At present the Bolsheviki and radical labor find their strongest moral support in the mistaken deeds, past and present, of Governments directed or controlled by the will or fear of the bitter-enders and militarists. Every revolution, born of rights wrongfully withheld, brings forth wild schemes that swing far beyond the line of reason, fairness or feasibility. Bolshevism is a case in point. Its insane, cruel and extreme methods and principles will ultimately bring about its own undoing.

In the struggle between the masses and the classes neither side, however, can win by strong-arm methods. In the long run neither a dying form of government or creed, nor a new one aspiring to take its place, could ever maintain or assert itself by the use of the sword or torch. Anarchism cannot effectively be fought by deportation, nor can it win by the use of dynamite. That form of government will ultimately prevail which most honestly lives up to the code of honor and ethics it professes and which goes furthest in observing the law, within and without the national lines, of loving one's neighbor as much, or at least almost as much, as one's self. It is not a test of strength, it is a test of morals that the world is faced with, and the sooner we realize that fact and attack our problems from that angle the sooner we shall emerge from our present difficulties.

The masses, harassed and distressed by the present trying conditions, will not be satisfied until some satisfactory solution is found. It will be one of the essential requirements of that solution to give labor a proper voice in the management of affairs, an adequate living wage and, if possible, a share in the profits. Furthermore, conceivably, at least, some sort of direct influence in the Government. The safest bulwark against Bolshevism is some practical experiment of this character which would go to the utmost limit compatible with the strict preservation of the principle of the sanctity of private property, the preservation of individual efficiency and of strict submission to the majority rule of a parliamentary government.

Germany is trying such an experiment at this time. She has enacted legislation making obligatory the organization of shop councils in every establishment employing more than a given number of hands. These councils have certain rights with respect to the working conditions of the employes. They also may have one or more representatives on the Boards of Directors of corporations. Representatives of these councils are grouped together in superimposed organizations in order to deal with questions affecting an entire industry or profession. And finally, members of these larger organizations are delegated to act on the economic council of the entire republic, which council acts as an advisory body to the Parliament. One can readily see the vast possibilities of such a plan, which, in effect, creates a second house of nonpolitical experts, on which all important unions, guilds and professions are represented. There would not be any possible call for "direct action," particularly if this body of experts in due course of time were endowed with the same rights to vote as the political chambers. It is not beyond the bounds of imagination to suppose that, instead of two political bodies, like the House of Commons and the House of Lords, or the House of Representatives and the Senate, nations in the future might Parliament, together deciding their Parliament.

From what I have been able to learn of President Millerand's plans, they appear to follow a similar trend of thought in that they contemplate making the French Senate more representative of the guilds, trade unions and chambers of commerce of France. It is realized, of course, that for the United States a development on these lines must be considered as entirely remote, but of all the interesting evolutions taking place in Europe at this time the progress in this direction strikes me as one of the most significant and one deserving of our closest attention.

Bolshevism seems dead one day and full of life and vigor the next. But whether Lenin and Trotzky retain their strangle hold on Russia or whether they go under, a practicable solution must be found which will satisfy reasonable demands of labor. Without some such settlement, labor, in many countries, will not quiet down and increase production sufficiently to arrest the fall of their exchanges. Nor may we expect that without such settlement labor will submit to the overwhelming burdens of direct and indirect taxation, without which increasing inflation and ultimate bankruptcy cannot be avoided. The more desperate the economic needs of a country, the weaker the authority of its Government, the greater must needs be the concessions to be made to labor. Italy is a case in point. It is significant, furthermore, that after Germany was compelled at Spa to concede to the Allies the monthly delivery of 2,000,000 tons of coal and the reduction of its army to 100,000 men, she had to embark at once on a scheme for the nationalization of her coal mines, with a profit-sharing plan for labor and owners, and with ultimate complete Government ownership. Failure to offer some such plan would at once have played into the hands of the Independents or Spartacides and, at the same time, would have exposed Germany to the dangers threatening her from non-fulfillment in the punctual delivery of the coal.

The inferences are obvious.

If Germany fails in these scientific and orderly attempts to solve her labor troubles, they will lead either to more Bolshevistic forms, or to reaction and civil war. If she succeeds, on the other hand, how long will it be until some other countries will find that they will not be able adequately to increase their production unless they, too, grant similar concessions to labor? Should not victorious countries take care lest a policy of driving Germany to extremes might prove a boomerang?

Nationalization, or socialization, is a thought that exercises a great influence upon the imagination of the laboring masses, even though from the fiscal, as well as the economic, point of view it has generally proved itself as an inadvisable, uneconomic venture, to be avoided wherever possible. But where economic and social conditions become desperate, or where just demands of labor have been neglected too long, nothing will satisfy the exasperated masses but the fetich of nationalization, and radical concessions in one country will at once affect conditions in others.

The great majority of the German people abhor Bolshevism. They are temperamentally an order-loving people with a passion for hard work, even though dishonesty, corruption and even barefaced robbery have made alarming inroads among the distressed masses. The great majority of the German people abhor reaction and are through with the militarists. They want to work out of their present distress and pay any reasonable indemnity that may be imposed.

Individually and collectively, however, they are at the end of their tether. They are undernourished; they still live on pitch black bread that, during my stay, contained only 20 per cent of flour, and tuberculosis is spreading at an alarming pace. Their death rate has increased tremendously. Taxation in a hundred different forms takes an amazing proportion of their capital and income, while the balance of their revenues command only a fraction of their one-time purchasing power. With all that, though the item of revenue from taxes in the latest budget provides for an estimated increase from 2,500,000,000 marks before the war to approximately 30,000,000,000 marks per annum, a Government deficit of some 60,000,000,000 marks still stares them in the face, which is being met by constantly printing more notes and Treasury bills. Their ships, their colonies, the bulk of their foreign investment and about one-third of their ore mines are gone; a scarcity of coal has laid many industries idle and keeps the people freezing in houses which the rich have to share with the poor; their country is disorganized through foreign occupation and internal troubles, their military protection against riots and insurrections is totally insufficient and unreliable.

How, on top of that, are they to pay fabulous indemnities and avoid bankruptcy and social disorder? With all the powers of a dictator, one would not know how to solve such a problem, and if any financier among the Allies or the neutrals could show how it can be done he should promptly step forward and give the world the benefit of his advice.*

* American papers recently carried a report from Paris to the effect that the French were disappointed that the Germans did not pay. As a matter of fact, they have paid the Allies in kind some twenty billion gold marks and they are paying every month two million tons of coal, amounting approximately to $30,000,000 per month. We have lost all sense of proportion if we do not realize the importance of these payments. It is

The danger of such a situation is that if driven to desperation even the sanest population might in the end surrender to the argument of the reactionary to the effect that if all hope for a brighter future is to be abandoned, it might be better to open the doors of Bolshevism, in spite of all its horrors, which then would engulf all Europe and give Germany a chance to start again on an equal level with her unforgiving victorious enemies.

Europe is at the crossroads of her destiny, and the decision whether she will sink or rise lies largely in the hands of France. In contemplating the present plight of France and Germany, I am led to compare poor France, with her devastated regions, to a man maimed in the war, showing the stump of a limb shot to pieces in the struggle. Germany, on the other hand, economically ruined, may be likened to a man infected to the core with tuberculosis, hopelessly doomed to death unless the disease is arrested, but, to the casual observer, showing no outward signs of the dread malady.

Can the poor French invalid expect to regain his strength by a transfusion of blood from so wretched a body? There are those in France who take the moderate and wise view that, if Europe and her present form of social order and civilization is to survive, countries must cease to carry on a war after peace, that they must stand together in removing the wreckage and in trying to salvage

---

sufficient to realize that $360,000,000 (that is some 30 billions in paper marks) a year is equal approximately to one-third of our pre-war budget. When we bear in mind what an effort it has been for France to pay off $150,000,000 of the loan, which fell due in October, while she still has command over a large volume of foreign securities owned by her nationals and while she has colonies, steamers and credit, while Germany has been stripped of all these, it becomes clear enough that Germany is making substantial payments at this time. Indeed, a close study of existing conditions may raise some doubts as to her ability to do much more, for, after all, it must be borne in mind that her Government must find ways and means to raise by taxation the equivalent of the coal that she surrenders every year, and it is this fiscal side of the problem that requires the most thorough examination.

We gain some insight into the significance of these facts when we read the recent statement of the German Minister of Finance, that in order to indemnify the German owners for foreign securities and properties, ships and other material turned over to the Allies (included in the above twenty billion gold marks paid in kind) the Government had to incur a debt of approximately 131 billion paper marks!

what still can be saved. Such men are at one with England and Italy in wishing the indemnity question settled promptly and on a reasonable basis. As against this school of thought, there are the "bitter enders," who partly from hatred engendered by the war and partly from fear—both easily understood—say that Germany must be so loaded down with debts and deprived of her coal to such a degree that she can never recuperate. This would imply the reduction of 60,000,000 people to 40,000,000. I do not believe that the world wants to shoulder the responsibility of seeing the fate of Austria duplicated. My own feeling is that the moderate elements in France ultimately are bound to prevail; her financial and economic difficulties and her genuine anxieties are, however, so real and so grave that it is most difficult for her to reach that conclusion.

Victorious Germany, under the leadership of her militarists, overreached herself in 1871, and thereby created a condition which ultimately led to the catastrophe of 1914. She overreached herself again at Brest-Litovsk and Bucharest. Poland did the same when attacking Russia, and Russia committed a similar blunder when attempting to overplay her victory before Warsaw.

The friends of France should help her in avoiding the pitfalls of a similar course. I hope that Hegel's saying, "We learn from history that men never learn anything from history," will not again prove true. No fair-minded person would deny that France is entitled to the most complete military protection against the risk of a military attack by Germany and that she is entitled to special consideration for her industries crippled by the destruction of war and as large an indemnity as the German Nation can possibly pay, but it is obvious that France stands in danger to lose these benefits to which she is fairly entitled unless Germany is given a chance to work and become reasonably prosperous. France, suffering, magnanimous, and wise, will enjoy the sympathy and active support of all the world. The opposite course, it is to be feared, will lead to a rift in the Entente and a continuation of uncertainty, intrigue and destruction, which Europe is in no condition to stand and survive.

Mr. Rowland F. Boyden, the United States "unofficial observer" at the Brussels financial conference, stated the case tersely last month when he said that "co-operation in Europe is an economic principle." Until this principle is applied, Europe, to use Mr. Boyden's language, is not "a good business risk for the United States."

The American people would be strangely lacking in a proper conception of self-interest and self-respect if, at this juncture, they were not moved by a strong impulse to assist Europe to the utmost of their ability. But a genuine and constructive peace between estranged nations and classes is an indispensable prerequisite. No matter how painfully we may ourselves be affected by economic chaos in Europe, a comprehensive action of relief on the part of the United States cannot be successfully undertaken as long as the Old World remains in the throes of bitter political strife and acute social unrest. America cannot save Europe until Europe saves herself.

Germany Transformed Within a Week; Socialist Deputies Leading Revolt

by George Renwick

AMSTERDAM, NOV. 10.—From all parts of the Kaiserless Empire come reports of the astonishingly rapid spread of the Socialistic revolution. It is in Munich, the capital of Bavaria, that matters appear to have moved with the greatest speed. There a Socialist Government, with Herr Kurt Eisner, a well-known Socialist at its head, has been formed, a republic has been proclaimed and the garrison has placed itself under the orders of the new powers that be.

The movement was rapidly successful at Hanover, where all the trains bound for the front were stopped and the soldiers and their officers were disarmed. The movement completely conquered Oldenburg, and at Schwerin the Grand Duke received the members of the Soldiers' and Workers' Council, who informed him that the whole province of Mecklenburg had gone over to the Socialist revolution.

Throughout the Rhine industrial region the movement is now

spreading like wildfire. From Essen and many other places many people in their alarm are trekking toward Holland. At the Krupp Works many thousands of foreign workers have been dismissed and thousands of others have stopped work. A council has also been formed there, and Socialist patrols are said to be surrounding the Krupp Works with a machine gun detachment.

At Crefeld a great Socialist meeting demanded that all munition factories immediately suspend work.

Sudden End to Autocracy

An astounding week in Germany is ending in a remarkable blaze of historic events. In seven short days the German people have effectively burst the fetters of the tyrannous, autocratic rule which had bound them for so many generations.

The Socialist revolution has swept with extraordinary success and remarkable rapidity through practically the whole country. That Germany which plunged Europe into war has, in short, been beaten far more thoroughly than even the most optimistic ever hoped would be the case. As this historic week ends it may be said to have been wiped out.

Kaiserism is dead. Today its great champion, Kaiser William II., abdicated, together with the Crown Prince. Prince Max of Baden will be Regent, and Herr Ebert will be the new Chancellor. An immediate general election will be held in order to bring together a national gathering to decide upon the future constitution of the country. There can be little doubt that a German republic will be called into existence.

The Socialist leader Sollman declared that a Soldiers' and Workers' Council had been formed and had established itself in the City Hall. He proclaimed the Council's demands to be as follows:

1. The immediate ending of the war.
2. A German Social Democratic Republic.
3. The release of all political and military prisoners.
4. The abolition of the military salute.
5. The army to be made a real people's army.
6. The abdication of the Hohenzollerns and all the German Princes.

Socialist Council's Demands

Some speakers, amid a good deal of applause, advocated Bolshevist methods.

While the meeting was being held disorders took place in various parts of the city, especially in the markets, where a great deal of food was carried off by the crowds.

In the afternoon the whole garrison announced its adhesion to the movement.

During the afternoon strong measures were taken to restore order, and these were successful. The Law Courts were shut down. Deputations from other cities arrived in the course of the day and had a tremendous popular reception.

The city presents a curious aspect, lavishly decked as it is with red flags and streamers. Soldiers and civilians have their caps and hats decked with red. Wherever crowds gather together loud cheers are raised for a Socialist republic.

The Chief Burgomaster has announced his agreement with the Council's demands.

In Hamburg the movement is reported to have taken one peculiar feature, in that very considerable enmity is now being shown against the more moderate Socialist elements.

The Red Flag, formerly the Hamburger Echo, organ of the Soldiers' and Workers' Council, prints an order issued by the Council warning people against adhering to what appears to be a countermovement by the Moderates. The Bourgeos press has been forbidden to print appeals from that quarter, which seems to consist mainly of trade union elements.

The Cologne Volks-Zeitung hints that it is probable that the extremists may be overcome by the older Socialist Party and by the trade unions, and the movement will have less revolutionary character.

In all other ports the movement continues in being.

Hamburg Crowds Cheer Wilson

Nov. 8.—Germany is in the throes of a revolutionary movement, which began early this week and which has spread and is still spreading with great rapidity, becoming more and more openly revolutionary in character. Both the Socialist parties have now been drawn into it. Berlin was quiet today, but action by the Socialists there is expected at any time.

A traveler arriving from Hamburg tells me that the movement there is frankly revolutionary. He heard the crowds cheering the Entente and President Wilson.

That the Socialist Majority Party has placed itself at the head of the German revolution is shown by a manifesto published this morning in Vorwärts. In the early hours this manifesto created a tremendous sensation throughout the capital, and the excitement is reported to have grown with every hour since. It is as follows:

"Workers and Party Comrades: Peace is assured. Within a few hours the armistice will begin, so let there be no thoughtless actions which may cause the bloodshed, now stopping at the front, to begin again at home. The Socialist Party is putting all its strength into the work of securing the speediest concession to its demands. To that end the executives of the Socialist Party and of the Reichstag faction of the Socialist Party have placed the following demands before the Imperial Chancellor:

"1. Permission to be given for holding those gatherings today which had been prohibited.

"2. Instructions to be given to the police and military authorities that they must exercise the greatest circumspection.

"3. Abdication of the Kaiser and the Crown Prince before midday of Friday.

"4. Strengthening of the Socialist influence in the Government.

"5. Reorganization of the Prussian Cabinet according to the policy of the Reichstag majority parties.

"If before Friday, Nov. 8, at noon, no satisfactory answer has been received the Socialist members of the Government will resign.

"Workers, wait for further announcement from us in the course of Friday afternoon."

The manifesto is signed by the executives of the Socialist Party and the Reichstag faction of the party.

I believe the Socialist terms were handed to the Chancellor yesterday afternoon about 4 o'clock, so that Prince Max had twenty hours in which to concede the demands.

At meetings all over the country resolutions have been passed demanding the Kaiser's abdication, and these resolutions have been pouring in upon the Government. Especially in South Germany has the demand for his going been of a particularly clamant nature, and press utterances on the matter became increasingly plain spoken. As far as can be gathered, a majority of the people favor a regency. But it cannot be denied that the demand for a republic is growing, especially since the ports burst into revolution. The Kaiserin is said to have been keenly in favor of abdication.

"Kiel is in the hands of German terrorists," says the Bremen Weser Zeitung, and the latest news shows that the statement is not exaggerated. A message dated yesterday says that the house of Captain Heine, Town Commandant, was entered at night by a naval patrol. The sailors demanded that the Captain should come with them. When he refused he was shot dead on the spot. The Soldiers' Council expressed regret for the incident, for which it disclaims responsibility.

The general strike which began Tuesday still continued yesterday. The patrols in the town have been strengthened and the red flag has been hoisted on the City Hall. Kiel is entirely cut off from the rest of Germany. The telegraph, telephone, and railway services of the town have been suspended. No letters are being delivered.

The Soldiers' Council issued another proclamation yesterday, reporting acceptance by State Secretary Haussmann, on behalf of the Government, of a large number of conditions. Some of them I have already reported, while others are that the fleet must not leave Kiel under any circumstances; that there must be complete freedom of speech; that the censorship of letters must be abolished, and that there shall be no more superior officers. There are several other terms by which apparently all power in Kiel passes into the hands of the Soldiers' Council.

Similar events have taken place at Hamburg, Lübeck, Flensburg, near Kiel, and Cuxhaven.

The trouble began on Tuesday in Hamburg with the arrival there of a torpedo boat, flying the red flag. Shortly afterward thousands of workers of numerous firms laid down their tools and began to demonstrate in the streets. At the stations they prevented the departure of soldiers whose leaves had expired, and many of these soldiers joined the demonstrators.

While this was going on a Soldiers' and Workers' Council was formed, patrols were placed on the streets, and guards put over the public buildings. Here and there fights took place, and altogether, it appears, about twelve people were killed and twenty wounded during the day.

In the afternoon all the ships in port were ordered to hoist the red flag, after which all the sailors left the ships. By this time the demonstrators numbered about 15,000, among them being a large number of women. Their next act was to disarm all the police and take possession of the barracks. At the infantry barracks there was a warm exchange of shots for a considerable time. Eventually the officers came out and surrendered the building.

In Altona, adjoining Hamburg, a Soldiers' Council also was formed, and the two councils entered into negotiations with the local military command, which, as at Kiel, agreed to the demonstrators' demands. The councils then took possession of the military command offices.

All military and naval prisoners in Hamburg and Altona have been set at liberty. The well-known Independent Socialist Deputy, William Dittman, is acting with the demonstrators there, while at Kiel Herr Noske placed himself at the head of the Soldiers' Council.

How Bremen Rising Started

Nov. 7—(Midnight.)—News late tonight from Hamburg shows that Hamburg and its suburb, Altona, are completely in the hands of the revolutionaries. Military posts, with red flags, hold all the important points with machine guns and all the soldiers wear red bands on their arms. It is reckoned that there are 18,000 soldiers in Hamburg alone, who placed themselves under orders of the Soldiers' Council.

So far the reports from Bremen are brief, but it is not thought that the revolutionaries there have the situation fully in their control. Matters did not move there until Tuesday. On that day a train brought 500 marines who were going to Wilhelmshaven to escort prisoners to a camp at Münster. They left the train at Bremen, however, and marched into the city in large numbers. The people joined them on their march to the barracks where the guards were disarmed. While this was being done, another crowd marched to the City Hall, and there from a balcony speeches were delivered, the burden of which was a demand for a Socialist Republic. A Soldiers' and Workers' Council was then formed, and the commander of the garrison was told that this body was assuming entire control of the city.

Yet another crowd marched to the prison with the intention of releasing all military and civilian prisoners, but these had been set at liberty before the revolutionaries arrived. Not many workers appear to have gone on strike, but discussions are reported to be proceeding between employers and workmen in Bremen.

Liebknecht is directing matters and the whole Independent Socialist Party appears to have linked itself up definitely with the movement. In the evening the revolutionaries had the city bells rung in token of the dawn of the new freedom.

Small demonstrations are just reported from the northern districts of Berlin.

The Congress of Tours

by Walter Duranty

PARIS, DEC. 26.—The radical element cracked the whip of mastery over the opening session of the Socialist Congress at Tours yesterday. They made it clear right away that the verdict must be in favor of adhesion to the Third Communist Internationale of Moscow, and even indicated the proportion of the majority—about two and a half to one—that will vote submission to Lenin and acceptance of the twenty-one points of the Bolshevist "creed."

According to the agenda drawn up beforehand, the first two or three days of the congress were to be devoted to discussion of the reports of the Secretariat, the Treasury Department and the parliamentary group. But hardly had the strains of the "Internationale," by which the proceedings opened, died away, when Citizen Dreint, Communist delegate from the Seine section, jumped up and proposed that discussion of the all-important question of adhesion to Moscow be entered upon immediately.

The Anti-Moscow Party, led by Renaudel and Paul Boncour, protested. So did the Centre, under Longuet and Blum, who would like to join Moscow with reservations, one of which is the lifting of the Bolshevist excommunication ban against Longuet himself. Both were promptly squashed by the adverse vote of 2,916 to 1,228. The radicals did not even bother to argue the point. Their delegates voted with a swift, silent solidarity that proved the Communist steam roller was geared up to full efficiency.

"It's all over, bar the shouting," said a disgruntled anti-Bolshevik afterward. "They might as well swing the axe right away and save weeks of time."

The radicals at Tours make no secret of their determination to obey the twenty-one points to the letter and force the expulsion on all who decline to follow them.

"No compromise," is their motto, and they add: "Lenin is right. If the social revolution is to succeed we must have perfect discipline and obedience to a central direction. The great war was won by unity of command. Lenin will be the Foch of our victory in the class war."

Such frankness, now that they are sure of getting a majority, is in marked contrast to the disingenuous propaganda by which the radicals obtained instruction of Communist delegates throughout the country. Their agents declare, especially in the country districts, that the real point at issue was not so much their adhesion to Moscow, but to give Moscow a pledge of their sympathy and support and to show the capitalist Governments that they were opposed to any further attacks on the Soviet Federation. By emphasizing this side of the matter and leaving the twenty-one conditions of adhesion in the background the radicals persuaded country section after section to instruct its delegates for Communism.

Any labor or Socialist party in the world would have—in fact, they all have—voted a resolution against further attacks on Soviet Russia. By tricking their peasant supporters—who, like the workers in small towns, are less familiar with the undercurrents of modern socialism than in any other big nation—into the belief that they were doing something of the kind, the French radicals are going to stampede a majority of the party into adhesion to Moscow, which has been rejected by majorities of England, Germany, Switzerland and America.

This manoeuvre explains the fact that is puzzling, annoying, or moving to indignant denial bourgeois newspapers today, namely, that delegates of the country districts yesterday at Tours in a brief review each delegate gave of his mandate announced much bigger majorities in favor of the Communist platform than delegates from the industrial sections. The same fact explains the success of an advanced Socialist in an election to the Chamber of Deputies held a few days ago in the agricultural département of Lot-et-Garonne, which previously had been a stronghold of conservatism.

The Temps and other leading newspapers were quite horrified and did their best to explain away the results by local intrigues, family influences, &c. But the fact was that in the case of the Tours Congress the peasants thought their choice of radical delegates meant a protest against attacks on Soviet Russia. As in England, even those who are opposed to Bolshevist ideas are still more opposed to any more war and voted accordingly.

PARIS, Dec. 31.—The French Socialist Party is like a worm that has been cut in half by the Tours Congress. Both parts are wriggling vigorously, and each is claiming that it is the head and the other the tail. When the congress opened there were three sections—radicals, who included two-thirds of the total delegates, instructed to vote for adhesion to the Moscow Centrists; the party of Longuet, who declined to vote adhesion without reservations, and opponents of adhesion, the party of Renaudel and Blum, who frankly put patriotism before Socialism.

As expected, the radicals carried adhesion by a big majority, pledging themselves to accept Lenin's twenty-one conditions, of which one provides that they abandon the name of Socialist Party and call themselves Communists henceforth. But the split which resulted was into two parts instead of three. Longuet and the Centre last night formed an alliance with Renaudel and the conservative element. They were quick to seize the advantage offered by the change of name enforced on the radicals. The new combined group tonight issues a manifesto in Longuet's newspaper, Le Populaire, which is now to be their official organ. They remind their followers that they and they only are the Socialist Party and declare that they intend to work as always for the unity of that party and to bring back the "dissident Communists" into the fold when they have learned the error of their ways.

A further point is made that they represent the French section of the Trade Union International of Amsterdam. Like the trade unionists of other European countries, those of France have been more hostile towards economic Bolshevism than the political side of the party. The French labor federations have not got over the effects of the abortive general strike of last Spring, into which they were forced by the theoretical element. That failure not only discredited the radicals individually and strengthened the conservative leaders, but it led to a very large number of defections in the union ranks. The result is that the workers' federations now regard Communism with a cold eye and the great majority of their adherents will certainly follow the Longuet-Renaudel group rather than the Cachin-Frossard radicals.

The latter also issued a manifesto today in their organ, l'Humanité. As previously stated, they are followers of Lenin more in the letter than in the spirit, and already they are doing their utmost to ignore the enforced change of name. They do not call themselves Communists at all, and claim that they are real Socialists, who support Moscow because the Bolsheviki have rescued the pure gospel of Karl Marx from the false interpretations of semi-bourgeois heretics.

The manifesto is headed "Socialism," and the only reference to their pledge to change their name to Communists is in a somewhat embarrassed use of the portmanteau term "Socialist Communists," by which they apparently hope to include this awkward point. Although they have at present a big paper majority, it is probable that from now on they will lose ground, as the mass of their followers come to realize what they have swallowed in accepting the twenty-one points.

Chief interest in the split lies in the possibility it opens up of a reconstitution of the Bloc Gauche (Block of the Left), by which France was governed from 1880 until 1914. This block consisted of all the liberal or advanced elements in Parliament—Radical-Socialists, as they were called, who formed the biggest group in the Chamber—together with the few Socialist fiery extremists, who correspond to the present Communist Party. Disintegration by the war and the refusal of the Socialist Party to participate in the Clemenceau Government hammered the lid on its coffin. The Socialist decision to hold aloof from any "bourgeois" Government prevented attempts at resurrection. But now it is thought likely that the Longuet-Renaudel combination, freed from control by the Radicals, will be willing to revive the old alliance with the Liberals.

The prospects before such an alliance are alluring, as, although the present chamber is controlled by the "national block" of Conservatives, it is doubtful whether they really represent the opinion of the country. For instance, the National Block three months ago was in favor of a strong attitude toward Germany and would probably have preferred not to reduce the army service to eighteen months. They found, however, that the country was all out for reduction and quite ready to see a trial of a compromise policy on the Germans. The recent bye-election in Lot-et-Garonne, when a Socialist captured a Conservative seat, showed how the tide of public opinion was turning, and there is a fair probability that within a few months France will be governed by a more liberal combination, whose platform will be peace abroad and internal reform and reconstruction.

Italy Rebels Against Rebellion

by Anne O'Hare McCormick

THE STATE of Italy is very aptly typified by an incident which occurred Easter Sunday afternoon during the first of three orchestral concerts conducted by Arthur Nikisch in the Augusteo in Rome. The audience was the largest and the most rapt I have ever seen at a symphony concert. They crowded every tier of the great amphitheatre built on the tombs of Augustus and the Roman Emperors, and followed with absorbed and breathless attention a masterly rendition of Beethoven's Heroic Symphony punctuated by the reverberations of the storm that shattered the top of the historic obelisk in front of St. Peter's. Mr. Nikisch himself received an ovation. It was his first appearance in Rome since long before the war, and even if there were not less hostility to the Central Empires in Italy than in any other allied country, the Italians are too artistic a people to let any political or national prejudice affect their enjoyment of art.

But it was the poignant death song of Isolde from "Tristan and Isolde," played with a feeling and finesse that wrung the last drop of beauty out of one of the loveliest passages in modern music, that stopped the performance. The "bravas" outdid the thunder and drowned the wash of the tempestuous rain on the glass roof, until finally appreciation got out of bounds and applause became something like pandemonium. For ten minutes the conductor could not proceed. The acclamation slackened only to gain force again, rising and falling as rhythmically as the orchestral crescendoes. The noisiest part of the audience was determined that the passage should be repeated. Their "Bis! Bis!" beat upon the air like the sharp hissing of exploding skyrockets. The other half, seeing that the conductor wished to go on with the program, was determined to restore silence. To that end they kept shouting "Basta! Basta!" with a vociferation that only increased the clamor and confusion. Mr. Nikisch made vain gestures of appeal for quiet, and at last, in a moment's lull in the racket, he started the orchestra on the Tannhäuser overture. But no sooner were the opening bars recognized than a "Bis!" as loud and imperative as a cannon shot stopped the players and in despair the conductor gave in and ordered the repetition of the "Mort d'Isolde."

This effort of Italian audiences to put themselves in order, usually with an angry hissing for untimely applause far more distracting than the original disturbance, is exactly what is happening in the national drama at the present moment. I watched the Roman crowd at the Augusteo with a fascinated sense that I was really seeing Italy itself in the same noisy and impassioned attempt to restore order and harmony. The country has a "Bis" contingent whose shouting for more has reached a point of violent insistence which threatens to break up the whole show. And while the Government makes more or less timid and ineffectual motions to silence them and go on with its business, there has risen up a "Basta" group which is so furiously bent upon putting down disorder that it is difficult to tell which is more out of bounds, the communists in their madness to destroy or the Fascisti in their zeal to save the existing machinery of government.

The same struggle between order and disorder is going on all over Europe, but it is more significant in Italy, not only because it is more spectacular, but because the Italians are the people who have taken into their own hands the fight against disruption and anarchy. Last Fall the traveler in Italy who was impeded by constant strikes, cut off from either going or staying by a paralysis of industry based on almost any pretext—a protest against the imprisonment of a Socialist leader or a punishment for some military "insult" to a member of the proletariat—was apt to be in a constant state of irritation against a feeble Government and a complaisant people. He grew a little tired of the patience of the submerged majority, more than a little skeptical of the mild threats of an apparently spiritless people. There did not seem much force or purpose behind an exasperation so diluted with forbearance. "We'll let them go as far as we can," was the common comment at a common occurrence, like a general strike that tied up a whole city. "But some day they will go too far, and then we'll do something."

The people seem at last to have reached the point of doing something. They have begun to shout "Basta" in no weak or uncertain voice. Represented by the Fascisti, a league of combatants something like the American Legion, they are defying both the Government and the communists in their drastic determination that their country shall not be dragged into the chaos of Bolshevism. Their long patience makes their action now more startling and more dangerous, since they are evidently resolved to have law and order if they have to murder every agitator in Italy to get it.

The result is a condition closely bordering on civil war, but the kind of civil war that takes place in the human body when the white corpuscles rally to resist an invasion of deadly germs. It is a desperate struggle for national health. As such, the actual hand-to-hand fight being waged in the teeming fields of the contado and in the narrow streets of nearly every town of Italy is a kind of reduction to ultimate terms of the conflict between the two forces that are disputing the mastery of the world. It is hardly too much to say that whichever side wins in Italy is likely to win everywhere else.

Having marveled at the patience of Italy, I was so eager to see the manifestation of its impatience that I hastened back when the news of the sporadic but almost daily risings south of the border began to cause a little uneasiness in France. The French Government has every appearance of security. The discontent that flares up in rebellion in other places in France is just now concentrated in a fierce resentment against the evasions and the insolences of the Germans. The eternal enemy on the doorstep has the effect of fusing French factions in a bitter anger that overpowers all lesser angers. But they watch Italy rather nervously none the less, with a disquieting fear that fires that are not quenched there are sure to leap across the frontier.

Coming into Italy one March evening by the port of Leghorn, and engaging at once in a little battle of my own with the boatmen and other bandits who infest all Italian ports, I was in a sufficiently martial mood before I discovered that it was impossible for any traveler arriving at 9 o'clock to dine or sup or lunch at Leghorn, because no one in the hotels would serve him, and every restaurant and café in the place was closed "on account of the revolution." The streets and squares in the centre of the city were practically deserted by civilians. Soldiers were gathered in groups here and there, lounging and chatting in the informal and unmilitary fashion of Italian troops. There was no disorder, but the unusual sight of an Italian city perfectly quiet and empty in the early evening did more than any number of sensational reports to convince me that the situation was really serious.

I do not know by what art a city that seethes and shakes and wrestles with itself more than any city in Italy always contrives to look the most dignified and tranquil of them all. Florence, when I arrived, was just recovering from three days of actual and ugly civil war, supplemented by hideous outbreaks of fanatic peasant hatred against the landowners throughout the surrounding country. There were the marks of a hail of bullets on some of the principal buildings. There was everywhere shattered glass, the result of the fire of machine guns and armored tanks. In the San Frediano quarter, where the communists were hunted to their hiding places by avenging Fascisti and soldiers, there were shattered doors, all kinds of wreckage, fresh red stains on old walls that often before had tasted blood. Piled up in an ancient church, under a strong guard, I saw some of the loot collected in these raids—provisions, guns, supplies, of a quantity and variety to prove that the revolutionists of Tuscany were prepared for a long siege. The bridges of the Arno were still guarded by soldiers and commanded by guns. The city was filled with soldiers, swarming with gorgeous officers whose swaggering light blue capes and boots, polished to a state of incandescence, sustained the reputation of the Italians for being the smartest and best-turned-out military men in the allied armies.

There was everything in Florence to suggest abnormal circumstances, and nothing in the least abnormal in the air and atmosphere of the city. I thought I had never seen anything more suggestive of ancient order, beauty and peace than a view of the domes and towers and steadfast walls etched by a golden dusk against a sky already silvered by early moonlight. There was something imperturbable in the glowing old profile of a city that has always evoked a kind of passion in her lovers, that is as used to bloodshed and revolt as to sunshine and rain, that has borne more turbulent, truculent and mighty spirits than almost any other town, and that remains forever cool, detached, smiling over her memories of glory and shame, serene in her almost cloistral loveliness. If one of her greatest sons had set out to paint a portrait of Florence in his "Mona Lisa" he could hardly have suggested more surely her wise and ineluctable charm. "If they have done anything to Florence!" was my first callous thought when I heard of the rising; and now it was as if Florence assured me how little she was shaken by the gusty contests of men, showed me how little she had been violated by the assaults of a thousand embattled years.

The streets were thronged, the tea shops and cafés full of sedate, untroubled crowds. The Florentines dismissed the trouble with a disdainful shrug of the shoulders; the visitors discussed it as if it were a spectacle staged for their benefit. I was told at the hotels that the guests had congregated on the roofs to watch the fighting in the streets below, just as in other days great ladies must have watched the battles between Guelfs and Ghibellines from the high windows of houses like fortress towers. "Our people really enjoyed the show," boasted one hotel proprietor, as proudly as if the opportunity to see a revolution enhanced the spectacular attractions of his city. A young English girl who had been caught in the San Frediano quarter during one of the hottest hours of the conflict described its excitements with sparkling eyes.

"Oh, it's too bad you missed it," she condoled with me. "I really saw the whole thing start, on the Sunday afternoon when a body of students, celebrating something or other, began to march through the streets carrying the Italian flag. It was just near here"—we were sitting in a tea room in the Via Tornabuoni—"that the military, fearing there would be trouble because of the pitch to which the people had been roused during the strikes by the Bolshevist agitators, and because all outbreaks in Italy follow some waving of the national banner, ordered the marchers to abandon their procession and to go home quietly. They were starting for home when they were set upon by the communisti. I watched them go up the street, a perfectly harmless and orderly group in a perfectly orderly demonstration. And a few minutes afterwards nearly a dozen of those nice, quiet, patriotic boys were dead—murdered without a chance, though they put up as stiff a fight as they could.

"Well, you can imagine what that outrage did to the Fascisti, already straining at the leash for blood. They broke loose then and started on a hunt for the Communists. They got the leader and shot him like a dog. Then both sides, with the soldiers joining in, started on the rampage and gave us three days of real war. On Monday morning, foolishly I suppose, but thinking the trouble was over, I started for the Piazza San Frediano, where every week I give a sort of dancing lesson to the poor children in a free kindergarten. I found the place full of soldiers and Fascisti on a man hunt. I was literally shooed into a doorway by bullets and only got a shaken, keyhole glimpse of the raids. They weren't pretty, some of the sights I saw. It was a little like the picture in one of your sobby war films of the capture of a French town by the Germans. It was deadly quiet, except for the sound of guns and an occasional scream of terror or agony.

"It was like that almost anywhere in Florence during those three days. Both sides were in terrible earnest, fighting to kill. It was the Fascisti who won out at last, mostly, I think, because they fought with a kind of cold and terrible anger. I am glad, of course; but don't think," added my young friend ardently, "that I don't realize that the revolutionists have a side. You know how the poor have been oppressed here in Italy. You know how the soil has been cultivated by the upper classes for Bolshevist propaganda. Why, after I've had those little children in San Frediano dancing all morning they are just as cold as when they started. They are bloodless, half-starved. I tell you hunger is the first cause of all revolutions, and these people listen to the agitators because they are hungry. What do they care for life when they have nothing to live for?"

A wise old Florentine banker shared her view. "In Italy we are reaping what we have sown," he told me. "The peasants have always lived too close to the starving line. The war propaganda of the Germans, which is the real root of all the present trouble, was successful here because it was so easy to mix truth with its lies. The people never had a fair deal. Now, of course, the Government has become panicky and is practically turning over the country to them, giving them everything they demand and bleeding all the rest of us. I suppose it's our turn," he concluded with a wry smile, "but while the present policy may turn the Bolsheviki into conservatives it is very likely to turn the conservatives into Bolsheviki at the same time."

Living is a luxury for all Italians nowadays, but the Latin prejudice against the principle of direct taxation makes the burden less heavy on the rich than in countries in which the Government helps itself out of big incomes. Everybody in Italy who buys a postage stamp or a railway ticket, a hat or a pair of shoes, who indulges in bread, sugar, meat or macaroni, who spends a night at a hotel or eats a meal in a restaurant, who goes to the movies or has his picture taken, has to pay a tax. He cannot do anything, or do nothing, without being taxed for it. Why a people balks at an income tax and accepts this outlay tax at a time when incomes are so impotent compared to expenses is one of the many mysteries of European finance. The only principle on which the Government can base its new luxury tax—aside from the fundamental one that it has to have the money—is that the cost of necessities is so high that there is nothing that is not a luxury.

The organized Socialists, with their powerful "bloc" in Parliament, are not at all responsible for the direct action of the revolutionists though they must have directed the general policy of strikes and obstruction which encouraged the extremists to proceed to further excesses. These excesses are greatly embarrassing the party since they have the inevitable effect of fusing and hardening the people against it, a fact which explains the present eagerness of the Constitutionalists and the unwillingness of the Socialists to submit the issues to the test of an immediate general election.

But while the reluctance of the Socialists to be judged by the people is evidence of their own conviction that they have lost strength since the last election, it would be a mistake to underestimate the power or desperation of the revolutionary forces. It is impossible to go to the remotest village in the land without encountering signs of their activity or their propaganda. In those aloof, unworldly, gray, Franciscan towns that crown the blue hills of Umbria, unchanged since the Middle Ages, kept alive today mostly by the sadly fading fame of saints and old masterpieces, it is startling to find vivas to Lenin and the Russian revolution painted on walls that have not been touched since the time of Giotto. Perugia is under as radical a Socialist administration as Bologna, and Assisi, which hitherto seemed to know no one but St. Francis, has now become well acquainted with Trotzky and Lenin.

Rome is the steadiest and least disturbed of Italian cities, but there is hardly a wall of a church or public building in the capital itself, under the eyes of Pope and King and Parliament and more soldiers than appear in any place in Europe, that is not blackened with slogans extolling the revolution and the advent of the Socialist republic. And while in Florence, when I was there, it was confidently believed that the rebels were completely disarmed and routed, several eruptions since prove that the volcano is by no means extinct. Every day in the newspapers there are accounts of pitched battles, killings and frenzied destruction of property in nearly every city and town in the north and in a few in the south. The frightful bomb outrage in the Diana Theatre in Milan, while it profoundly shocked the country and was bitterly denounced by the "Avanti" and the entire Socialist press, has been followed by more bomb-throwing elsewhere.

Also, it must be remembered that if the Bolsheviki are embarrassing the Socialists, the Fascisti are also rather embarrassing to the Government. While they are now, of course, doing the Government's work in a manner more thoroughgoing and direct than would be possible for the Government, their activity is a pretty resounding rebuke to the policy of the Administration. They mean to save the country, but if their power and popularity continue to grow there is no telling that they will not save it at the expense of the present Government.

In the plebiscite at the Augusteo concert, the Oliver Twists won because they were more noisy and insistent than the majority of the audience. Also they knew exactly what they wanted. But the "Bis" group in the national amphitheatre are striking out blindly, filled with nothing more purposeful than a fury to make somebody suffer for their accumulated wrongs. They will not win the country because the "Basta" element has ceased being complaisant and because the very blindness of the anarchist aim has made their blows too wild. The peasant proprietor, the most conservative man in Italy, has seen them at work, with the result that he is everywhere joining forces with the Fascisti. The women, though still a very feeble national force, are thoroughly roused. I first heard of the Milan catastrophe from an old peasant woman who stopped me in front of a church in Rome the morning after the event for no other reason than to tell me the news. She was so ablaze with horror and indignation that she had to talk to somebody.

"I tell you, Signora," she declared, pushing a ragged shawl back from a weatherbeaten face, "men are beasts since the war. I think the devil is the only king they follow now. I do not know the world at all. It is like living in a madhouse."

She blessed me copiously because I agreed with her, and went off cursing, with a generous inclusiveness, all agitators, wars, pescecane, writers and dogs of Russians. I think her maledictions pretty justly distributed the responsibility for the troubles of her country; and that they express a gathering wrath in the hearts of the people against wantonness in the name of any tyranny, high or low, that will be the best hope and fortification of a wise constitutional Government. Italy is uncomfortable for the moment, but there is nothing in Europe healthier than her rebellion against rebellion.

British Labor's Era of Reason Forestalling Rage of Rioters

by P. W. Wilson

IT IS NOW one year since the Labor Party in Great Britain became the official Opposition in her House of Commons, and perhaps it is not too early to consider how a situation, so unusual and so challenging to society as now constituted, has worked out.

There is one respect and only one respect in which Labor has established what looks like a new precedent. Even today no Labor members sit in the House of Lords and when Bonar Law's health failed it was held, therefore, that the Prime Minister must belong to the elected Chamber. Labor as an official Opposition has thus meant the difference between the Marquis Curzon as the proudest of peers and Stanley Baldwin as the richest or one of the richest of capitalist employers. It is possibly evolution, but assuredly not revolution.

Assisted by the discontents arising from a fall in wages, a lack of houses and unemployment, there were three courses that the Labor Party, as it gathered momentum, could have pursued.

The first of these was to appeal frankly to a proletariat, already trained to the use of arms, and so to overturn society by force.

The second was to adopt what may be called industrial Sinn Fein —in other words, to withdraw all Labor members from a Parliament declared useless, and to develop a new authority, a Soviet, outside the Constitution which would reflect the aims of the workers.

The third course was to enter Parliament, accept its rules and capture its machinery for the ends which Labor has in view. It is this third and least violent policy that Labor is pursuing. The presiding officer of the Trade Union Congress is this year a woman, Margaret Bondfield, of the Shop Assistants' Union.

There is in the House one and only one Communist member, John Turner Walton Newbold of Lanark in Scotland. He has declared that "there is no country in the world where there are as many precedents for civil war as in this country"—that is, Britain. But he said this inside as well as outside the House of Commons.

His more orthodox colleagues are orderly in debate and accept the decisions of the Chair. It is true that the sessions have included the usual percentage of "scenes," and that on one occasion four Labor members, infected like Newbold with Scottish irreconcilability, were suspended while there has been sung the Red Song.

But in the House of Commons such incidents are nothing new. Half a century ago the late John Redmond was suspended on the very day he entered the House. Lord Hugh Cecil once helped to howl down Asquith, who was Prime Minister. And Ronald MacNeill, now Under Secretary for Foreign Affairs, not only threw an order book at Winston Churchill, but hit him with it on the face. It is these occasional ebullitions of high spirits that make Parliament interesting, both to itself and to the country.

And the offending Labor members have been welcomed back again to the green benches. In their excesses there has been nothing that could be mistaken for an attempt to break up the parliamentary system. Indeed, when David Kirkwood of Dumbarton, in Scotland, declares that he has "come through the fiery test" and has been "in prison several times," and has even been "deported," he is addressing a public opinion that measures these somewhat mild and temporary experiences by the standard of Ireland, to say nothing of continental Europe. After all, John Burns, the most conservative of Labor statesmen, who was pensioned by Andrew Carnegie, and John Dillon, the most conservative of Nationalists, were at one time political prisoners.

Why Labor members from Scotland should be more extreme than others is a problem in national psychology. At the General Assembly of the Church of Scotland a minister said that these members brought "scandal and disgrace" to Westminster, but the Moderator promptly apologized for the use of such language. Indeed, in March, no fewer than 500 Episcopal clergy, supposed to be the most cautious of all British Christians, signed a manifesto supporting the Labor Party and based on "direct knowledge of the suffering, deprivation, mental, moral and physical, to which millions of our fellow-citizens are subjected in our present social and industrial order, to find a remedy for which is the chief purpose and aim of the Labor movement." British labor is thus by no means bereft of ecclesiastical benediction. For many of its theses, it claims, indeed, a scriptural sanction.

It is true that the Labor Party began its career as official Opposition by electing as leader "a pacifist and pro-German," as he was called, Ramsay MacDonald, so deposing J. R. Clynes, a Privy Councilor and former Coalitionist Minister. But the whole point of Ramsay MacDonald's dislike of the war lay in the conscientious objection to the use of physical force. He stands for government by persuasion, which means through Parliament. The tone of his speeches, let us say on the Ruhr, does not differ in any essential from the tone adopted by Grey, Baldwin, Asquith, Lloyd George and other "capitalist" statesmen. With other leaders of his party he was invited by Lady Astor to meet the King and Queen, and he dines at Buckingham Palace.

It is fair to the Labor Party to add that no Opposition, thus working loyally with the Parliamentary system, can initiate serious legislation or new expenditure. To complain that the Labor Party has achieved nothing at Westminster is to display an ignorance of the Standing Orders of the House. The Government of the Day controls both the time of the House and the public purse and only the Government of the Day can "achieve"—let us say, a levy on capital.

The real question is whether Labor has exerted a new influence on national affairs, and here undoubtedly the answer is in the affirmative. The Labor Party may succeed or it may fail, but, beyond all controversy, it has provoked in Britain a momentous argument over the very foundations of happiness, wealth, production, wages, employment. Capitalism on the one hand and constitutional communism on the other have been dragged into the daylight of an unfettered discussion. Bolshevism and bourgeoisie have met, face to face, and battled, not with bayonets but with bluebooks.

The rage of rioters has been forestalled by an era of reason. And it has been noticed that a logician like Asquith has been heard much more attentively in the new House of Commons than in the preceding House, where "coupon members" were in so marked a majority.

But the verdict of public opinion on the discussions cannot be claimed as yet by the Labor Party. While the situation is uncertain and subject to sudden changes, Stanley Baldwin and his Die Hards appear at the moment to have recorded a distinct improvement on the prestige which they inherited from Bonar Law. They hold only one-third of the votes in the country. But as long as the Progressive forces are divided between Labor and two unreconciled Liberal Parties, Toryism must continue to be entrenched.

The real question before Labor is whether it is holding its own in the constituencies. At the last general election the votes recorded were:

Conservative	5,474,533
Labor	4,312,030
Liberal	4,079,665
Others	302,244
Total	14,168,472

It will be seen that the Conservatives polled more than one-third and Labor less than one-third of the votes recorded. In the by-elections of the last twelve months the votes recorded have been:

Conservative	123,507
Labor	92,725

Liberal	92,549
Others	11,248

From these figures it is plain that Labor is no nearer to sweeping the country now than it was a year ago. In fact, the Conservatives have increased their proportionate lead and the Liberals have drawn level.

What Labor has to face is an electorate of which two out of every five voters are women. Last year only 14,000,000 votes were recorded out of a possible 21,000,000, or two-thirds; and the wire-pullers of all parties have to reckon with the unpolled margin of 7,000,000 votes, most of them belonging to the sex least accustomed to politics.

The Labor Party on the whole opposes conscription. In fact, the party has proposed a resolution in the House favoring disarmament. But from the minds of hotheads within the party, who still look to Moscow as their Mecca, a commune backed by a Red Army is not entirely absent.

It is the social condition of Britain that explains these outcries of sudden folly. The Labor Party includes James C. Welsh, the miner poet, whose novel, "The Underworld," created some sensation. In his maiden speech he described the opening of Parliament by the King as an Aladdin's Cave of wealth and color in which "nothing more beautiful ever came from the hand of God than a well-formed woman or man." But he added as contrast:

"I saw a miner's row—about four or five hundred houses, all of them single apartments. There were two holes in the walls for beds. It was certainly a happy home, as happy as it could be made under the circumstances, but in one of the beds lay an injured parent, brought home from the mine, writhing and groaning in agony, and in the other bed lay a dead child, and at night time, during the period of death and burial, the dead child had to be lifted out to allow the living ones to get in."

In such an appeal, there is not only sentiment but substance. Yet what the Labor Party finds is that it has no monopoly of this genuine emotion. In Viscount Astor's paper, The Observer, Lord Milner, once a prancing Proconsul in South Africa, has been arguing that the workers "are entitled to have their say about the conduct and policy of the business on which their whole existence depends"—a view elaborated by the Quaker family of Rowntree. And on the State ownership of industries, Lord Milner holds that "each case should be judged on its merits."

In November, Parliament will again assemble. The menacing prospect of another Winter with more than a million unemployed must then be faced. And while the evil is palliated by schemes of work and doles, there is an increasing nervousness, especially among Conservatives. As long as unemployment persists on such a scale, no administration is safe and no social order is entirely secure. Hence the anxiety to arrive at a tranquil solution of the Ruhr crisis, and hence, too, the attention paid to the now world famous resolution on socialism proposed by Philip Snowden. Of that resolution two opinions may be entertained. One is that it was an assertion of socialism which divided the House, as Ramsay MacDonald put it, into "only two parties"—namely, "the capitalist party and the Labor and Socialist Party." But another view is that the resolution really applied the soft pedal.

Inside the House, however, this blunt avowal of "the Socialistic Commonwealth" was smoothed into the opinion that "legislative effort should be directed to the gradual suppression of the capitalist system by an industrial and social order based on the public ownership and democratic control of production and distribution"—which sounds, at least, startling.

Writing in the Tory newspaper, The Morning Post, Philip Snowden, so recently hailed as the English Robespierre, tells us that "the Labor Government will then proceed, tentatively and gradually, to nationalize those industries and services which have reached the most advanced stage of monopoly and concentration"—but not more than one or two of such industries will be so handled in the course of any single Parliament (of about four years' duration). Snowden also mentions land, mines, railways, electric power, banking and insurance as instances of possible State ownership. In every one of those industries, except perhaps mining, Great Britain and her empire are today busily engaged! Nor is there one the State purchase of which or State control has not been advocated at one time or another by capitalists and employers themselves.

Moreover, labor is careful not to advocate confiscation of these enterprises. They are to be bought out by the State, and, to be frank, in some cases the proprietors would not be at all sorry to unload their liabilities as well as their assets on to the public. More than once in Great Britain an embarrassed capitalism has found salvation by selling out to the State at a figure which afterward embarrassed the State not a little.

In fact, the largest single industry in Britain is today already owned and run by the State. The Post Office includes the telegraphs, the telephones, the pensions and a bank. But there is no reason to suppose that the workers in the Post Office are more contented than many workers elsewhere. The Labor leaders, therefore, are evolving a new kind of socialism, based, as they put it, on the idea of a guild, in which labor would be included in the management and capital would be organized as in a co-operative society. In a sentence, the old time-honored "bureaucratic socialism" is now out of date—employment by high-salaried officials with a past that includes the university being regarded as distinctly unpalatable. But even in co-operative societies there are strikes, which, again, is discouraging, while it is not easy to derive hope from labor management of industries in Russia.

The fact is, of course, that labor is today up against the hard realities of commerce. In the year 1920 the membership of the unions rose to nearly 8,500,000. That membership has now fallen by more than 3,000,000. One reason is doubtless unemployment. But a contributory cause is disgust. The funds of the unions, painfully accumulated by weekly contributions, have been recklessly depleted by strikes which have brought 100 per cent loss to the workers. And the rigid demarcation of skilled and unskilled workers into two castes has involved a denial of opportunity to the unskilled man. In the building trades, where labor is apt to be seasonal, the workers are in some cases rebelling against rules which prevent them earning high wages for overtime when the going is good. And throughout the unions the man who is ready to work is asking why he is to be held back by his comrade who is less ready to work and why his output is to be used to pay for somebody else's slackness. There is thus growing up a demand for payment by results or by piecework, which labor has often opposed. And the argument of the older unionists that the employer fixes piece rates by the output of the most efficient carries less weight than formerly.

Labor is thus in the melting pot, and many accepted unions are apparently breaking. The union that covers a trade—there are about 1,500 of them, and many overlap—is challenged by the union that embodies an industry with many trades. While the open shop is, of course, resisted, there is a strong desire for more ventilation in the closed shop.

Once Again British Labor Takes the Helm

by P. W. Wilson

AGAIN LABOR has taken over the reins of government in Britain. After weeks of electioneering Stanley Baldwin and his Conservative Cabinet are out and the King has called James Ramsay MacDonald, leader of the Labor party, to form a government—the second administration for which Labor has been responsible. Thus the whole political stage at Westminster is reset.

As in 1923, MacDonald is in office but not in what is usually called power. This does not suggest simply that he has to fear a regular vote of censure. It means that, day by day, he has to carry a House, on balance politically hostile, on the innumerable issues, including side issues, which require a vote in the lobby. Under the circumstances, it is by no means certain that, on a first or a second defeat, MacDonald would take action. The House itself, though defeating him, might wish him to carry on.

At the same time much will depend not only on the measures proposed and the policy adopted but upon the handling of the House itself. In 1923 Labor was accused of antagonizing even friendly Liberals and forcing a strategic issue. If that procedure be followed with Lloyd George as the objective, there will be lively incidents and a certainty of parliamentary crises.

The situation at Westminster is always a reflection of the mood of the country. The description of the election just concluded as "apathetic" has been belied completely by the results. If ever there has been a revelation of awakened citizenship it is here. Many constituencies polled 90 per cent of their electors and the women turned out en masse.

Whatever view be taken of the Labor party, its achievement has been little short of a miracle. In the Conservative and Liberal sense of the term, it has an empty war chest. It distributes few, if any, honors to its supporters. Its candidates are often persons of limited private means. Yet by the sheer enthusiasm of voluntary workers, it has made itself the largest party in the House of Commons. Labor has conducted, not a campaign, but a crusade.

Policies of the Cabinet

It is, then, under conditions fairly to be described as stalemate, that the King's Government has to be carried on. The question arises, therefore, what is to be Labor's policy, at home and abroad?

From both spheres of statesmanship, Ramsay MacDonald has excluded whatever is meant in Great Britain by communism. This means that the Communist relation to Labor is similar to Labor's own relation to the Liberal party, say, in the later '90s. It is quite possible—some would say probable—that, as a result of Labor's moderation, there may develop a Communist party, the apparent violence of which will be merely an expression of irritation. On the other hand, a vigorous economic policy by Labor would be a sedative to this discontent on the Left.

As a dogma, Labor still believes officially in the nationalization of all means of production, distribution and exchange. In that sense, MacDonald is as much a disciple of Karl Marx as Lenin used to be.

But MacDonald has laid it down that every step toward the Socialist State must be approved by public opinion, constitutionally expressed in Parliament. In other words, it must not be forced on the country by any method of coercion like a general strike. The cry of "socialism in our time" is thus interpreted as not much socialism for the time being. Also, MacDonald rules out sheer confiscation.

The result of this consideration for private property is that railway nationalization, to give an instance, loses something of its charm. In Great Britain the railways are already consolidated into great systems, and an ownership by the State, though involving an important change, would not mean that capital charges were eliminated, but merely that they were placed under a national guarantee, as in India.

An examination of Labor literature, used in the late campaign, thus indicates that there is hardly an item or even an argument which has not been regarded for years as orthodox Liberalism. In finance, the party and especially Philip Snowden himself, the accepted Chancellor of the Exchequer, is still free trade and opposed to "safeguarding" industries by protection. In effect, Labor has abandoned a levy on capital and talks rather of raising the death duties yet further, of differentiating further the scales of taxation on higher and lower incomes, and on incomes earned and unearned. There are the usual promises of a free breakfast table which have been made, many times in the last thirty years, and depend for their fulfillment on the surplus available for such relief.

The social program involves housing, national insurance, health and education, with all the paraphernalia of associated topics. To enter into details is here impossible. Broadly, the position of Labor is that there should be more housing, a higher rate of insurance, an increased attention to health and a more abundant opportunity for education. In all these avenues of effort there is nothing essential that, given the occasion, might not be brought forward, let us say, by a sympathetic and progressive Conservative Minister, like Neville Chamberlain, or by Lloyd George and his "experts."

The whole of these schemes have to be translated into terms of cost. It may be taken for granted that, under Labor, the British budget will continue to be balanced. Hence, every concession to old age pensioners and mothers with babies—whatever be the concession—will have to be referred to the Treasury. Quite the most dangerous cry that a socially active government has to face is that it has sacrificed economy to expenditure.

An instance is education. In Great Britain, public education has always been something of a Cinderella. What the eager intellectuals in the Labor party wanted, even in 1923, was a raising of the school age to 15 years, and free "secondary" or high schools, with a maintenance grant for the children affected. Among local authorities, this is a serious proposition, and it will be seen whether the new government is ready to take its courage in both hands.

Unemployment Proposals

It may be assumed that Labor will not be able to hold office or to retain its unity without dealing with unemployment. In broad outline the issue is here simple. The unemployed already receive what is called "the dole"—really an insurance—which yields some kind of a maintenance. The question is whether the credit of the country shall or shall not be pledged to the extent of at least a billion dollars for the provision of work on roads, housing and other outlets for labor, still demobilized.

To that question Prime Minister Baldwin returned a negative answer. But the scheme of David Lloyd George was based on the use of public credit. The logic of the situation lies, then, in pursuing such a plan—quite the most definite yet put on paper—and on this issue MacDonald would be assured of Liberal support, which would at once raise his majority—we repeat, on this issue—to about eighty, even if, which is unlikely, all the Conservatives were to be against him.

The pledge of Lloyd George that his plan, if adopted, would end abnormal unemployment within a year is not a pledge to which Labor is a party. But there is strong economic backing, including the views of J. M. Keynes, for the claim that the interest and sinking fund of the unemployment loan, reckoned at 6 per cent, can be met without extra taxation by economies and the use of betterment on land developed.

The second urgent subject is the reorganization of the coal trade. Here again Labor is in a fortunate position. The entire problem has been worked out in two reports, the one standing in the name of Mr. Justice Sankey and the other standing in the name of Sir Herbert Samuel. The charge advanced by Labor and Liberalism against Prime Minister Baldwin has been that, with these documents in his hands, he did nothing. The question is now whether positive action is to be taken.

That the Prince of Wales was terribly shocked by what he saw in the northeastern coal fields is an open secret. That Prime Minister Baldwin objected to his visiting the coal fields in Wales is in substance the fact of the matter. It is thus inconceivable that Labor will be able to hold its forces intact unless it applies remedies to a situation admittedly deplorable.

At the same time let there be no mistake as to the magnitude of this or, indeed, of any of these problems. In the case of the mines, it is not merely a more or less nominal transference at a price of the landowner's royalties to the State that is involved. It is the closing of uneconomic pits, the consolidation of neighboring but separate companies, the provision of new machinery and the simplification of production and distribution that has to be undertaken. Also the displaced miners, numbering, let us say, 200,000 men, have to be transplanted, no easy or popular job, to unfamiliar surroundings and occupations at home and abroad.

In pursuing such a policy MacDonald would be in the same position regarding the Liberals as in the case of unemployment. Sir Herbert Samuel regains a seat at Westminster and it is the plan that he worked out which, in general terms, must be the basis of whatever is attempted.

If education, unemployment and the mines are handled with courage and good feeling, labor will be kept busy and will earn a solid prestige. The party includes many men and women who have given their lives to social service and are thoroughly versed in these complicated problems. The real weakness of the former Labor government was that, intent on gaining experience of office, it was self-educated rather than socially constructive.

About British foreign policy, there has always been a certain continuity, based on a strongly organized diplomatic service. But it is expected that the present change of administration will result in a real change in the international outlook. Whatever else happened during the election, it is at least certain that public opinion passed a vote of censure on Sir Austen Chamberlain. In Birmingham, the stronghold of his family, his majority of 7,643 was reduced to an odd 43 or thereabouts—this despite the fact that his brother, Neville, did very well. It is, indeed, a piquant circumstance that, at the Foreign Office, the most aristocratic of departments, Ramsay MacDonald rapidly established a high reputation.

In certain respects there appears to be no difference between the position of the new government and the old. Both administrations advocate peace, disarmament, the League of Nations, the Kellogg treaty and Anglo-American friendship. The question has been and is what should be the content of meaning included in these words. On the whole, it is alleged that Sir Austen Chamberlain emptied the words of practical significance. Certainly, the supporters of Ramsay MacDonald, at any rate, expect him to translate the words into achievements. Such optimism, of course, must be held subject to the obvious consideration that in diplomacy it takes two to arrive at an arrangement.

Faith in the Kellogg Pact

The Labor party includes many pacifists and even conscientious objectors. To the party as a whole the Kellogg pact is not simply something that may do good and can do no harm. It is the agreed basis of the new international order on which diplomacy should proceed to build the logical superstructure of a permanent peace throughout the world.

Coming to close quarters with a situation, admittedly of the utmost delicacy, we may point out that MacDonald not only endorses the pact of Locarno, but claims that it is the logical result of his own policy as Foreign Secretary. Toward France he is friendly. He has studied the French point of view and France has a definite place in his international sympathies. What he insists upon is, however, the right to be not less friendly with nations other than France, including Germany; and this is undoubtedly the attitude of Great Britain as a whole. The country considers that the war is over forever and that the peace should be a real peace.

In particular, MacDonald stands for the conviction that, whatever else happens, the telephone between Paris and London shall not cross lines with the telephone between London and Washington. Whatever the relations may be between Great Britain and the United States, at least they must be direct relations. It was the belief that Sir Austen Chamberlain allowed Paris to be included in his route to America, which was the real reason for the misgivings, well founded or ill-founded, during his term of office.

Hitherto the discussions of Anglo-American parity have been devoted to the size of navies, including cruisers. MacDonald has indicated his readiness to reopen the discussions with a consideration of the use of the two navies, whatever their size may be. In other words, he is prepared to examine what is meant by freedom of the seas and the right of blockade.

His argument is simple. Under the Kellogg pact, any war in which conceivably Great Britain could be engaged, is to be a war with "a mad-dog" nation, breaking its pledge to peace. It is only in such a war that, according to this reasoning, the British Navy could be used. Evidently Mr. MacDonald holds that an agreement along these lines might be usefully considered, in which event the problem of cruisers, dealt with later, might be seen in a somewhat different perspective.

The Labor party is unanimous in its support of President Hoover's appeal for an actual reduction of armaments. Indeed, it is held that Great Britain herself might save a large sum of money on her navy, army and aircraft. One reason why a better understanding with the United States has been so prominent a subject during the political campaign just concluded is a strong desire that nothing in British policy shall divert the force of President Hoover's initiative.

In the question of debts and reparations, it should be made clear, first of all, that under a Labor government the word of Great Britain, applied to her financial obligations, must be her bond. If there was anything in a recent speech by Philip Snowden that was capable of a different interpretation, it has been counteracted by other pronouncements.

Subject to these conditions, it is undeniable that Labor, in its heart of hearts, would like to see the whole tangled edifice of debts and reparations swept into the discard of a war that is remembered only as a nightmare. It is assumed that, at Washington, Stanley Baldwin might have obtained easier terms than he did obtain, and in many responsible quarters, Conservatism included, this opinion is repeated. At the same time, the policy of the Labor party, as disclosed up to the present, does not imply an association of the debt question with the question inherent in naval parity.

In 1923, Ramsay MacDonald recognized Russia and sought to negotiate with her a trade agreement. On taking office the Conservatives ceased to recognize Russia and the idea of a trade agreement lapsed. Again to recognize and develop trade with Russia is now an accepted plank of the Labor program. During the disarmament meetings at Geneva, Russia met the other powers, including Great

Britain and the United States. It is axiomatic that, after the lapse of four years, she has become not more revolutionary in her attitude toward society but less revolutionary. It is scarcely conceivable that Labor will be again embarrassed by an artifice like the publication of the Zinovieff letter. The whole atmosphere in Great Britain has changed. There is now no general strike, either pending or possible, and temperature is much reduced.

A problem now imminent is Indian reform. Here, again, the determining document, expected about November, will stand in the name of a Liberal, Sir John Simon. The Indian Communist, Saklatvala, has lost his seat, but there is here, none the less, a possibility that the Left wing of Labor will be vocal. Prime Minister MacDonald's attitude toward India and Egypt has been made unmistakably clear. He is a progressive, but he stands for British sovereignty or influence.

It must be remembered, in conclusion, that this is not the first Labor government, but the second. The position in 1929 is very different from the position in 1923. When first he took office Ramsay MacDonald knew that, compared with the Conservatives, his party was in a minority. Today he holds a majority over the Conservatives. In 1923 he was confessedly marking time. Today he has no choice but to attempt positive tasks. The budget of 1923 was merely correct. A Labor budget, if submitted next year, must be constructive. It is in order that things may get done that MacDonald has been returned to power.

Labor's Opposition

That the Conservative party will remain a solid and, on the whole, a hostile and formidable opposition, goes without saying. No mistakes made by Labor will be allowed to pass unnoticed. It will be an immense achievement if, despite the attrition of votes which usually afflicts a party in office, MacDonald is able to keep up the increase of Labor votes in the country and prepare the way for winning, at the next election, a clear majority over all parties in the House. Hitherto the rule has always been that a government is strongest on the day that it assumes official responsibility.

With a vote of 5,000,000 to their credit, the Liberals cannot be ignored. In the United States the third party, led by Theodore

Roosevelt, disappeared after its defeat. But it would be very dangerous to argue that the precedent applied to a third party in Great Britain. The persistence of the Liberals—be it futile or useful—is astonishing and thoroughly characteristic of national obstinacy. Believing that they have been the victims of an electoral grievance, they may be trusted, though at bay, to put up the usual fight. The period on which Parliament now enters is transitional. All that can be said is that, according to all the historical parallels, it will result in an ultimate realignment according to the two-party system, on which the normal working of the British Constitution has always depended.

Part 2

SOCIALISM AND FASCISM IN THE 1930's

THE MULTIPLE CHALLENGE of internal and external fascism, the depression, political disintegration, and a civil war dominated Socialist concerns in the 1930's. Socialists rarely seized the initiative, and were controlled by events much more than they cared to admit. The first two articles in this section deal with the failures of British Labor and German Social Democracy, the third and fourth with the Popular Front in France, and the final two with the Spanish tragedy.

P. W. Wilson examines the split within the British Labor party in 1931, the consequence of the collapse of the MacDonald Labor government over depression policies and its replacement by the MacDonald "National" government, which was in fact a Conservative government. MacDonald's rival, Arthur Henderson, the leader of what was left of the Labor party, is portrayed as a practical, bureaucratic politician, while the apostate MacDonald is seen as an idealist whose idealism was sapped by his encounter with the realities of British politics. Long-standing division within the Labor party widened into a chasm, argues Wilson, and the collapse of the party was almost inevitable. Simeon Strunsky, commenting upon his recent visit to Germany (in the summer of 1932), demonstrates how Socialists and workers had become too successful: they had benefited from the Weimar Republic without showing enthusiasm for it, at least in their official ideology, but were now its chief defenders at the very moment when it was being deserted by the middle classes and by youth. While it may be an exaggeration to claim that the educated classes had rallied to Hitlerism, it does indicate that Socialists and their followers were left on a sinking ship, and that they insisted upon following ordinary procedures when emergency measures were clearly necessary.

Emil Lengyel and P. J. Philip wrote about Léon Blum, Socialist Premier of the Popular Front government in France: Lengyel just prior to Blum's assumption of office, Philip after six months of the Blum experiment. Lengyel is concerned with the extraordinary tasks that faced Blum, whom he sees as a man of integrity and humanity, a "practical idealist." Lengyel emphasizes Blum's deep commitments to peace and to the fight against fascism, recognizing that a dreadful choice might have to be made between them, and he demonstrates that Blum's conception of the Popular Front was definitely not a revolutionary one. Philip, who had observed Blum's government through the summer of 1936, shows that the Premier had virtually reached an impasse by the fall when anything he did would be found wrong. Strikes, political turmoil, the impact of the Spanish Civil War had taken their toll, and the government was then "at the mercy of events."

Herbert L. Matthews was one of the most celebrated journalists of the Spanish Civil War, and Luis Araquistain was a major figure on the Left of the Spanish Socialist party. Both recognized that Spain during its civil war of 1936–1939 became an international battlefield where foreign powers cynically sought to manipulate events after their own selfish interests. Matthews wrote of the appeal of anarchism to Spaniards at a time when it was being severely criticized by Communists and other leading groups in Republican Spain; anarchism was later to be attacked and virtually crushed by these same elements. Arguing that anarchism derives from the Socialist ideal, Matthews presents a vivid account of the anarchist experiments in collectivization in 1936 and traces the history of anarchism's appeal in certain sections of the Iberian peninsula. Araquistain, who served as Ambassador to France while Largo Caballero was in power, wrote these three articles—grouped here under a single heading—after the defeat of the Spanish

Republic in the spring of 1939. For Araquistain, Largo Caballero was being cast for the role of tool of the Soviets when he resigned in the spring of 1937, unwilling to carry out their design to crush the Spanish revolution. His successor, the Socialist Juan Negrin, was a sorry dupe of Moscow, according to this former Socialist, and he denounces the subservience of the Spanish government to foreign instruction. Araquistain's is a powerful accusation, but its tragic truth has not been refuted by most historians.

MacDonald and Henderson: The Rivals

by P. W. Wilson

DEPRESSION MAKES strange bedfellows, but even amid the economic crisis, there was one change in the kaleidoscope of British politics that no prophet was so audacious as to foresee. James Ramsay MacDonald, the Socialist, sits as Prime Minister, with Stanley Baldwin, the Conservative, and Sir Herbert Samuel, the Liberal, at his side. That other Socialist, Arthur Henderson, leads an embittered Opposition.

It is no mere reshuffle of the cards. Lifelong loyalties are rent asunder. The protagonists in the duel that has begun under circumstances thus dramatic, have been at once comrades and contemporaries. Henderson's age is 68, MacDonald is 65. Together, they began their careers; together they achieved success. It is a tragedy, indeed, that, of such an association, this estrangement should be the end.

By birth, the rivals are Scots; yet with a difference. No one talking with Henderson, would detect the ominous fact that he was cradled in Glasgow. He migrated early to the Tyneside where he was apprenticed as a molder to the aristocracy of organized engineering and so became what England calls a north-countryman.

MacDonald was bred a clansman of no mean clan. Like Henderson, he may have agreed with Dr. Johnson that the most attractive scenery for a Scotsman is the road to England. But, with other Scots, he would accept no Tyne as his frontier. His river must be the Thames itself—what John Burns called liquid history—and it was mind, not "mud" of which he would be the molder. Like Barrie, like "the heids o' departments" where Caledonians enjoy a monopoly of promotion, MacDonald was the "lad o'pairts" who, wearing his old dominie's watch, might starve, but would read, write and dream his dreams.

Both men have been mystics first and only politicians as an expression of their mysticism. Henderson enrolled himself as an officer in the Salvation Army, and emerged a Methodist local preacher which he continues to be unto this day. MacDonald married an outspoken evangelical and brooded over the somber glories of Presbyterian psalmody.

MacDonald was the idealist. A theologian and economist, he absorbed John Knox and Karl Marx in parallel columns. His was a spacious internationalism and his friends were Jaurès of France, Bebel of Germany, Vandervelde of Belgium and Branting of Sweden. He sat at the feet of John Morley, collected intellectuals like a connoisseur, and traveled to the ends of the earth.

Henderson was the practical man. As an official, he became the complete trade unionist. His college was the municipality. At Newcastle he was a member of the City Council, and at Darlington he served as Mayor. If the workers called him "Uncle Arthur," it was not alone because of his rectitude and total abstinence. It was because he was one of themselves and did not want to be anything else. His abilities developed, his influence spread; he has worn a silk hat. But within his class he has not changed, and it is his class that, the other day, gave him a medal. It was Labor's order of merit.

In the language of Calvinism, both men desired that their election should be secure, not only in the heavens but on the earth; and they owed their start in politics to the friendly assistance of Liberals. MacDonald's patron was the once redoubtable "Tommy" Lough who sat for Islington; Henderson was the protégé of the great industrial family of Pease. But there was a new spirit abroad; and, in many MacDonalds, many Hendersons of the later 1890s, it was justified of its children.

Dark eyed, black haired, loose limbed, rich in voice, MacDonald, with his pocket poetry, was by far the most picturesque figure in the movement. The Lloyd George of Scotland, he was gifted with a superb sense of strategy, and as the architect of the Labor party, his plumb-line was never in doubt. It was independence. A man might believe what he liked. But he must stand pledged to one tabu. Under no circumstances must he appear on the capitalist platform, whether it be Liberal or Conservative. The ban was absolute, and it was recognized that the chief inquisitor, the most vigilant guardian of the distangling orthodoxy was not Snowden, not Thomas, and certainly not Henderson. It was MacDonald who, in his secretarial capacity, dotted the line along which authorized candidates must inscribe their names.

Steady, solid and companionable, Henderson, with his serious face and his genial smile, was among the trade unionists who submitted. But within the new party, thus formed, there was a cleavage of sentiment. The Socialist intellectuals, led by MacDonald, were few and were suspected of being the tail that wags the dog. In 1908, therefore, it was Henderson who, as a typical man among the many, was elected leader of the party in the House of Commons. MacDonald was his second in command, and, in the strictly industrial field, that position has continued to this day. During the succession of labor disputes which culminated in the general strike of 1926, MacDonald was swept aside and only consulted as a courtesy. If anybody at all made a difference it was trade unionist leaders like Thomas, Hartshorn, Barnes and, last but not least, Arthur Henderson.

In the House of Commons, men are judged as men. Manifestly, it was MacDonald who displayed that elusive, indefinable quality called the Parliamentary gift. As a critic of Sir Edward Grey's foreign policy, as a student of India and South Africa, he looked beyond the narrow horizon of the workshop and surveyed the world itself. In 1911 the Labor party decided that, for the peculiar job of talking in dialectic with capitalists on the two front benches, MacDonald was, perhaps, the best equipped of the competitors. He was chosen leader and, a little flushed, it was Henderson who now sat in the second seat.

For twenty years the game of seesaw has continued, and the play included two supreme emergencies. In August, 1914, there was the war, and in August, 1931, there was finance. On both occasions, the political issue was essentially the same. Was it or was it not the duty of independent Labor to join a national government? In 1914, MacDonald said No, and Henderson said Yes. In 1931, MacDonald has said Yes, and Henderson has said No. In both cases, MacDonald voiced a statesmanship which depends on the inner light, and in both cases, Henderson carried the trade unions.

In August, 1914, there was, frankly, an agreement to differ, and within the Labor party, a severance of personal and political relations was avoided. Indeed, events rapidly drew Henderson and MacDonald once more into their former alliance. Over Russia, they have always seen eye to eye. As a Minister in the War Cabinet, Henderson was convinced that MacDonald should be sent to the conference at Stockholm, there to negotiate in 1917 with the Bolsheviki.

The men shared a common humiliation. Even Henderson could not persuade the Seamen's Union to provide MacDonald with a passage, and on a well-remembered occasion Henderson himself was left by his colleagues in the Lloyd George Cabinet, waiting "on the doormat." It was an insult that Labor resented, and Henderson's Canossa became his salvation. In the pacifist swing to socialism of which MacDonald was the martyr in resurrection, Henderson also became a certainty. By "showing him the gate" the capitalists had supplied him with precisely the credentials that he needed.

But with Labor reunited, there arose again the former question that now involved the most glittering of all political prizes within the British Empire. For the leader of the Labor party might expect to be sent for by the King. He was Prime Minister-elect.

As a compromise a third man, J. R. Clynes, was selected, and the trade unionists assumed that his position was unassailable. They reckoned without their MacDonald. In 1922 he mobilized every doubtful Labor member, caught the other side napping and beat Clynes—it was said by the narrowest of margins. Such are the chances that direct the fate of nations.

In the first of Labor's Cabinets MacDonald insisted on serving not only as Prime Minister but at the Foreign Office. Henderson was thus no more than Home Secretary, a post that requires great judgment but seldom affords an opportunity for a brilliant success.

When, therefore, Henderson was appointed in Labor's second administration to MacDonald's office of Foreign Secretary, there were those who assumed that he would be merely the rubber stamp in the master hand. They were much mistaken. As diplomatist, Henderson has been in every respect the equal of his predecessor, and MacDonald's monopoly of international acumen was brought, somewhat abruptly, to a definite end. He ceased to be his own Richelieu.

It was darkly hinted that MacDonald did not love the proletariat quite as fervently as in earlier days. His tweeds began to look ducal. In order to spend one day at Lossiemouth, he would risk two trips in an airplane. Like the automobile that a Scottish neighbor gave him, it was all suitable enough for a Prime Minister in a capitalist party. But plain working men who had been warned by MacDonald for years to mistrust such capitalist politics, did not understand a leader who, as they thought, was apt to hobnob with peers. It may be said that such details are mere trifles. They are. But it is these trifles that contribute to the small talk of a nation, and it is the small talk that matters to the small-town mind.

When the test came the trifles turned many a scale. A split was inevitable. But it was not inevitable that the split would leave Henderson with the entire rank and file of Labor solidly at his back. For reasons, admittedly urgent, MacDonald joins the select company of those who, accused of turning the coat, are cast out by their friends as renegades and applauded as heroes only by their foes. This is the disillusion that has rallied a stricken party to the leadership of his opponent.

After all, nothing in England happens for the first time, and there have been precedents. We may recall Thomas Wentworth, the Puritan friend of John Hampden who advocated the Declaration of Right, yet turned Cavalier, and as Earl of Strafford was beheaded by Parliament. There was Charles James Fox, who assailed Lord North for years over his treatment of the American Colonies, only to join "the enemy of mankind" in a coalition with the Tories. There was Sir Robert Peel, the Protectionist, who allied himself with Bright and Cobden in what Disraeli denounced as an "organized hypocrisy" and so secured free trade in food. There was Joseph Chamberlain, who, "a Home Ruler before Gladstone," yet joined the Unionist party which smashed Home Rule. So famous, so infuriating are the somersaults of sagacity.

For MacDonald had not seemed to be merely a politician. It was as an apostle of a social gospel that he appealed to the people, and when he preached the downfall of capitalism there were millions who really believed him. Henderson never said as much about all this as MacDonald, and had the great renunciation fallen to his lot, there would have been the less to unsay.

Whatever may be the verdict of history, there is no doubt as to Labor's judgment, here and now. It can be expressed most politely in the language of the immortal lament which Robert Browning dedicated with such terrible scorn to his "lost leader"—the Wordsworth who became poet laureate. Socialists say of their "Mac" how they

> * * * *had loved him so, followed him, honored him,*
> *Lived in his mild and magnificent eye,*
> *Learned his great language, caught his clear accents,*
> *Made him their pattern to live and to die.*

On a champion of Labor who—as these stalwarts suppose—"breaks from the van and the freeman" the immediate verdict has been

> *Let him never come back to us,*
> *There would be doubt, hesitation and pain,*
> *Forced praise on our part, the glimmer of twilight,*
> *Never glad confident morning again.*

Yet Henderson's task is none the easier for that. What he has to do is to deal with the hopes that MacDonald aroused, the suspicions that he insinuated, the theories that he promulgated; and already the disciples who, in good faith, accepted the gospel, are saying with Maxton that if such a prophet as "Ramsay" cannot be trusted at Westminster, it is time for direct action. To keep the Maxtons within the Parliamentary system is Henderson's urgent business. The pound sterling has been saved but, on a different plane, confidence has been shaken.

It is a century and a half since the House of Commons began to furnish the ring where rival statesmen could fight out their duels till death do them part. For twenty years, Pitt, the Prime Minister, and Fox, the leader of the Opposition, confronted one another as MacDonald and Henderson confront one another today; and in a splendid simile these Titans of debate were compared by Byron to mountains in Greece—"Athos and Ida with a dashing sea of eloquence between." In such conflict did an enraged Gladstone thunder imprecatory perorations at a cool and cynical Disraeli, while thus it was that a forensic Asquith overcame a dialectical Balfour and his bodyguard of gilded nobility.

To Parliamentarians of the old school, if any are left, there has been, obviously a break with the past. The debate is like Shakespeare in modern dress. Speech is plain, brief, direct, and there are no quotations from the classics. But if the costume is changed, the parts in their essence, are the same. The Montagues still fight the Capulets. The ins and the outs are unreconciled.

It is beneath the surface that the drama fascinates. In a land where the King and Queen still reign, where princes and princesses still open bazaars and lay foundation stones of useful edifices, where dukes, marquesses, earls, viscounts and barons are still ranged according to the five orders of the peerage, where cities are ruled by a Lord Mayor and dioceses are blessed by a Lord Bishop, where Admirals and Generals and viceroys and judges glow in the glory of their uniforms, their velvet and ermine, their stars and garters and ribands and medals, who would have thought it conceivable that the titular leadership of the Commons on both sides of the House should pass out of the hands of the older parties, whether they be Liberal or Conservative, and that the accepted spokesmen of Parliament, once the best club in London, should be two Socialists who have devoted their careers to proclaiming the failure of what they described with inflammatory scorn as the capitalist system? The irony of it is completed by the insinuation that it was the bankers, of all people, who conspired to achieve an incredible result.

German Democracy's New Test

by Simeon Strunsky

ADOLF HITLER, after a Reichstag election which netted him only a little more than one-third of the popular vote instead of the majority confidently predicted, nevertheless felt justified in demanding of President Hindenburg that he be placed in control of Germany with the full powers of "a Mussolini." Apparently the Nazi leader believes that votes should be evaluated qualitatively rather than quantitatively. His 37 per cent of the German electorate, consisting of resolute, patriotic, "real" Germans, would by this test far outweigh the anti-Hitler majority consisting of outlaw Communists, traitorous Socialists and bigoted and misguided Centrists. From the Nazi viewpoint there can be no denying that of the people who count, or ought to count, in Germany, an overwhelming majority is lined up behind Hitler.

In this selective sense, rather than by the weighing of absolute majorities, it is indeed true that German democracy has suffered a decline. To be sure, measured by the votes for the various parties in the Reichstag election, the shift in power from Left to Right is far from revolutionary in extent. If we omit the Communists, who will make trouble for any government but who obviously will stop short of joining with Hitler to overthrow the German Republic, there is a possible anti-republican majority of less than fifty in a

Reichstag of more than 600 members, and that majority is by no means sure.

By the test of numbers, then, the decline in the fortunes of German democracy is not alarming. But what is much more disconcerting is the fact that the democratic cause does not enjoy the support of any but a small fraction of the German middle classes. The republican bloc—Socialists, Centre and minor groups—consists of workingmen, peasants and small traders, with a remnant of democratic elements from the middle and upper classes. It is regrettable, and it may yet turn out to be ominous, that the German Republic has failed to win to itself that section of the German people from which should come its principal leadership. The educated classes and the principal bearers of German culture have, unfortunately for the cause of popular government, rallied in overwhelming numbers, according to all reports, to the Hitler brand of fascism.

For the historian the alignment of classes in present-day Germany constitutes an anomaly, or, at least, a reversal of the record that amounts almost to revolution. Historically, the rise and development of democratic institutions and parliamentary government have accompanied and characterized the rise of the middle classes to power. Representative government is the form in which the emerging business classes have everywhere asserted themselves against the old feudalism. On the other hand, until very recently the prevalent Socialist doctrine showed no exceptional fondness for the democratic parliamentary State, which it was the custom among Socialists to describe as only a device for the defense of the capitalist system against the exploited working classes. Bernard Shaw still holds to this opinion, and that is why he is all for the dictatorship method of putting across the proletarian revolution against a middle class entrenched behind the institutions of free, representative government.

But in Germany today the principal champions of free government are the workers, as represented in the Socialist and Catholic trade unions. They are outspoken in the defense of what a very few years ago used to be regarded by Socialists as a "bourgeois" set of values. The basic democratic liberties and privileges—freedom of speech, press and assembly and the franchise—which Socialist orators were in the habit of making quite secondary to the economic interests of the working class, now occupy the most prominent place in the Socialist agenda. The chief task of the moment is the safeguarding of the German Republic, even at the very serious sacrifice of their immediate class interests.

This is by no means pure idealism. The German workers have prospered under the republic. Their material condition shows the same enhancement in the main that has been recorded elsewhere among the industrial workers. Real wages in Germany since the war are from 10 to 15 per cent higher for the skilled trades and probably 25 per cent higher for unskilled labor. If we go back an entire generation, to the beginning of the present century, we shall doubtless find the gain in German living standards to be very much what it has been found to be in the United States and Great Britain.

A recent study by the London School of Economics, in continuation of Charles Booth's monumental "Life and Labour of the People in London," asserts that in the space of a generation the well-being of the British people has increased by one-third. This is very nearly the same rate of progress reported by Paul H. Douglas for the United States over approximately the same period. If the actual gains in Germany should turn out to fall somewhat short of this figure, there would be enough reason for the difference in the economic consequences of Germany's defeat in the World War. And in Germany, as in the other countries mentioned, by far the greater part of the gain achieved in the course of a generation was registered in the years after the war.

It may sound a bit odd to speak of the well-being of the German workers at a time when the unemployed in Germany number 6,000,000. But normal conditions of once upon a time cannot obviously be compared with the highly exceptional situation today. It is not yet established that the future norm for German labor is 6,000,000 men and women out of work. If the comparison is made between the status of the German worker, say, in the year 1911 and his position as late as the Fall of 1930, the gains will be very nearly as they have been described above.

And for that matter, even in the face of the staggering burden of unemployment today, and the mass of human privation which it connotes, it may be argued that the well-being of the German working population as a whole, counting the employed and the idle, is higher than it was before the war. The average basic weekly "dole," as a result of the drastic cuts promulgated in President Hindenburg's decree of June 16, now stands at about 9 reichsmarks; and it is hardly necessary to expatiate on what a subsistence level of $2.25 a week must mean. Yet this unemployment allowance of 32 cents a day is nearly one-half the average minimum wage in German industry in the years immediately before the war. In general, it might be said for Europe as a whole that unemployment relief averages up to 40 per cent of pre-war wages.

The comparative arithmetic of the whole situation is simple. You have in Germany today more than four-fifths of all gainfully occupied persons still at work, at wages that are 33 per cent higher than a generation ago. You have the remaining workers living on unemployment relief that leaves them only 40 per cent as well off as they were a generation ago. The total income of all the German workers is still higher than it used to be a generation ago—even with 6,000,000 persons idle today.

That this arithmetic is not altogether fantastic, that it portrays a very real element in the economic and social situation the world over, is shown by one simple fact: and that is an absence of industrial and social unrest that may well be called extraordinary after three years of acute crisis. In the face of 6,000,000 unemployed and the recent sharp slash in unemployment pay—and quite putting aside Hitler—the gain of about half a million Communist votes in two years is not astonishing. Actually the Communist percentage in the recent election was just about what it was two years ago, before the full force of the economic crisis had developed.

The temper of the German Communists today is noticeably less militant than it was two years ago; the Communists were actually willing to discuss an alliance with the Socialists before the election. In general, it may be noted that the word "revolution" today comes most often out of non-labor mouths. The direst forecasts for our capitalist civilization are promulgated by bourgeois seers. There is a strong belief among Socialists the world over that the college presidents are altogether too pessimistic about the future of capitalism.

When the German workingmen, in the great majority, fervently dedicate themselves to the defense of a democratic régime under which 6,000,000 workers are without employment, the reason must be that even under such extreme conditions the workers find their situation to be not intolerable. In Hitler and reaction they discern a threat to the gains which they have made over a long period of years and which have by no means been wiped out in the present crisis. Nor is the progress made by the German workers under the Weimar régime to be measured solely in wages and other immediate material advantages. Democracy has meant for the German masses, in kind if not in degree, that Opportunity which American democracy has connoted for a hundred years, which has made America and Opportunity synonymous. The children of the German working classes have won access to the institutions of higher education which before the war were regarded as the exclusive possession of the upper classes; the elementary Volkschule was for the children of the poor. Higher education in turn is the doorway to the government service, which since the war has to some extent been democratized. And in general the years since the armistice have brought to the German working class a fuller individual existence and a larger share in the nation's life.

The rally of the German middle-class parties to Hitler is largely due to the feeling that the gains made by the German masses under the republican régime have been attained at the expense of the rest of the nation, and particularly of the bourgeois elements. The argument, as commonly stated, is that the German middle classes have been the heaviest sufferers from the war and its aftermath. They were ruined by the currency inflation of 1922–23 which wiped out investments and savings. They were victimized by emergency rent laws which came near to being confiscation. They have been the victims of a set of circumstances which Hitler has characterized as The System but which may be more justly described as an inevitable displacement of power and prestige inevitably following upon the disasters of the war. The republican régime is associated in the average German middle-class mind with defeat, national humiliation, economic decline and, in general, a life of straitened opportunity.

German university students are in overwhelming majority with Hitler because, it is said, high-spirited youth is impatient of the low estate to which Germany has fallen among the nations. But it is not denied that student sentiment also reflects present economic difficulties and an uncertain future. The professions are overcrowded. So is the government service. Business opportunities are not what they might be if business were not staggering under the burden of taxes piled up by a socialistic government to pay for its class policies. In short, the middle classes have been voting Hitler in protest against the unhappy condition to which they have been reduced by the dominant German democracy. That is the familiar case.

Now, it would be idle to deny that war, defeat and subsequent internal disorganization have imposed heavy sacrifices upon the German middle classes. In the collapse of the currency and the destruction of investment values it is obvious that they must have been peculiarly the sufferers. Germany in defeat obviously does not offer the same opportunities for useful labor and personal achievement and distinction that prevailed when Germany dominated the Continent. Yet all this does not explain why the movement away from the republic and toward Hitler should have seized upon the German middle classes, not when things were at their worst, but when things were very greatly improved.

It is probably true that in 1930 the material condition of the country was still in some respects below the pre-war level. But there is no denying that conditions in 1930 showed a vast improvement over the situation half a dozen years earlier. Yet in 1924–25 a large section of the German middle classes followed Gustav Stresemann in adhering to the Republican régime. In 1930 they flocked to Hitler. How is this to be explained?

It will be a help to finding the answer if we first dispose of the argument that economic distress and a general decline in well-being have been chiefly responsible for the defection of the German middle classes from the democratic cause. There is no intention here to enter upon an appraisal of German prosperity, of the celebrated German "capacity." Yet it should be possible in a very rough way to check up on some of the items just cited, in respect to the unhappy condition to which the German middle classes have been reduced.

1. It was no doubt true in the years immediately after the war that many middle-class parents could no longer afford to send their

sons to the university, or could do so only at the most extraordinary sacrifices. But what are the latest available facts? University attendance has almost doubled since the war. In 1911–12 the students numbered 68,000, excluding foreigners. In 1930–31 they numbered nearly 113,000. To some extent this increase will be explained by the larger number of students from working-class families, as part of the democratization process at work since the war. But in the great mass the swollen university enrollment means a rush of students from middle-class families. This suggests a more cheerful financial condition in middle-class homes than we have been asked to visualize.

2. Many of Hitler's recruits are said to be young men who see no chance to establish themselves in the professions; these callings, together with the government service, constituting in every country the principal field of opportunity, for children of the middle classes, after business. The German census of 1907 recorded 1,328,000 persons in the government service and the "free" professions in a population of 55,000,000. The census of 1925 enumerated 1,502,000 persons so occupied in a population of 62,000,000. It is exactly the same proportion. The field of opportunity for the educated youth of Germany in this respect does not seem to have been reduced. To be sure, the rush to the universities has unquestionably thrown upon the intellectual labor market more workers than the country can absorb, but that is a condition which prevails everywhere.

3. The collapse of the currency in 1923 and other vicissitudes destroyed the savings of the German people. By 1931 the process of building up new reserves had made considerable progress. In that year the savings banks had 11,000,000,000 marks on deposit as against 18,000,000,000 in 1911. In describing the "impoverishment" of the middle classes, it is not always mentioned that savings were back to two-thirds of the pre-war level.

4. The German national income in 1929 was officially estimated at $17,500,000,000. This would make the national wealth in that year somewhere between $80,000,000,000 and $90,000,000,000, which is above every estimate of the national wealth before the war. It is twice the wealth of Germany in 1924 as estimated by Dr. Luther, then Minister of Finance. In other words, Germany

was nearly twice as rich two years ago when Hitler scored his first big successes as in 1924 when the moderate Stresemann policies were dominant.

5. Great Britain's exports in 1913 were worth £635,000,000 and in 1930 were worth £658,000,000, an increase of about 3 per cent. German exports in 1913 were worth 10,000,000,000 marks, and in 1930 12,000,000,000 marks, an increase of 20 per cent.

6. The census of 1907 recorded 1,622,000 persons in domestic employment. In 1925 there were 1,643,000 persons so employed. Relative to the population this is a decline of 10 per cent, but an impoverished middle class should have cut down much more sharply on a luxury which is among the first to suffer in hard times.

7. It may not be altogether irrelevant that the number of visitors at the German spas and health resorts in 1929 was about 30 per cent higher than in the year before the war. More than nine-tenths of such visitors, contrary to the general belief, are Germans. Allowance should be made for a larger number of patients than before the war at the public sanatoria and drawn from the working classes. It is also likely that fewer Germans spend their vacations abroad than before the war. It would still be true that the German middle classes, from which the resorts draw most of their visitors, seem to be in a position to seek health and recreation as they did before the war.

8. More than a separate chapter might be written about the extraordinary development of sports, athletics and the outdoor life. This will be true of every country on earth since the war, but it is the impression of at least one recent visitor that nowhere has the vogue grown faster than in Germany. Two years ago the athletic and sports organizations had between 7,000,000 and 8,000,000 members. The gymnastic societies (Turnvereine) alone accounted for 3,000,000 members. The German Football Association had 1,000,000 members. It would be rather difficult to say how many of these millions come from the middle classes and how many from the working classes. But it is impossible to take note of the ardor with which the German people has gone in for play and outdoor recreation and reconcile it with the theory of an economically prostrate and spiritually bankrupt nation, driven by bitter circumstance to register its protest against the existing democratic régime by voting for Hitler.

There would thus seem to be scant justification for the familiar theory that about the year 1929 the German middle classes turned definitely away from the republican régime and toward the Fascist standard under the pressure of material circumstance. At that time the prosperity of the German people, and of the German middle classes with others, could stand comparison with pre-war records. What is of greater moment in making a people contented or discontented is the question whether things are going up or going down, and in 1929–30 German affairs were decidedly on the upward grade. This would be true, also, for Germany's position in the world. The middle classes were supposed to be driven into Hitler's arms by their bitter economic condition at a time when they were really growing wealthy. So they are described as turning to Hitler in resentment against Germany's inferior position among the nations, at a time when Germany's rehabilitation in the international sphere was making rapid progress.

Is not there, in Germany's returning prosperity, the real explanation? The middle-class majority may have lined up with Hitler against the democratic system not because the republican régime kept them poor and weak, but because under the republican régime by the year 1929 the middle classes were growing strong and well-to-do. It is not really a case of their seceding from democracy but of their never having been converted to democracy. Only they needed to recuperate from their undeniably harrowing experiences in the years after the war before asserting themselves against the dominant democratic influences. By the beginning of 1930 they seem to have felt themselves strong enough to make their bid for power, and Hitler came forward to formulate the challenge. Whether, as a result of the election and the stopping of Hitler, middle-class sentiment will try to find a truce with democracy or will carry on the war, is among the issues to be resolved in Germany's highly complicated immediate future.

France Tries Another Pilot

by Emil Lengyel

FRANCE ONCE AGAIN moves in an atmosphere of crisis. She stands guard over an old civilization, yet her own future remains uncertain. Only one thing now appears relatively sure—that in the months ahead the Third Republic will be guided by Léon Blum, leader of the Socialist party. That much was decided in the recent Parliamentary elections when the anti-Fascist Popular Front, composed of Radical Socialists, Socialists and Communists, won a majority of the seats in the Chamber.

Blum is thus taking command of the forces aligned against fascism. His will be the task of representing France in her dealings with Hitler and Mussolini, and under his leadership France must attempt to restore the prestige of the League of Nations. He will have to meet the problems of the franc and the gold standard. On him will fall the burdens of unemployment, of an unbalanced national budget. Not since the days of Clemenceau and Poincaré has a French Premier been forced to wrestle with so many or such critical issues of statecraft.

The man who faces all these problems is neither in temperament nor in program the traditional "strong man." On the contrary, he is an intellectual. His is an analytical mind, interested in first causes and ultimate effects—the mind of a scholar and also of a practical idealist.

At the Chamber of Deputies, in the Salle des Pas Perdus, Blum may be easily recognized, for he is always surrounded by people who seek his advice and help. His youthful step does not betray his 64 years. His dark eyes still look upon life with interest and curiosity. To the host of caricaturists who are constantly picturing him, his walrus mustache is an unmitigated delight. As a speaker Blum is sparing in the use of gestures, although he knows how to use his hands expressively. His voice is dramatic, well modulated, but there is nothing in it of the theatrical. He is the picture of alertness, this man who, despite his boundless energy, is a master of conversation which recalls the grand style of nineteenth century drawing rooms.

The Chamber always listens to Blum in hushed silence—its greatest compliment—and Socialist assemblies regard him as their unrivaled star. Spurning oratorical flourish, he is careful not to insult his audiences by talking down to them. His speeches always are loaded with arguments and, even when a bit heavy, are as logical as mathematical deductions.

Blum is often twitted for being a "millionaire Socialist," but all France knows that his affluence does not prevent his championing the little man, of whose problems he has deep knowledge.

His apartment on the Boulevard de Montparnasse, where I called not long ago, bears the marks of unobtrusive wealth. In a salon reminiscent of the early days of the Third Republic I could admire his taste. The carpets were well matched, the heavy furniture reflected the spirit of serious study, but a few Sèvres vases lightened the generally ponderous effect. On Blum's long desk stood a statuette of his friend and mentor, Jean Jaurès, the great Socialist leader who was assassinated at the outbreak of the World War. The room was crammed with books on sociology and economics, but there were also some volumes of the Greek and Latin classics and fine editions of poetry, from Homer to Paul Valéry.

Blum spoke about war and peace, the subject closest to his heart. Although he realizes that humanity is confronted by a world crisis, he does not despair. He was willing to answer a question about the French attitude toward war.

"You may canvass all members of the Chamber," he said "beginning with the Royalists and coming around to the Communists, without finding a single one who favors war. On this point all Frenchmen compose a common front. War has become so abhorrent to us that even our former jingoes oppose it. Nor do we seem to have the type of extreme radical who wants to see the way to a new social order lighted by a world conflagration.

"War has taught us a great lesson, for the resulting poverty and moral breakdown disturb the social order which is the Frenchman's ideal. If we are to accomplish the change advocated by socialism we must fervently hope for peace, which is an indispensable prerequisite."

When Léon Blum speaks of peace his eyes sparkle and his words resound. He likes to quote Goethe: "Let us rather suffer from injustice than from war."

"One of the serious problems of our time," he continued, "is a sort of war psychosis—and it seems to be gaining ground. Many people talk about war's inevitability, thereby talking themselves into a state of war-mindedness. There's the real danger. They are creating an atmosphere of fatalism which leads to indifference in the face of the war menace. We must combat this attitude with all our might."

In the Populaire, the chief paper of the Socialist party, Blum has affirmed his unshaken belief in collective security. He wants peace based on a general limitation of armaments and enforced by a vigorous League of Nations. He wants full agreement between Britain and France.

During the course of a long Parliamentary career, Blum has often had things to say on international problems. His general solution is given by what is called the Blum formula—security through arbitration and disarmament. And here he dissents from Edouard Herriot, whose more popular formula is security first, then arbitration and then disarmament.

Since the elections Blum has made it clear that he hopes to meet the Fascist danger by establishing a strong government. In a recent address to the Socialist party's executive council he declared: "The Cabinet will be under your control, but it must have full power." Foreseeing an attempt by the Right to seize power, Blum warned solemnly: "We are not an isolated few. Behind us are massed the millions and they will not tolerate any defiance of their will."

Blum has outlined a vast public works program to take care of unemployment. Since he is anxious first of all to stimulate business activity to a point where all will have opportunities for work, he scoffs at the thought that he might undertake revolutionary change, thus precipitating tumult and disorder. He is definitely opposed to devaluation of the franc, perhaps because he is in constant touch with the masses and knows how depreciation of the franc would injure millions of thrifty Frenchmen. He has also announced that he would like France to reach an understanding with America in regard to the war debt.

Does M. Blum regard socialism as feasible in our own time? He admits frankly that he cannot perceive the maturity of socialism which he considers essential for its practical application. In capitalism he sees a rich uncle whose estate socialism will inherit, and thus he refuses to endanger an inheritance of the future.

Socialism is democracy, he says, and the democratic idea means equality. But true equality depends upon both political and social equality. "Socialism knows the dangers of victorious but sterile movements, victorious in that they have gained political power, sterile in that they cannot use it for social change."

Blum has often stated that the success of a collective society is dependent upon a definite Socialist majority in Parliament. Accordingly, a heterogeneous majority of Radicals, Communists and Socialists such as Blum must use is not the proper mechanism to inaugurate a socialized State.

It was a sheltered life into which Léon Blum was born in 1872. His father, a wealthy silk merchant of Paris, came from a Jewish family of Alsatian origin. The son, though a precocious youth, was, after all, a patriotic French boy who shouldered his toy gun and led his gang into battle against the "Prussians" with "Revanche" on his lips.

At school he was particularly brilliant in classics and mathematics, subjects in which he sometimes excelled his teachers. He not only delighted in translating Greek and Latin verse into French, but he tried to compose verse in Virgil's language. As a youth he stood aloof from politics, and it was only with half-amused indifference that he watched the early struggles of the Third Republic.

At the Lycée Henry IV, Blum was a scholastic leader. One of his schoolmates was André Gide whose rise to literary prominence was even then predicted. Blum placed his own literary efforts in La Conque, a not-too-modest magazine of poetry of which he was an editor. His editorship was in part due to his ability to meet the demands of an insistent printer for money. One of the contributors, Paul Valéry, was later to be hailed as the greatest French poet of the day.

When La Conque died prematurely Blum had to find another outlet for his work. Fate brought him to Marcel Proust, then far from fame, who placed his stories in a magazine of the advance-guard, Banquet. Later he began to contribute to the Revue Blanche, which on occasion listed the name of Anatole France in its table of contents.

Ultimately Blum was graduated from the Ecole Normale Supérieure, the most difficult school in France, and the traditional school for famous Frenchmen. Apparently he was cut out for a literary career, and he was in fact well established in literary circles when a storm broke, opening a new period in his life. It also marked a turning point in French history.

For three years Captain Dreyfus had been on Devil's Island, his case all but forgotten. Blum, who remembered it but vaguely, suddenly had his interest aroused by a friend. He studied the evidence: suddenly he believed that Dreyfus was innocent. There had been a monstrous miscarriage of justice.

France at the end of the century was dominated by the Dreyfus Affair. Into its quarrels and debates Blum plunged with all the enthusiasm of youth. He thrilled to Zola's tremendous indictment in "J'accuse." He fell under the spell of the Socialist, Jean Jaurès, whose place he was destined to inherit.

Blum's fate was now decided, although for a while literature still laid claim to his energies. He worked as a dramatic and literary critic, then obtained a government job at the State Council. He began to earn a reputation as an unusually eloquent lawyer.

Since the World War Blum, except for a brief period, has led the French Socialists. His daily editorials in the Populaire are probably commented upon more than any newspaper articles in France. Although one of the most powerful members of the Chamber, he has in the past consistently refused to enter or lead a government, contending that premature participation might compromise the future chances of socialism. His foes have called him a Cabinet-wrecker because he has done so much to overthrow conservative Ministries.

While few Deputies have been so exposed to attack as Blum, the number of his admirers has steadily grown. When he returned to the Chamber a few years ago after a short absence Poincaré, a political opponent, welcomed him with the words: "We need your light and counsel, Monsieur. It is well for France that men like you should sit in the Chamber."

The affection of millions was dramatically demonstrated last March after Blum had been attacked and wounded by a group of Royalists. Not only the Ministers, the Chamber and the Socialists, but countless other Frenchmen expressed their sympathy and admiration.

Now Blum is about to take over the government, for he has come to believe that conditions today demand sacrifices from the head of the largest party in Parliament. Whatever record his administration may have, it is certain that there have been few statesmen in the Third Republic whose work has been anticipated with such keen interest as that of Léon Blum.

Blum Navigates a Rough Political Sea

by P. J. Philip

PARIS

OUT OF Spain's civil war has sprung an ominous threat to international peace. Half of Europe has taken sides, however much the dictators may protest their intention not to intervene. Berlin and Rome have openly recognized General Francisco Franco's government. Moscow is helping Barcelona and Madrid all that it can—although perhaps much less than is alleged. London is trying desperately to keep clear and at the same time maintain enough authority to stave off for a little time the break of the war clouds which seem to be gathering even more ominously in the Mediterranean than on the Rhine.

English opinion is divided. Communism is disliked there; so is anarchy; so is the disturbance of business. Most Englishmen are inclined to argue that fascism of either the Italian or the German form is better than Russian or any other kind of communism. But Mussolini's conquest of Ethiopia, his disregard of the League of Nations covenant and other engagements and Hitler's reoccupation of the Rhineland and his rearmament program are equally unpleasant matters for thought.

Fortunately for Prime Minister Baldwin and Foreign Secretary

Eden there is little public sidetaking—far less than there was last year over Ethiopia. Disgust with both parties in Spain is perhaps responsible. So Baldwin and Eden can wait for others to make mistakes.

In France it is different. Opinion here is far more clamorous, far more insistent. "Airplanes for Spain—action by Blum" was the refrain which masses of people shouted as they marched through the streets of Paris last Sunday in tribute to the memory of Premier Léon Blum's colleague, Roger Salengro. Even within the Cabinet there are elements which keep pressing for intervention, for France to throw her hat into the ring on the side of what is called liberalism and democracy.

Only those who, if any other government than Blum's were in power, would be calling for stern notes and menaces to Berlin and Rome are hesitant and keep preaching non-intervention. They have discovered that they are anti-Bolshevist first and only anti-German afterward.

Prime Minister Baldwin can do almost anything he likes so long as he does not allow the British flag to be trampled on. Premier Blum is in this quandary: that almost anything he does will be found wrong, both by a section of his supporters and by all of his opponents.

Bruised in spirit by the suicide of his friend Salengro; harassed by internal difficulties which seem to keep surging up like waves, however actively he plies his broom; opposed bitterly by those on both wings who refuse to put the interests of France before their private quarrels and doctrines, his task of keeping the peace and insuring it is ten times more difficult than that of those others who are playing this enormous game of bluff with Barcelona as its center, disregardful of whether war may come. And perhaps on him more than on any of these others will depend whether war can be avoided.

In a portrait gallery of contemporaries the face and figure of Léon Blum might pass for insignificant. He has none of the commanding aspect of Mussolini or Stalin and does not go in for the pageantry of Hitler. His long, lean legs, his out-thrown feet and his wide-brimmed black felt hat of somewhat Latin Quarter fashion are good cartoon material. The drooping corners of his mustache give him an air of melancholy; his eyeglasses, which are always precariously perched on his long, straight nose, contribute a suggestion of awkwardness.

Any one seeing him for the first time and noting casually the fineness of his features would set him down as a scholarly man, somewhat of a dreamer, who would be likely to be hesitant and unreliable in emergency. And such, during most of his twenty years in French politics, was his reputation, at least, among his opponents. But even they respected him and admired the clarity and precision of his thinking and public speech.

When, having been beaten at an election, Blum returned to Parliament after a two years' absence, Poincaré, who was then Premier, halted the speech he was making to turn toward him and welcome him back. It was, as it is so often, a time of crisis in the Chamber, and although Blum's return had been at the expense of one of Poincaré's own Nationalist supporters he paid this generous compliment: "This house needs minds like yours and men like you."

It was the tribute of one honest man to another. They might differ in doctrine, for Poincaré was one of the last great defenders in France of the bourgeois régime. He believed in it, in the middle classes from which he had sprung, in the virtue of accumulated wealth and of the laws protecting wealth.

Blum is just as "middle class" in his origins as his predecessor. But he joined the ranks of the Socialists twenty years ago because he believed that the day of that régime was over, that it no longer gave justice to the mass of men, because it seemed to him inept and inefficient. Something in his tidy mind rejected it because, he reasoned, it had made a world of inequality, of extreme luxury and extreme poverty, of class distrust and hatred, of national and international insecurity.

At times with Poincaré as with others he indulged in oratorical duels when their doctrines clashed. But these duels were always marked by the same respect which Poincaré showed him on that day when he welcomed him back to the Chamber. There has never been any question at any time during his whole political career of either the moral or the intellectual integrity of the present Premier, and every one concedes his brilliance.

And yet during all these years very few, either among his opponents or his supporters, believed that Léon Blum would come to power or would in power show as great ability in leadership as he had done in opposition. There was something in his attitude, in his appearance even, which suggested the dilettante. It was remembered that he had been a theatrical critic and it was known that art was one of his dominant interests.

In France these "weaknesses" do not count against a man as in some other countries. Clemenceau used to go to the Louvre every now and then and stand in front of the "Joconde" in silent contemplation. What in Blum's case was perhaps most in doubt was his courage. It was one thing, it was argued, to believe this world was out of joint, but it was quite a different thing for Hamlet to set it right.

Where everybody erred was in underestimating the strength and fire of the faith that was in this wealthy intellectual Socialist. Those strongholds of capitalism, the Bank of France and the Havas Agency, secure in their traditional monopolies, were only mildly perturbed when the Left Popular Front swept to victory last May with a majority which was comparable to that of President Roosevelt in the recent election. They had withstood attack before and they were confident that within a few months, long before the Popular Front leaders could put their program of reform into operation, the ranks of the majority would be broken, that the Communists and the Radicals would pull in such different directions and that Blum and his Finance Minister Auriol would make so many mistakes that their coalition would collapse.

When the government took office the country was already rent by the stay-in strike movement. If it did not meet shipwreck on that rock it certainly would meet disaster in the fog of devaluation.

What was least expected was that Blum would take advantage of the high tide of his success and push through Parliament, at a pace that had never been equaled, and dazzled even his supporters, reform after reform; that within five months he should have reorganized the whole status of labor, transformed the Bank of France, met the necessity of devaluation frankly and pushed it through under cover of an international agreement; put the manufacture of armaments under government control, begun the reorganization of the army and air force so as to increase their efficiency, and passed in all over sixty laws, many of which were of almost as revolutionary importance as those passed by the United States

Congress during the Roosevelt administration, but with this difference, that they cannot be upset by any Supreme Court and are the law of the land.

In dealing with diverse groups among his supporters, the Premier has relied entirely on persuasion. He does not threaten. It is an essential part of his belief that men can be better swayed by argument than by menace, and the furthest he has gone in coercion has been to remind the unruly that they were elected on a common program and that his task is to apply that common program.

He is not, he insists, a Socialist Premier and his is not a Socialist government. He is the head of the Common Front government, strictly bound to carry through only the reforms outlined in the Common Front program last Spring. If any member party of that Common Front breaks away, it will be its responsibility. He himself will loyally abide by the joint election promises of all three parties and go no further.

Probably no one has been more surprised than Blum at the success which he has had. "Our problem," he said, "is to find out if it is possible in the present social order to prepare men's minds and the course of events for passage to a better organization of human life. We will not ruin but also we cannot cure and save this bourgeois society. Its ruin is already real enough, for that régime is ruined which is in contradiction with human intelligence and morality."

That condemnation of the existing order was uttered over five months ago and Blum has in no way changed his position. He is still a Socialist preparing, he insists peacefully and in friendly fashion, to mold this world, or his country at least, nearer to his heart's desire. But his strength lies in the fact that throughout these five months he has never put his socialism in front of his duty as head of a combined majority to play fair by all parties.

It is in this absolute loyalty to his followers that his force of leadership lies. He towers above most of them intellectually, but these five months have proved that it is his moral courage, which few people suspected him of having, on which the authority of his government has so far endured.

Accidents may, of course, happen. That perennial source of trouble, the French budget, must be negotiated through Parliament during the next two months. In the Chamber there will be no difficulty, although there may be much noise. In the Senate, however, there is likely to be a stiff conflict of wills, for the French Upper House regards itself as the last rampart in the defenses of that bourgeois régime which Blum considers to have already perished through incompetence.

Then there is the Spanish situation. If Blum had followed his natural desire, and perhaps if he had been in opposition, he would have been among the first to urge that France should go to the defense of Madrid.

But being at the head of the government of one's country is a different matter. One sees all around the problem, and from the outset Blum has recognized and insisted that France alone can do nothing to help the Left parties in Spain. Just as at home he has to work with a coalition of three parties and set his pace somewhat to the mean of all three, he feels that in international affairs he must also keep in step with Great Britain and with the popular and governmental sentiment in the United States.

He is far too alive to the dangers of the situation in the Mediterranean and their accentuation by the Spanish war to risk the isolation of France. There must be no break, he argues, in the solidarity of the democracies of the world and no separate action if that curious political religious movement called fascism is to be finally checked.

In his secret mind the French Premier is among those who hope and believe that democracy can finally win without war. As a student of history and human evolution he believes that finally the attempted totalitarian States must break down because they are not founded on the broad basis of popular support but depend on the authority of single men.

And it gives him satisfaction to think that one of the most curious features of the Fascist movement is that it is a kind of rank growth of democracy. His fellow-Premiers—Mussolini and Hitler and Stalin—are men of far more humble origin than he and, although he does not insist on it, of far less education. The systems of which they are the heads are less systems, except perhaps in Russia, than phenomena born of the too hasty effort to reach order after the chaos which resulted from the collapse of all the old systems at the end of the war.

They are in his opinion stages of evolution without any deep root, destined to perish with the men who have led them. In France he is building differently, believing that, even if he dies or disappears, the movement of the organization of life for greater justice toward all men will continue.

Perhaps he is an idealist, but he is a very human idealist and a very clever one. It took him nearly forty years of preparation, of which twenty were spent in Parliament, to reach the point at which he could put some of his idealism into practice. And although he has worked fast he has avoided being extreme. He knows that men cannot be rushed into new ways of thinking and doing too fast; that it is better to build slowly and solidly than to seek to convert a whole system overnight.

If he needed an example to prove the wisdom of his case he has certainly had it in these last months in Spain. It was the attempt to rush matters there that begot violence, and violence is above all what Blum is anxious to avoid. He is not afraid of it. He warned his opponents, both at home and abroad when he took office, and has done so again several times, that if they tried it they would be met by even greater violence. But he will not begin it either at home or abroad.

Perhaps this strong trait of patience derives from the fact that in race and blood he is not wholly a Frenchman, although he is entirely French in culture and in love for the country in which his family has lived for several generations.

He himself, at the beginning of the new session of Parliament, declared confidently that his government would last far longer than its opponents and even most of its supporters believed likely. He based his confidence on the undoubted fact that the government still had the entire support of the mass of the French people and that it had avoided offending its adversaries too deeply.

It is, however, only to be expected that sooner or later the Right will seek to react, for in politics no Frenchman ever admits defeat.

So, very quietly, Blum has been preparing, by way of anticipating a defeat or a forced resignation, for a dissolution and a new election in the hope that he will get the same, or an even better majority. If this plan worked out, and he got a second term, he might be able to say as President Roosevelt did at Madison Square Garden on the eve of his re-election:

"I should like to have it said of my first administration that in it the forces of selfishness and lust for power met their match. I should like to have it said of my second administration that in it these forces met their master."

Many more analogies might be found between what Blum is trying to do in France for the renovation of his country peacefully and what President Roosevelt is doing in the United States. They both believe in democracy, in the power of men to live decently by common consent, with justice toward all.

But all Blum's work is at the mercy of events. He is in reality engaged in trying to do what his old leader, Jaurès, was trying to do when a pistol shot at Sarajevo set the world on fire and destroyed its whole structure. The fiery doctrines of communism and fascism have to some extent taken the place of the old beliefs in liberty and democracy, and in the face of what has been happening in Spain, and may happen on a much wider scale, Blum's mild socialism has today an almost old-fashioned flavor.

Anarchism: Spain's Enigma

by Herbert L. Matthews

BARCELONA

SPAIN IS A symbol and a battlefield for a war of classes and ideologies. Democracy, republicanism, socialism, communism, anarchism—these are the movements whose fates are at stake here on the peninsula in greater or lesser degrees. But Spain is the country par excellence of anarchism, and this war, which is changing the face of the earth in so many more ways than people realize, is, among other things, a turning point in the history and development of that movement.

A majority of Loyalist Spain has turned on the Anarchists and is seeking to dominate them and nullify their force in the conduct of government and the prosecution of the war. The Negrin Government is the negation of what the Anarchists are seeking. It is democratic, moderate, even bourgeois, in its policy, although the controlling force, or at least the strongest single force behind it, is communism. Spanish communism is bourgeois at the moment, paradoxical as that may seem. But that is another story; the important thing is that the Communists here are waging a powerful campaign of propaganda against the Anarchists, and the Anarchists, after lying low for a few months, are now showing signs of fighting back. The political development of republican Spain can almost be explained in terms of this conflict; even the outcome of the civil war may depend on its results.

It has been said that every Spaniard is an aristocrat. Certainly he is a being apart from his fellow-beings. He is egocentric, not social; practical, not idealistic. His response is to something which has a direct, personal appeal, such as anarchism, rather than to a call for submergence of his individualism in the State as the Fascist demands, or to an authoritarian society such as communism. There is a deep religious substratum to his character. It compels him to project his personality like a sharp silhouette against "the white radiance of his eternity."

He is not at home in any of what Salvador de Madariaga calls "the middle stretches in which social and political communities lie." Anarchism catches him at the individual end of those two poles, ego and universe, and his response to its appeal is instinctive. Of course, when the time comes to give reality to anarchism's objectives he is only too likely to find out that, despite everything, society impinges on his individuality and he cannot live in a vacuum. Nevertheless, the philosophical appeal is deep and haunting.

To be an Anarchist you must believe that men are essentially good. Hence, it is government, political leaders and institutions which must be bad. Get rid of them and let man be natural and free, the Anarchist philosophy urges. It is a noble ideal, with a mystic and spiritual content that is more suitable to the Spanish temperament than communism seems to be. This is particularly true in respect of the Catalan, the Valencian and the Andalusian.

The philosophical appeal of anarchism to the average Spaniard is through that strong individualism which is at the base of his character. The Spaniard does not naturally merge into a society or a State. His instinct is to absorb, not to be absorbed. You cannot make an automaton of a Spaniard. For that reason neither Moscow's authoritarian communism nor the dictatorial fascism of Rome and Berlin suits his character. Whatever happens in Spain, neither of those things will have any chance of lasting here.

The numerical strength of anarchism in Spain varies according to who is doing the claiming. The Anarchists themselves say they have 2,000,000 members, while their opponents are unwilling to credit them with much more than half so many.

In the early days of the rebellion a number of Anarchist experiments were started in the provinces of Aragon, Catalonia and Granada. Most of them were short-lived, for the majority of the peasants opposed efforts to anarchize their communities and some sanguinary struggles resulted. In certain towns the experiments proceeded and are only now being liquidated by the Negrin Government, which is determined to maintain general control under war conditions.

One of the more successful efforts occurred at Bujaraloz in Aragon. There 14,000 peasants collectivized 11,000 hectares of land, of which 9,000 hectares were wheat-growing and 2,000 were in pasture. Last Autumn they had a crop of 2,150,000 kilos of wheat valued at 7,000 pesetas. Money was abolished and the surplus wheat was used instead, after deduction of enough for local needs and valorization at current market prices.

That was the basis of the group's barter, and each member of the community had an equal share. Tickets were given out representing the values, and to each person was allotted a certain number for food, clothes, education, hygiene, and so on, while what was called a "prudential reserve" was set aside for emergencies. Every family received ration cards and food was distributed cooperatively. The aged, invalids, widows and orphans were reported well cared for.

On the whole, the experiment seemed to work well for a while, but friction of all sorts apparently was developing. Federico Urales —one of Spain's veteran Anarchists, who is much respected in Anarchist circles—recently issued a blast against all such communities. He asserted that not a single one of the agricultural or factory communities had proved a success; only the transport services in Catalonia had done well.

Anarchism, like communism, derives from socialism in so far as it advocates the community of property and is identified with the class struggle. However, it is libertarian, not authoritarian. It seeks the realization of its ideals not in Marx's democratic State or in Lenin's dictatorial one but in the free and voluntary organization of communes and workers' federations. According to the classic formula of communism, "each one gives according to his capacities and receives according to his needs"; but according to anarchism "each one gives and takes what he wants, and that presupposes abundance and love."

Anarchism in Spain began to gain ground in 1868 (the year of the liberal revolution which ousted Isabel II), when the first emissary of the International, a follower of Mikhail Bakhunin, named Farinelli, appeared on the Spanish scene. He found fertile ground for anarchism. The year before that Bakhunin had drawn up a loose program for the International Alliance of Socialist Democracy. "The alliance," he said, among other things, "desires the definite and absolute abolition of classes. * * * It desires that the land, the instruments of labor and all capital be the collective property of all society, to be utilized only by workers. * * * It holds that all presently existing States, political and authoritarian * * * must disappear in the universal union of free associations."

Bakhunin's final open break with Karl Marx a few years later had its repercussion in Spain at the Congress of Saragossa in 1870, where occurred the profound split which still divides the country. The split centered around Barcelona, which opted for the individualistic, direct action of anarchism, and Madrid, which chose the democratic, political action of socialism. To this day Madrid is the center of socialism and communism, while Barcelona is the fountain of anarchism; but the disciples of the latter philosophy have always been in a minority and have always been persecuted.

Oppression of anarchism and the reaction to it have caused the movement to be firmly identified in all minds with violence. Anarchism in popular opinion is synonymous with strikes, bombings and assassinations, and there is good reason in Spanish history to make that identification. However, theoretically anarchism abhors violence.

There are no really important Spanish exponents of the anarchist philosophy, for the movement here has always been in a process of ferment in which the leaders were actively struggling, rather than formulating theories. Among the few worth mentioning are Juan Serrano y Oteiza, his son-in-law Ricardo Mella; José Llunas Pujols and, above all, Anselmo Lorenzo, who died in 1914.

The theorist who seems to have made the greatest impression on Spaniards was the Italian Errico Malatesta, whose long and turbulent life permitted him to be in the movement from Marx's days until after the formation of the Second Spanish Republic in 1931.

Malatesta, like all Anarchists nowadays, was a "voluntarist." The program was to be achieved by direct action and was realizable only in proportion as men desired it. Here is a synopsis of that program as Malatesta formulated it at the time of the Second Congress of the Italian Anarchist Union in Bologna in 1920. It contains the essence of what anarchism is striving for:

> Abolition of the private ownership of land, raw materials and the instruments of labor.
>
> Abolition of government and all power which the law assumes and imposes on others; therefore, abolition of monarchies, republics, parliaments, armies, police, magistrates and all institutions endowed with coercive powers.
>
> Organization of social life by means of free associations and federations of producers and consumers.
>
> Guaranteed livelihood for all.
>
> War against religion.
>
> War against patriotic rivalries and prejudices. Abolition of frontiers. Fraternity among all peoples.
>
> Reconstruction of the family in that form which results from the practice of love, freed of all legal bonds, of all economic or physical oppression and of all religious prejudice.

There you have the final goal of anarchism, which modern theorists call "libertarian communism." However, like all social ideals, it is not capable of achievement all at once. You need preparatory stages and, in the case of anarchism particularly, you need some practical, organizational expression to act as a channel and weapon in the struggle toward the goal. That is where syndicalism comes in.

Spanish workers took so naturally to the syndicalism of Georges Sorel, brought over from France in the latter half of the nineteenth century, that virtually all of them in time became members of syndicates—as they still are today. To the Anarchists it gave immediate fulfillment to their need for organization and collectivization, so that the movement here is always more properly identified by calling it anarcho-syndicalism.

According to Sorel, the producers by industrial not political methods were to organize the economic world. Direct action was to take the form of an industrial war in which the workers of the same industry in syndicates were to be the soldiers who should fight a class struggle with the weapons of the strike, boycott, sabotage, union label and the like. It was syndicalism also which brought the conception that property should be appropriated for the workers. Hence you get your violence, although Malatesta always protested against the identification of anarchism with violence.

The period of particular Anarchist violence was during the minority of Alfonso XIII, when there were bombings, assassinations, incendiarism, strikes, terrorism of all sorts and even revolutionary movements. It came to a particularly severe climax in the Barcelona riots and fires of 1909, after which Francisco Ferrer was arrested and executed along with other revolutionary leaders.

It was two years later that the now all-powerful C.N.T. (National Confederation of Workers) was first formed. It was promptly suppressed, but revived in 1915 and by the time of the Second Republic had a million members. Now it claims something like 2,000,000, of which 1,200,000 are in Catalonia. The C.N.T. is the Spanish organization of anarcho-syndicalism.

Held firmly in check under the dictatorship of Primo de Rivera, it burst out into violent opposition against the republic and for the next five years, until the civil war started, it fostered many strikes and even revolutionary movements.

The more violent and determined members had formed a militant organization at Valencia in 1927 called the F.A.I. (Iberian Federation of Anarchists), which joined forces with the C.N.T. early in the republic and from then on dominated its councils.

The role of both organizations in the civil war has been unfortunate. The Anarchists have been accused, with only partial justification, of placing the social revolution before the rebellion—of trying to achieve their particular program instead of joining with Republicans, Socialists and Communists in prosecuting the war. In some places in Catalonia and Valencia Province they tried to impose independent communes and collectivization against the will of the townsfolk and peasants. Violence and loss of life resulted in towns like Puigcerda, Bellver and Fatarella.

Meanwhile, the Communist-Socialist U.G.T. (General Labor Union) was cannily backing the peasants. Spain has a predominantly agricultural population which the old governing classes and large landowners were unable to save from misery. The farmer in many sections such as Catalonia and Andalusia was more often than not a desperate, starved, ignorant man, with nothing to lose and an easy prey to propaganda for violence.

At the beginning of the republic, and again when the civil war started, farmers seized the latifundia (wide areas under single ownership) and divided them into strips, thus, with true Spanish individualism, showing a preference for private ownership. The Communists are supporting them against the Anarchists' effort to collectivize the farms, and in that struggle lies one of the fundamental reasons for the present antagonism of the two organizations.

What are the Anarchists going to do now? Loyalist Spain's chances of winning the war depend partly on the answer. They are still a very powerful element—far too powerful to be suppressed. They have pledged themselves to help win the war under all circumstances. But they are apparently determined not to fight a war that will end without a social revolution. Will their ideas on how to win coincide with the Government's?

Socialism and Communism in Spain

by Luis Araquistain

PARIS, MAY 18.—Soon after the beginning of the military insurrection against the Spanish Republic in July of 1936, the name of Francisco Largo Caballero, the most popular Socialist leader of Spain, was being acclaimed in workers' meetings and at the fronts with the addition of "the Spanish Lenin." The order to use this qualifying phrase came from Moscow.

The Communists needed a figurehead with prestige in Spain. In their own party there was not one outstanding intellectual, political or labor personality. The mental or moral level of its own best-known men and women—José Diaz, Jesus Hernandez, Vicente Uribe, "La Pasionaria," Margarita Nelken—was too low. They aspired to be directors of the Spanish tragedy on the Republican side, while other men, of other parties, would be the visible actors.

The chief role in the cast was assigned to Señor Largo Caballero. They gave him a grand title: that of "the Spanish Lenin." That was the greatest honor they could bestow upon a man who was not a Communist.

An Idol "Made of Clay"

A few months later, at the beginning of 1937, the Communists started to pull down the man they themselves had raised to the clouds. The idol they had manufactured was made of clay. The man they had chosen for his diamantine character, for his energy as a ruler, for his popularity as a leader of the masses became exactly the opposite—a weak old man, vacillating, without roots in the working class.

Why this sudden change? Nothing could be simpler. "The Spanish Lenin" had turned out to be excessively Leninian, too personal and independent, a Spaniard who wanted to govern his country according to the spirit and the interests of his fatherland and not to the dictates of a policy placed at the service of a foreign nation.

That and no other was the meaning of the May, 1937, crisis, in which Dr. Juan Negrin replaced Señor Largo Caballero in the Premiership. It meant the triumph of the Communist policy in Spain. But the day of that crisis was the day the war was lost for the republic.

The Spanish war has been lost through the fault of the Communists. Did they really want to win it?

The first conflict between Señor Largo Caballero and the Communists hinged on the political commissars of the army. One day, Premier Largo Caballero learned that, without consulting him, though he was also Minister of War, the commissar-general, Julio Alvarez del Vayo, who was also Foreign Minister, had appointed hundreds of political commissars in the Republican Army. The majority were Communists. The idea of the political commissars had also been imported from Soviet Russia.

The Communists wanted to have a monopoly on commissars, not to educate and inflame the soldiers, but to compel them to enroll in the party, offering them advantages and promotions if they did and persecuting them by every means—including attempts against their lives—if they refused. From the first moment the Communists were the most privileged part, the aristocracy of the Republican Army. For that they made use of the political commissars and for that Señor Alvarez del Vayo appointed them.

Señor Largo Caballero canceled those appointments, which had been made behind his back and in favor almost exclusively of the Communist party—that is to say, of Soviet policy in Spain. On that day the Socialist leader signed his death warrant as head of the government. The Communists wanted a "Spanish Lenin" not of flesh and blood but of straw.

It will surprise some that Señor Alvarez del Vayo, a Socialist, should lend himself to this policy of favoring communism. But for those of us who know him from long ago there is nothing surprising in it. Since much before the war his conduct was that of a perfect "libellatic." (In the early days of Christianity the word "libellatic" was applied to those who, being already Christians, displayed a "libel," or certificate, attesting that they worshipped the pagan idols.) That is, he was a Communist without officially having ceased to belong to the Socialist party. His body belonged to this party; his heart, to communism. The Soviet witches found in him an easy Macbeth.

All of us who have had some contact with the Communists know this tactic of stimulating the ambitions and flattering those they want to seduce. When I was Ambassador in Paris a certain agent of the Comintern used to come every day to offer me I don't know how many political and social kingdoms in Spain. Finally, one day, tiring of so much adulation, I ended by saying to him:

"Don't tire yourself. Neither am I Macbeth, nor do I believe in witches."

Señor Alvarez del Vayo lent an ear to the witches of communism and offered himself as the Macbeth of the Spanish proletariat. He would sacrifice his own party and the Spanish people, if necessary, to serve Soviet Russia. He would be the king of revolutionary Spain, the political and labor heir of Señor Largo Caballero, the supreme leader of the Spanish workers united in a single labor party controlled by the Communists.

Youth Groups Sought First

This labor of unification—that is to say, of absorption of the Socialist proletariat by communism—had its start in the youth groups. One had to unify the Socialist and the Communist youth.

The preparatory operations were conducted in the home of Señor Alvarez del Vayo. I lived in Madrid one floor above Señor

Alvarez del Vayo and could witness the daily visits made to him by young Socialist leaders with the purpose of interviewing the Comintern agent then operating in Spain, one Codovila, who used the false name of Medina and spoke Spanish with a strong South American accent. There it was that a voyage to the Muscovite Mecca was organized for them; there it was arranged to deliver the Socialist youth, the new working generation of Spain, to Soviet communism.

That happened during the first few months of 1936. Communism being the chief reason for the disaster of Republican Spain, the responsibility of Señor Alvarez del Vayo, instrument of the Communist party, is one of the greatest.

PARIS, May 20.—From my vantage point of the Paris Embassy I could notice with surprise that already at the beginning of 1937 some liberal newspapers of London, which let themselves be inspired more or less consciously by Communists or Communist sympathizers, began to print pictures and eulogies of Dr. Juan Negrin, then Minister of the Treasury, without any visible reason. The hidden motive was that in Moscow he had been selected as successor to Spanish Premier Francisco Largo Caballero.

Dr. Negrin held the chair of physiology at the Madrid School of Medicine and belonged to the Socialist party. But, as he was neither politically nor scientifically known outside of Spain—and in Spain only within a very limited university circle—they had to prepare international opinion and manufacture quickly a statesman's reputation for him. The Communists are masters in the art of artificially creating representative men.

Once it was proved that Señor Largo Caballero would not consent to be a docile instrument of Moscow's policy in Spain, it became urgent to put him out of the way. The final proof of his independence was had by the Communists when, after the May, 1937, insurrection in Barcelona, they invited him to dissolve the P.O.U.M. (Workers' party for Marxist Unification), accused of Trotskyism. "I won't dissolve any workers' party!" Señor Largo Caballero replied categorically.

Military Operations Planned

There was another reason for throwing him overboard. For months Señor Largo Caballero had been preparing a military operation in Estremadura, in the west of Spain. The idea was to cut the line of communication of the Rebel army with the south, whence it received constantly reinforcements of Italian and Moroccan troops.

The success of that operation, splitting the enemy into two unconnected parts and depriving him of the foreign troops and war material that entered through the ports near the Strait of Gibraltar, could have changed completely the course of the campaign. The north could have been saved, all Andalusia could have been recovered. In any event, General Franco's victory could not have been so quick nor so decisive, and there would have been time and propitious circumstances to negotiate a diplomatic peace.

Everything was ready for the drive, scheduled for the middle of May. At the last moment some army resistance had to be overcome. General José Miaja, who was ordered to send some of the Madrid troops to the Estremadura sector, refused at first. His disobedience was inspired by the Communists, who were then General Miaja's real chiefs and who made of him—an officer of very limited ability—a great international figure. In the end General Miaja had to desist of his undiscipline in the face of the energetic attitude taken by Señor Largo Caballero, and the required troops were provided.

But, suddenly, very shortly before the day scheduled for the offensive, in the midst of a Cabinet meeting, the Ministers of Education and of Agriculture, Communists both, submitted their resignations under some excuse or other. Señor Largo Caballero went to see President Manuel Azana and submitted the resignation of the whole Cabinet. At the same time he told him about the operation that was being prepared, lamenting the fact that the Communists provoked a crisis at such an inopportune moment.

Continues as Government Head

President Azana begged Señor Largo Caballero to continue at the head of the government until the operation was carried out, saying that if the Communists insisted on resigning the Cabinet would be reorganized without the help of that party. Señor Largo Caballero accepted and returned to his office, resolved, like President Azana, to eliminate the Communists from the government. If this plan had been successful, the fate of the war would have been changed entirely.

Having heard—perhaps through President Azana himself, who used to be in constant communication with Indalecio Prieto, Socialist Minister of the Navy and the Air—about President Azana's conference with Señor Largo Caballero, a few hours later two Socialist Ministers presented themselves at the latter's office. Dr. Negrin was one of them. They told him that, in view of the attitude of the Communist Ministers and bearing in mind that under the circumstances the government could not do without the Communist party, the two of them, and Señor Prieto also, were resigning.

The manoeuvre was clear. The three Centrist Ministers (that was Señor Prieto's affiliation) were declaring their solidarity with the Communists for the purpose of eliminating Señor Largo Caballero. It was necessary to stop his Estremadura operation, lest it be successful. This state of mind was expressed by Simeon Vidarte, a Socialist Deputy who belonged to Señor Prieto's group, with these candid and criminal words: "If Largo Caballero is successful in that offensive, nobody will be able to throw him out of the government." That is the way they thought they would win the war.

Señor Largo Caballero had no alternative but to resign definitively. Before that they proposed to him that he remain as President of the Council of Ministers, with the excuse that that post and the one of Minister of War were too much for one man. That this was a pretext was shown by the fact that later Dr. Negrin accumulated in his hands the Presidency of the Cabinet, the Ministry of Defense (in which had been consolidated those of war, navy and air) and, practically, that of the treasury, nominally headed by an old functionary of that department.

Communists Held in Control

The three Under-Secretaryships of defense (War, Navy and Air) were held by three Communists, who were the true masters of the army. Apart from this submission to the Communists, Dr. Negrin did not tolerate at his side any but insignificant men. On one occasion, when Julio Alvarez del Vayo again held the Foreign Relations portfolio, after a few months of estrangement, President Azana, who had a very poor opinion of Dr. Negrin's intelligence, asked the latter why he had appointed Señor Alvarez del Vayo. Dr. Negrin replied, "Because I haven't found any one dumber than he." That was the way the war was conducted in Republican Spain.

Señor Largo Caballero understood that the idea was to make of him a figurehead for the Republican ship of state, a kind of Kalinin or Molotoff, and, as he is not a man for that sort of decorative role, he resolutely insisted on his resignation. Thereby was destroyed forever the kind of sacred union which, around Señor Largo Caballero and on his initiative, when organizing his Cabinet in September, 1936, had been instituted by all the parties and labor organizations. The war was lost. Was that what the Communists wanted when they split the Republican forces through their frantic struggle for domination over the government and the army?

It may be asked, "How did the Spanish people, especially the working class, tolerate the fact that the man who had been president of the Socialist party and was still secretary of the formidable U.G.T. (General Union of Workers), with over two million members; the idol for many years of Spanish workers, especially since 1933; the man with the best qualifications of intelligence, will-power and purity that there was in Spain for the conduct of the war—the granitic and incorruptible Largo Caballero—was thrown out of the government like a disloyal domestic, without a protest from any one but a half-dozen friends?"

Explanation Is Twofold

The explanation is twofold. On the one hand it was not possible to inform the people about what had transpired and about the tragedy toward which the Communists were dragging them, with the help of agents in other parties. Señor Largo Caballero spoke in a Madrid theatre in the Summer of 1937. His speech was the first of a series he planned to deliver throughout Republican Spain. But it was also the last. The Negrin government forbade him to continue his campaign, and, one day, when he was on his way from Valencia to Alicante, Dr. Negrin had him arrested and confined to his residence in Valencia.

The whole press was in the hands of the government, which is to say of the Communists, or gagged by official censorship, a function also controlled by the Communists. We had a newspaper in Madrid, Claridad, founded by myself: it was expropriated at the suggestion of the Communists. We had another in Valencia: it was seized by the Minister of the Interior, the Socialist Zugazagoitia.

The most vital Ministries, from the point of view of the war, were dominated by the Communists. I have pointed out before how the Ministry of Defense, nominally headed by Dr. Negrin, was in fact directed by the three Under-Secretaries of War, Navy and Air, all Communists. In the one of foreign relations, held apparently by Señor Alvarez del Vayo, the principal departments were directed by Communists.

In the Under-Secretariat of Propaganda, more than 90 per cent of the functionaries—and they were about 500, most of them hiding there to avoid serving at the front—were Communists. The propaganda carried out abroad only sang the praises of Dr. Negrin, Señor Alvarez del Vayo and the Communists. The chief of the Cypher Bureau was a Communist, so that all the secret communications received by the republic from abroad were known sooner to the Russian Embassy than to the Spanish Government itself.

Communism was a State within a State, at the service, naturally —and this is the gravest part of it—of a foreign country.

"Blackmail" Constantly Used

Besides, if any labor group criticized those acts of dictatorship, it was silenced by telling it that, above all, "the war had to be won" and so all personal differences and all freedom of opinion had to be sacrificed. The Russian-help blackmail was constantly used. So that the Soviet Union would continue sending us war material, it was necessary to eliminate the men on whom the Communists placed their veto. In fact, in the last months of the Largo Caballero government, supplies arrived scantily and in bad condition.

Once the Negrin Cabinet was organized, Russia resumed her shipments with regularity. Months later this trick was used again to shake off Señor Prieto, the Defense Minister, who saw thus repaid his services to communism during the crisis of May, 1937. Señor Prieto is another of the great reasons for the defeat. In the last weeks of his tenure of office, Russian supplies also began to be scarce. As soon as he was fired—like a maid who talks back—in the Spring of 1938, Russian materials began coming in as usual.

But, really, the Soviet war material was never sufficient. Why? This is an enigma that only future historians will be able, perhaps, to clarify. Russia's policy in Spain during the war was anything but clear. It can only be interpreted through conjectures.

One hypothesis, if correct, would confirm the suspicions that some of us Spaniards had as early as 1937, that Joseph Stalin did not want us to win the war because that would have exasperated Chancellor Hitler—otherwise his help would have been more copious and efficient. Nor did he want us to lose it too soon, because, once the Spanish conflict was liquidated, Herr Hitler would have greater freedom of action to carry out his policy of aggression in Eastern Europe and even against the Soviet Union itself. Mr. Stalin simply wanted to prolong our war sine die, to keep Premier Mussolini and Hitler busy and force the latter, in the end, to come to an understanding with the U.S.S.R. In the Spanish war he only saw a strategic diversion.

PARIS, June 3.—The probative testimony concerning control by the Communist party—that is to say by the Soviet State—over the Spanish State (during the civil war) forms an immense mass of verbal and written matter.

At least 90 per cent of the Spanish Republicans can vouch for this fact, which was tolerated because of the cunning argument (really a form of blackmail) that, unless the policy favored by Russia was adopted by Spain, Russia would cease selling war material to the republic, as actually was done whenever Russia wished the dismissal of members of the government or military or civil officials in the bad graces of the Soviet.

This personal testimony has started to appear and will continue to appear in the press and in books, and the world will be amazed at the truth of what happened in Republican Spain. I suppose that some day the same thing will be done with regard to the happenings in Fascist Spain, and then the amazement of the world, which has been so incompletely informed hitherto, will be doubled.

Documentary Proof Scarce

On the other hand, documentary proofs of this policy of interference by a foreign State in Spain are still extremely scarce, and we shall have to wait for internal political changes and the pacifying action of historical time to permit the opening of the archives and a search for the truth more or less derived from diplomatic instruments and the confidence of special agents.

By good chance I have come into possession of two documents which clearly prove Soviet interference in Spanish affairs and which may be unique in their class, because their authors are distinguished by extreme caution in their dealings and relations with other countries. These documents are two letters signed by Joseph Stalin, Premier Vyacheslaff Molotoff and War Commissar Klementy Voroshiloff and sent by those gentlemen to the then President of the Spanish Cabinet, Francisco Largo Caballero. But their significance and transcendency would not be correctly understood without an explanation of the antecedents giving rise to these letters and the intimate sense of their wording.

The first letter, dated Moscow, Dec. 31, 1936, was brought to Spain by the Soviet Ambassador, Marcel Rosenberg, on his return from a journey he made to Russia, no doubt to inform his government of the political and military situation in Spain. The relations between the two countries were even then extremely strained, precisely because of the interference, discovered more and more each day, by the Russian civil and military agents in the affairs of the Spanish Government, especially where its head, Señor Largo Caballero, was concerned, in the conduct of the war and, to an even more marked extent, in the control of the army.

Señor Largo Caballero did not disguise his distaste for this importuning. On one occasion he was obliged to break off violently an interview with Mr. Rosenberg and virtually to dismiss him from his office for his impertinent insistence on the dismissal of General José Asensio.

Envoy Visited Moscow

Mr. Rosenberg went to Moscow shortly before this scene, evidently to give an account of the tenseness of this situation. The spontaneous letter from Messrs. Stalin, Molotoff and Voroshiloff was the reply to the information carried by Mr. Rosenberg. The blunt question whether the Ambassador was or was not to continue to be persona grata to the Spanish Government proves that Mr. Rosenberg, or one of the numerous Soviet agents in Spain, had given the Russian rulers full details of the Spaniards' discontent.

It is probable that Mr. Rosenberg described Señor Largo Caballero as a man who, by his personality and character, would never lend himself as a docile tool of Russian policy. The former Soviet general, W. G. Krivitsky, relates in The Saturday Evening Post (April 13, 1939) that as early as December, 1936, the Soviet authorities had agreed to dispense with Señor Largo Caballero as head of the government. If this is true, there is every inducement to believe this decision was reached as a consequence of Mr. Rosenberg's visit to Moscow in that month.

The Russian rulers assert in their letter that the Soviet forces in Spain had been sent in compliance with the repeated requests of the Spaniards sent through Mr. Rosenberg. They do not state who made these requests. It was not Señor Largo Caballero. Shortly after his government had been formed in September, 1936, the Russian Ambassador presented to it a serving Soviet general, stating that he was the military attaché of the embassy and offering his professional services.

Later on fresh "auxiliaries" sprang up spontaneously, without being asked for, and introduced themselves motu proprio into the military staff and army corps, where they gave orders at will. This caused much disorganization and discontent among the Spanish forces, not only because they were foreigners but also because of their manifest and immense incompetence.

The authors of the letter state that the categorical orders received by the Soviet soldiers who had gone to Spain were to act simply as advisers to the Spanish forces, and nothing more. It is doubtful, to say the least, whether such orders existed. In view of the iron discipline of the Russian soldiers, they would have obeyed implicitly, instead of behaving, as they did, in constant and open insubordination and independence, not only toward the Spanish military leaders, but even toward the highest authorities of the republic, throughout the war.

The air forces, directed by the Russians, operated when and where they pleased, without any coordination with the land and sea forces. The Navy and Air Minister, Indalecio Prieto, cynical and humble, made fun of his office to any one who visited him, declaring he was not Minister of anything, because he received no obedience from the air force. The real Minister for Air was the Russian General Duglas.

Many operations of disastrous consequences, like those of Brunete, Teruel and others, were carried out through the imposition of the Russian "advisers" against the opinion of the more competent Spanish soldiers. And when the Spanish Government prepared an operation that was not to the liking of these advisers, or which they claimed conflicted with their interests, they boycotted it, as happened in the case of the action planned at Merida.

Miaja Refused to Cooperate

Because he would not agree to use in this action units commanded by Communists, Señor Largo Caballero, then Minister of War, was unable to obtain the dispatch of the brigades that he desired by General José Miaja, who at the time was a Communist and obeyed only the orders of the Russian staff. The air force, entirely under the control of the Russians, likewise refused him its cooperation. Thus the Soviet soldiers obeyed Moscow's "instructions" both before and after December, 1936.

As a last resource they threatened to abandon Spain. I have here the unchallengeable testimony of Señor Largo Caballero himself, as related by him in a book as yet unpublished:

"The Spanish Government," he writes, "and, in particular, the Minister responsible for the conduct of operations, as well as the general staff, particularly at headquarters, were not able to proceed with absolute independence because they were obliged to submit, against their will, to irresponsible outside interference, without being able to free themselves from it under pain of jeopardizing the assistance that Russia was giving us through the sale of war material.

"On some occasions, on the pretext that their orders were not being carried out with the punctuality that they desired, the Russian Embassy and generals permitted themselves to acquaint me with their displeasure, declaring that if we did not consider their cooperation necessary and helpful we should tell them so plainly, so that they could notify their government and take their departure."

This threat was also implied in Mr. Stalin's first letter.

Russian Staff in Charge

The last and fatal action in Catalonia, which was rather in the nature of a gift, the suspicious end of which is not yet fully explained, was directed by a Russian staff.

The [Mr. Stalin's] letter is knowingly misleading: the soldiers that arrived from Moscow were not obliging advisers, but despotic dictators—plus, as already stated, an astounding incompetence. Such mental war equipment was not the most suitable for winning the war, or even for prolonging it for long.

But all the blame must not be thrown on the Russian soldiers. Behind them were the innumerable political figures who were disguised as commercial agents and were in real control of Spanish politics. Nothing is said of them in the letter, and their presence was also not requested by any government in Spain. They came alone, and few Spaniards were aware of their existence and of their operations in the dark.

They directed the Russian soldiers, the Communist party and Mr. Rosenberg himself, who in reality was only an ambassador of straw. The real ambassadors were these mysterious men who entered Spain under false names and were working under direct orders from the Kremlin and from the Russian police.

Señor Largo Caballero was able to advise a change of scene for Mr. Rosenberg; but it was these men, the pseudonymous agents of Mr. Stalin, who prepared the downfall of Señor Largo Caballero and his replacement by a man more amenable to the advice expressed in the letter and to much other tacit advice, or to counsels conveyed in other circumstances and through other channels. This man of tragic destiny was Juan Negrin.

At the very beginning of the letter Señor Largo Caballero is addressed on the policy that Spain is to follow. The Spanish revolution must not imitate the Russian; it must be parliamentarian.

Four Counsels Professed

Then follow the four counsels, likewise not requested by anybody: attract the peasants, whom nobody was driving away; attract the small and middle-class bourgeois, avoiding confiscations and not following Russia's example on this point; pacify the Republican leaders in order to get them to collaborate in the government and to make it impossible for any one to say that Spain is a Communist republic; appease foreign capital. To sum up: a policy of the Popular Front; an apparently democratic policy controlled by a dictatorship, more or less effective or concealed, by the Communist party.

The second letter, dated Feb. 4, 1937, is more reserved for the reason stated in it: because the Spanish Ambassador in Moscow, Marcelino Pascua, offered to take to Señor Largo Caballero particulars of his conversation with the Russian leaders for the purpose of a reply by the head of the Spanish Government to the first letter. I am inclined to believe it was these leaders who ordered him to make the journey to Spain, in order to avoid the risks of indiscretion and loss of a fresh letter. Consequently the Spanish Government did not recall him and, so Señor Largo Caballero told me, this journey was made on Mr. Stalin's instructions.

Señor Pascua went to Spain mainly to discuss with Señor Largo Caballero the questions of gold and of the unification of the Socialist and Communist parties. The Russian plan, passionately adhered to throughout the war, was to fuse the two parties. The new party would be called the United Socialist party, as was done in Catalonia; but in reality it would be a Communist party, controlled and directed by the Communist international and by the Soviet authorities. The name would deceive the Spanish workers, and it was hoped that it would not alarm the Western powers.

Stalin Urged Parties Unite

Mr. Stalin fervently desired Señor Largo Caballero, in view of his power and his enormous authority in the Socialist party, to bring about the absorption of the latter by the Communist party. Señor Largo Caballero replied that he did not think the moment had come for unification, owing to the proselytic efforts of the Communists, which were so troublesome to the Socialists. Señor Pascua carried this categorical reply to Moscow.

This was one proof more that Señor Largo Caballero did not suit the purposes of Moscow. The failure to unite the two parties rendered impossible the complete domination of Spain by the Communist party. That was the reason the Spanish people could be stirred up against the Negrin government in the last stages of the war, owing to the decisive intervention made in this movement of independence by the Socialist party of Madrid.

There were no more letters. What purpose could they serve? But those now published, together with the foregoing explanations, may give grounds for reflection to those who read them. For a long time to come the Spanish war will provide ample and invaluable instruction to those individuals and to those nations who are not desirous of compromising the sovereignty, the blood and the wealth of their country.

Following is a translation from the French—the language of diplomacy—of two letters signed by Joseph Stalin, Premier Vyaches-

laff Molotoff and War Commissar Klementy Voroshiloff of Soviet Russia and addressed to Francisco Largo Caballero at the time he was Premier of Republican Spain:

CONFIDENTIAL

To Comrade Largo Caballero

VALENCIA

Dear Comrade:

Comrade Rosenberg, our representative plenipotentiary, has transmitted the expression of your fraternal feelings to us. He has told us, also, that you are always inspired by an unchangeable faith in victory. Allow us to thank you fraternally for the feelings you have expressed and to tell you that we share your faith in the victory of the Spanish people.

We have deemed and we shall always deem it our duty, within the measure of our possibilities, to go to the aid of the Spanish Government that is directing the struggle of all the workers, of the entire Spanish democracy, against the military and fascist clique, which is only an instrument of the international fascist forces.

The Spanish revolution plots its course, different from many viewpoints from the course followed by Russia. This is determined by the difference in social, historical and geographic conditions and by the needs of the international situation, different from those the Russian revolution had to contend with. It is very possible that the parliamentary way will show itself to be, in Spain, a more efficient means for revolutionary development than in Russia.

But, having said that, we believe that our experience, especially the experience of our civil war, applied in accordance with the peculiar conditions of the Spanish revolutionary struggle, may have a certain importance for Spain. Following this premise, we have consented, on your repeated demands, which have been transmitted to us at various times by Comrade Rosenberg, to send a number of our military comrades to be placed at your disposal. These comrades have received from us instructions to serve, through their advice in the military field, the Spanish military chiefs to whom you will send them to help.

They have been categorically ordered not to lose sight of the fact that, despite all the consciousness of solidarity with which are imbued at the present time the people of Spain and the peoples of the U.S.S.R., a Soviet comrade, being a foreigner in Spain, can only be really useful if he limits himself strictly to the functions of adviser and only of adviser.

We think that it is precisely in this manner you will employ our military comrades.

We beg you to inform us, as a friend, in what degree our military comrades fulfill with success the tasks that you entrust them with, because, of course, it is only if you judge their work favorably that it will be useful to let them continue their work in Spain.

We beg you also to communicate to us, directly and frankly, your opinion of Comrade Rosenberg: Is the Spanish Government satisfied with him, or is it necessary to replace him with another representative?

Here are four friendly pieces of advise that we submit to you:

1. It would be necessary to take into consideration the peasants, who have a great importance in an agrarian country like Spain. It would be well to issue decrees relative to the agrarian question and the questions of taxes, which would further the interests of the peasants. It would be well also to attract peasants to the army, or to create detachments of followers at the rear of the fascist armies. Decrees issued in favor of the peasants could facilitate this.

2. It would be necessary to attract to the side of the government the small and middle bourgeoisie, or, in any event, to give them the possibility of taking a neutral position, favorable to the government, protecting them against attempts at confiscation and guaranteeing them, within possible limits, freedom of trade. Otherwise these groups will become fascist.

3. The chiefs of the Republican party should not be repulsed, but, on the contrary, they should be attracted to the side of the government and made to attach themselves to the common task of the government. It is above all necessary that the government should be assured of the continuance of [President Manuel] Azaña and his group in power, doing everything possible to help them overcome their hesitation. This is necessary in order to prevent the enemies of Spain from considering her as a Communist republic, and to forestall thus their open intervention, which constitutes the greatest danger for republican Spain.

4. The occasion could be found to declare in the press that the

government of Spain will not let any one attempt against the property rights and legitimate interests of foreigners in Spain who are citizens of nations not supporting the rebels.

Fraternal greetings.
Friends of republican Spain.
K. VOROSHILOFF,
V. MOLOTOFF,
J. STALIN.

Moscow, Dec. 21, 1936.

Later Communication

MOSCOW, Feb. 4, 1937.

To Comrade Largo Caballero,
President of the Council of Ministers of the Spanish Republic,
Valencia.

Dear Comrade:

Comrade Pascua has delivered your letter to us. We have had a long talk with him about the questions that did not seem entirely clear to us. We are not writing anything about the nature and the results of this conversation, because Comrade Pascua has offered to go to see you at Valencia and to report to you personally.

We wish you and the Spanish people a complete victory over the external and internal enemies of the Spanish Republic.

We deem it our duty to continue to help you in the future, within the measure of our possibilities.

We shake your hand as your friends.

V. MOLOTOFF,
K. VOROSHILOFF,
J. STALIN.

Part 3

LIBERATION AND COLD WAR, 1940–1960

THE FIRST TWO articles in this section have been selected in the hope that they capture the rise and then deflation of the spirit of the Liberation. The first, written in 1944 by Harold Callender, speaks of a mood of invincible hope that characterized the Resistance and Liberation era; the second, written in 1949 by Francis Williams, explains why Socialists had to be content with compromise and only partial fulfillment of their expectations. Callender was persuaded that the leaders of the "new" France would not tolerate a return to an old-fashioned and discredited capitalism, a fact he believed was demonstrated by their appeal for social experimentation; indeed, the more confident men of the Liberation expected to reweave the whole fabric of human activity. Williams, a Laborite, former editor of the *Daily Herald,* Labor's newspaper, and an adviser to Prime Minister Attlee, surveyed the ruins of the Liberation and found solace in Socialist strength in Britain and Scandinavia as well as despair in its weakness in France and Italy. Williams argues that Socialists had to embrace cooperation with the United States out of brutal necessity, owing to the threat of communism and Soviet imperialism. Thus Socialists could go no further than to reaffirm their commitment to democracy, legality, and constitutionalism, i.e., to the political status quo. Caught between a resurgent right and the strength of communism, Socialists pursued a middle way, which in fact was exactly what they had been doing in the years 1918–1939.

The second group, composed of three articles, is devoted to the Labor party, in and out of power: the first by Francis Williams, written in 1947, defends the work of the Labor government; the second by Barbara Ward of *The Economist,* written on the eve of Labor's defeat in the election of 1951, mildly criticizes Labor's record; and the third, written by Hugh Massingham of *The Observer* just prior to another Labor defeat in the election of 1955, analyzes the profound division within Socialist ranks. Williams sees Labor's policy of nationalization of key industries as a reassertion of the validity of democratic socialism and finds it consistent with respect for human freedom. Barbara Ward also emphasizes the consistency of Labor's aims, but finds this a fault. The aims were laudable, but she laments their staleness, the fact that much of Labor's program seems to be left over from the 1930's. This apparent refusal to update policy, and the fact that nationalization may produce few political rewards because of the slow rate of economic growth, heavy taxation, and the general discomfort it has caused worked to the disadvantage of labor. Massingham returns to the theme of the article by P. W. Wilson written in 1931 concerning the division in the Labor party between union leaders and intellectuals—the former pushing for immediate reforms, the latter retaining a desire for a profound transformation of society. Massingham reports on the leading party personalities, including Harold Wilson, describes the decay of the party since its eviction from office in 1951, and holds out little promise for its future.

The last two articles concern themselves with post-1945 socialism in West Germany and France, where Socialists were much less successful than the Labor party in Britain. Flora Lewis, correspondent for the Associated Press, discusses the personality and aspirations of Kurt Schumacher, leader of the Social Democrats, a man whose influence weighed heavily upon his party to the end of the 1950's. If a believer in democratic socialism, Schumacher continued the old and unfortunate practice (at least politically) of masking the Social Democratic program in Marxist language, while in practice his Marxism extended no further than the call for a capital levy. Schumacher also was staunchly anti-Communist and nationalistic, qualities that should have attracted patronage from the United States in the formative years of the West German state, except that Washington gave its support to the Christian Democrats. Miss Lewis described Kurt Schumacher as "the leading politician of his country." She was in error: she mistook Schumacher for Konrad Adenauer. Robert Doty, Paris correspondent for the *Times,* offers a brief history of Socialist difficulties in France since the Liberation in an article written as Guy Mollet came to power in 1956. Doty notes the pivotal place of the Socialist party in the Fourth Republic, gives testimony to Mollet's political maturity, and expresses some confidence in the prospects for his government.

The New French Revolution

by Harold Callender

PARIS

A WAITER IN the most conventional of tail coats gracefully poured wine into a glass. It was Château Latour 1938. One of the discoveries of the liberation period is that this was a fair wine year. Napery and silver were as choice as they had been under that roof in the time of the Third Republic or Second Empire. The waiter's movements were framed against the rich browns and blues of Aubusson tapestry hanging on the wall behind. By a slight displacement, one's eye fell upon a smooth green lawn and symmetrically placed trees seen through a huge plate-glass window of an eighteenth-century mansion. One might have imagined that nothing much changed in France, or that "plus ça change plus c'est la même chose." (The more it changes, the more it is the same thing.)

But a girl opposite was telling, while the level of the Médoc rose in glass after glass, how her father had been captured and tortured to death by Germans because he was a Resistance leader. As the waiter discreetly offered excellent Armagnac, a young man on my right described how he escaped madness when in solitary confinement by pacing diagonally from corner to corner of his cell while he composed a series of sonnets without pencil or paper. He was one of the many intellectuals who joined up with the workers to form the Resistance movement, and came out of it a changed man.

The setting in which we conversed seemed to carry one's mind back to the eighteenth century. But the stories my French friends told harked back to the worst periods of the Middle Ages, or even of barbarism. Yet these youths who had fought and suffered had faces turned to the future in a more hopeful mood than that of French intellectuals since the year 1870, at least.

The mentality of France today cannot be understood unless one begins to examine it by studying the Resistance movement—all of it—including university men who forsook their studies to slink up on Germans in the darkness or plant dynamite beneath trains, factory workers who skillfully bootlegged machine guns, youths who fled to the Maquis and lived a gangster existence. Like the great French Revolution, this one had its Encyclopaedists and its tough guys. It could have dispensed with neither.

In the intimacy of darkness and common peril the two groups became acquainted and got on together. The intellectuals grew tough, while the toughs were at least somewhat affected by what may be called the ideology of Resistance. Especially in France must men have an idea to justify fighting and dying. Out of privation, struggle, destruction and death there has arisen something greater than liberation or victory—something which in the minds of these tried and tested youths lends additional significance to those words.

The French often say that those who have not been under the heel of the Germans cannot conceive of what it was like. Many fail, at any rate, fully to understand that what the French were fighting was not only German power. It was the Vichy regime, which to them stood for something even worse—French acquiescence and participation in the German oppression of Frenchmen. The people of the Resistance were fighting against this national shame, as they call it. Also they were fighting against the humiliation of defeat in 1940. Thus they fought to regain for France her self-respect and pride as a nation. They have washed out the stain of defeat with their blood, and every Frenchman holds his head higher in consequence.

But behind the defeat which let the Germans into France, and behind Vichy which played their game, was something else—the defective political and social system which the Encyclopaedists of

Resistance hold to have been ultimately responsible for France's downfall and for the suffering which it entailed.

It was inevitable, therefore, that in the cells and torture chambers where the Gestapo and its French agents put captured patriots, in the secret cellars where the faithful met and plotted as Christians met in the catacombs, in caves and camps of the Maquis, there germinated and grew what I have called an ideology of Resistance —a social philosophy which sought to take account of the causes of France's ordeal and to insure against their recurrence. Consequently, for these men liberation is not merely the negative achievement of getting rid of the Germans. It has more positive, and indeed revolutionary, implications. Liberation is to be a new chapter in French history, introducing, perhaps, a new French social structure, or at least one greatly changed and economically democratized.

Since coming to Paris a few days after the departure of the Germans, this correspondent has met many Resistance veterans from the President of the National Resistance Council to the boys who have matured in the underground struggle. Some of these are Catholics, others are without religion. Some are conservatives, others are Communists. But on this point all agree—that democratic capitalism as France knew it in the years before her downfall must never be restored.

Emerson wrote that in the New England of his time nearly everybody carried a design for Utopia in his vest pocket. One is reminded of this remark by what one sees in France today. Nearly every Resistance organization has a program for restoring to the French people control over their economic life and consequently over the physical sources of their national strength.

These programs have been neatly embraced, necessarily in generalized terms, in a plan adopted by the National Council of Resistance on March 15 last. A direct reflection of them is seen in the Government's action in taking over control of the coal mines and in Gen. Charles de Gaulle's speech at Lille, urging a planned economy under the supervision of the State.

The direction in which France is moving seems clearly marked. But her precise path remains to be determined. Between various groups there are differences of what French call nuance. But often a French nuance assumes the proportions of the Grand Canyon.

Far more noteworthy than an agreement upon the need of social changes is the new sense of virility and confidence that animates the French, or, at least, these youths emerging from darkness and the Battle of Resistance. The feeling of weakness and frustration so conspicuous among intellectuals and university youths in the Nineteen Thirties, and the paralyzing pessimism over the future of France and democracy which caused so many bright youngsters to turn Fascist, seem to have been washed out, as the humiliation of defeat was washed out, by the ordeal and struggle from which the French have emerged.

The French, as represented by this élite that has gone through the fires of struggle, have acquired a new sense of their country, a new devotion to it, a new confidence in its destiny. It is as if the trace of degeneracy which had stained the French society of the Third Republic had been removed by a surgical operation.

Many now contend, as François Mauriac puts it, that "the former ruling classes now accept willy-nilly the Socialist experiment," which France seems destined to undertake as a new test of democracy.

It is probably difficult for Americans to appreciate the French aversion to their pre-war capitalism. Let it be noted that this French capitalism was very different from its American counterpart in that it did not bring to the working class anything like our standard of well-being, nor did it provide the State with anything like our industrial equipment for peace and war. Above all, it failed to unite France socially or to see her through a war; some say that it led her to defeat.

In this new French mood, suggestive in many ways of the utopian spirit of the seventeenth and eighteenth centuries, when human perfectibility seemed a natural assumption, one finds traces of a new and also of an older France. A passion for legality and order exists side by side with potent revolutionary impulses. The individualism of the past seems to have accommodated itself more or less to the hope or acceptance of socialism in the future. A proud nationalism to which the wartime struggle has contributed does not exclude a sense of the limitation of even France's renewed national strength or recognition of the need of powerful allies in building a less illusory peace.

Giving full weight to whatever qualifications may be imposed by judicious cynicism, there is a new spirit abroad in France. There is a new élite coming to the fore which is far younger than the elderly statesmen dominant in the Third Republic, and if less experienced, this élite is also less resigned to the evils and inequalities of the past. It is fired by faith in the future of the country which they have saved from defeat and humiliation.

To many Americans, as to this writer, France will seem little changed. Décor is still here, as in that room with the Aubussons and the Château Latour and the sedate lawn. But as familiar wine trickles into familiar glasses in a familiar Old World setting, I shall never quite forget those who sat there with me or the new France which is their vision and their aim.

An Appraisal of European Socialism

by Francis Williams

LONDON

RELATIONS BETWEEN Western Europe and America are today governed by a paradox—a paradox upon whose satisfactory resolution depends the success of the Atlantic pact and of ERP.

This paradox is that success of the current approach to world problems depends upon the ability of two opposing concepts, American free-enterprise capitalism and European socialism, to work together in checking communism.

The extent to which this is true can be seen from a quick look at the political map of Europe. Such a look makes clear that, however strange and even unnatural such an alliance may seem to many on both sides of the philosophical and economic line that divides the two, it is nevertheless a practical necessity. So much so that both sides should realize the value of the alliance without delay and make the considerable adjustments in thinking that flow from it.

Whether European Socialists like it or not, they cannot check communism without cooperating with American capitalism. And, however much many Americans may dislike the idea, they must accustom themselves to the fact that strong Socialist movements are now an absolutely essential element in European stability.

In Western Europe there are three areas in which economic and political stability has been maintained despite post-war difficulties and Communist pressure from the East. In these areas the clash between the extremes of the Right and Left, which elsewhere on the Continent still provides a grave and potential threat to the future, has been kept within safe bounds. The areas are Great Britain, the Scandinavian countries of Norway, Sweden and Denmark, and the Benelux countries, Belgium, the Netherlands and Luxembourg.

The significance of this lies in the fact that in all three of the areas there exist strong Socialist parties. Equally significant is the fact that in the Western European areas of political instability, particularly in France and Italy, the Socialist parties are weak and divided.

Socialist strength is greatest in Britain, Norway and Sweden, where there are majority Socialist governments, and in Denmark, where the Social Democrats (or Socialists) are the largest single party. Socialist strength is hardly less important in Belgium, Holland and Luxembourg, in each of which the Socialists are the second largest party and are strongly represented in coalition governments.

In both France and Italy the Socialist parties are not only weak and divided but without effective roots among the industrial and agricultural populations. And it is in these two countries that the Communist parties are most active and that the danger of political and military instability is greatest—even though this danger has been reduced by Marshall aid and the Atlantic pact.

Looked at from across the Atlantic the close relationship between socialism and political and economic stability may seem curious, particularly as all the Socialist parties concerned are pledged in varying degree to radical social and economic changes. It is this situation which makes an assessment of the strength and character of the Socialist movement in Europe, the purposes and principles for which it now stands and the role it is capable of playing in the struggle between the extreme Left and the extreme Right, a prerequisite of an objective understanding of the European political scene.

In seeking such an understanding one has to ask in the first place how far European socialism can in fact properly be described as an international movement. What are the common principles which the European Socialist parties support and what are the political and economic forces which have given them their present key position?

In the strict formal sense a European Socialist movement does not exist. There is no Socialist international comparable to the Communist Cominform.

There have taken place during the last two years four conferences of European Socialist parties and a conference of all the Socialist parties in the sixteen nations which are cooperating in the European Recovery Plan. On the initiative of the British Labor party similar conferences of European Socialist parties are now to be held each six months.

These conferences are to confine themselves, however, to the exchange of information and the discussion of common problems. They will not, as the Cominform does, establish a central political and economic strategy which all members must follow. They will not do so for the simple reason that the Socialist parties are constitutionally and organizationally completely independent of each other. They owe no such deference and obedience either to a central executive or to the Government of another nation as the Communist parties do to the Cominform and the Soviet Government. The doctrines, traditions, methods and political environments of the Socialist parties differ considerably, and each is strongly influenced in its day-to-day policy by national backgrounds and national loyalties.

They are, however, linked by certain common principles. All of them are democratic and constitutional parties looking to electoral support for success, and pledged to maintain free parliamentary institutions. They have all adopted programs which, while giving a high place to economic planning and the public control of the primary means of production, aim to combine economic socialism with complete political and religious freedom. They all envisage the existence of a considerable area of economic activity in which individual companies will operate as privately owned units subject only to moderate planning directives from the central government.

Politically they are all the product of middle and working class cooperation and although they exist to secure greater economic and social equality and are strongly opposed to a completely free capitalist system, they do not, for the most part, accept the Marxian interpretation of history or the Marxian belief either in revolution or in the dictatorship of the proletariat.

The Socialist parties are revolutionary in the sense that their political existence depends upon, and their political purpose is expressed by, the advocacy of sweeping social changes directed to securing a greater equality of incomes, the establishment of social security services and national control of banking and of the basic industries.

They are non-revolutionary in the sense that they are opposed to any attempt at seizure of power by force or to a one-party system of government. They believe that the social changes they seek can be secured by parliamentary means or through the normal channels of negotiation between trade unions and employers' organizations.

Although all the Western European Socialist parties have long histories of political campaigning and working-class organization behind them, their present key influence stems directly from the generally leftward swing throughout Europe after the war and particularly to the rising demand on the part both of the industrial workers and the peasants for substantial economic and social reforms.

It was this leftward swing which the Communists hoped to capitalize on throughout Europe as they were able to do in Eastern Europe. But in Western Europe, and more particularly in Britain, Scandinavia and the Benelux countries, the existence of strongly organized democratic Socialist parties which possessed strong working-class roots and backing from the middle classes stopped the swing to communism by offering an alternative more acceptable to men and women nourished in the democratic tradition.

In France and in Italy, where the democratic Socialist parties were split by internal factions and where, moreover, the Communists had obtained considerable support by their part in the Resistance, the leftward swing went farther.

These differences have inevitably produced—where they were not to some extent caused by—varying reactions on the Right. Where strong democratic Socialist movements existed, forces on the right have been prepared to abide by constitutional methods. But in France, for example, the existence of a strong Right Wing that is prepared to fight radical alterations has increased communism's strength among the workers. This, in turn, has increased the intransigence of both Left and Right and the danger of a social conflict which is only held at bay by a Catholic, liberal and Socialist coalition which, although it has made remarkable advances, suffers from some inherent instabilities.

Much the same situation exists in Italy, where the exploitation of the peasants by absentee landlords in the South and the suicidal selfishness of many rich families with Fascist histories has enormously strengthened the Communist appeal. For the time being the Communist advance is being held by the De Gasperi Government and the hard fact of American economic aid, but no objective observer can doubt the continuing strength of communism in Italy. That strength can only be diminished by substantial social reforms.

Through Western Europe, as a whole, the existence of strong Socialist parties in present circumstances actually has become a prerequisite of political and economic stability. This does not mean that stability is only possible where there are Socialist Governments. What it does mean is that a prerequisite of economic and military security at the present time is almost certainly the presence of sufficiently strong Socialist movements to offer a satisfactory and effective alternative to communism in political elections and in trade-union organizations. And these Socialist parties, if they are not themselves in the Government, must be in a position to exercise some influence on social policy.

The Socialists stand directly in the way of Communist advance and are under heavy and persistent Communist attack for that reason. Outside Britain—where Communist strength is practically negligible and where the constitutional tradition is so strong that there is no serious threat to it—this fact inevitably affects Continental attitudes and must be taken into account in considering American policy.

Most of the Continental Socialist parties outside Britain include strong groups brought up in Marxist tradition within the organized working-class movements. (The Scandinavian Socialist parties, which do not share this Marxist tradition to anything like the same degree, are affected in their attitude to Russia by their geographical nearness to it.) As a consequence the European Socialist parties, although they oppose any attempt at Russian interference in their internal affairs and strongly support the Atlantic Pact as a defensive measure, are not to be regarded as potential allies in a preventive war against Russia.

Undoubtedly also there still exists among many of the Continental Socialist parties some suspicion of "American dollar imperialism." This suspicion has been very much reduced by the terms of Marshall aid and by an increasing understanding of the genuine American desire to assist European recovery as a step toward world political and economic stability, but it remains as a state of mind still likely to emerge from time to time as a factor in Continental policy.

Despite their difference in economic principle there is no reason why a satisfactory and cooperative accommodation should not be reached between the European Socialists and American capitalism, for they are not concerned, as the Communists are, in trying to disrupt and overthrow the economic and political systems of other countries but with economic and social reforms within their own countries. They desire both as a matter of principle and urgent practical necessity to develop international trade. By learning American production techniques wherever they can be applied successfully within the conditions of their own countries, they hope to increase their own exports and raise internal living standards sufficiently to buy more from abroad and particularly from America if American economic and exchange policy permits it.

How far European socialism will be able to succeed in establishing the middle way it seeks it is not yet possible to say.

In Britain and Scandinavia, where the Socialist parties are strong and where there is a long constitutional tradition which affects all parties, the prospects are bright. In Holland and Belgium the outlook is reasonably good—although by no means certain—and so also is it in Austria, where the Socialists are now the largest party and are well and moderately led. In Germany one cannot yet estimate the future with any assurance, but social democracy is bound to play a significant part.

In both France and Italy there is still considerable danger that unless strong democratic Socialist movements can be built to blunt the Communist appeal to workers communism will spread. This is particularly the case where, as in Italy, Marshall aid has not so far been accompanied by social and economic reforms which are overdue, so that American assistance to Europe appears to many as assistance to the privileged in maintaining the status quo.

American capitalism and European socialism can cooperate in stopping the westward spread of communism. But they can only do so if their cooperation is allowed to lead to a quick, demonstrable improvement in the social and economic conditions of the mass of the people.

The Basic Question in Britain

by Francis Williams

LONDON

THE MEASURES TAKEN by the British Labor Government to meet the economic crisis have brought to the forefront a question which has always existed in the minds of many men and women in America, in Europe and in Britain itself. It is a question of the most profound significance; one indeed of cardinal importance in attempting to assess the contribution that British socialism can make to a solution of the world's moral and economic problems at this time.

It is the question whether the system of controlled and centrally planned economy to which the British Labor Administration is pledged and which has received a new impetus in many of its crisis measures is compatible with the maintenance of the essential human freedoms upon which the whole conception of democracy rests.

Can Socialist planning and essential individual liberty run in harness or are they mutually incompatible? Is democratic socialism a possibility or is there represented in that phrase not, as British Socialists assert, an extension of the idea of democracy but two alien philosophies which must sooner or later clash?

The answer which British Socialist leaders—and particularly the

Prime Minister, Mr. Attlee—would give is clear. It is emphatically that the system of economic controls which they believe to be necessary for Britain's industrial recovery and future stability are completely compatible with the democratic freedoms and so far from weakening the foundations of individual liberty will strengthen them.

The philosophy of the British Labor leaders is a democratic philosophy, although not all who call themselves Socialist fully accept it. Thus the Prime Minister in a recent speech to old comrades in the Labor movement, after praising the pioneers of British socialism who, he said, had fought not merely for material improvement but for "freedom of speech, for freedom of conscience, for the right of every individual to think as he pleased and express these thoughts without fear," uttered this warning:

"I am concerned that there should be people in this country, and people who profess to be Socialists, who appear to condone things that are done by Governments that call themselves left when they would protest vigorously if precisely the same things were done by Governments of the right.

"It is of vital importance to the health of the Socialist movement that it should uphold absolute moral values. Justice must be done whatever may be the views of the individual concerned. Freedom of speech, freedom of conscience and personal freedom are the right of the individual whether he is a capitalist or a worker, a Conservative, a Liberal or a Socialist. Wherever you find the right of opposition denied, there is no true democracy, there is no true freedom."

To this it may be said by some that the moral and philosophic utterances of statesmen have not always been duplicated in their actions and that even a man of great personal integrity and democratic conviction, such as Mr. Attlee is universally acknowledged to be by his opponents, as well as his supporters, may find himself driven by the inner logic of the political and economic creed upon which he has embarked to adopt courses alien to the moral principles he quite honestly believes to be true.

In other words, is it not possible—some would say inevitable—that the path of economic controls which British socialism has chosen and which is fundamental to its philosophy and political administration will compel it to enforce such limitations on individual freedom that it will cease to be democratic in any sense of that much abused word acceptable to Western thought? Can there be freedom within a Socialist planned society or will Britain be faced sooner or later with a choice between the two? And is that choice, if indeed it is inevitable, being brought rapidly nearer by the magnitude of the economic problems which Britain now faces?

These are not rhetorical questions. They are of the most pressing practical importance. They concern all those outside Britain as well as inside it, who understand not merely the national but the international significance of the vast experiment that Britain is undertaking.

And because they are practical questions they can only be satisfactorily answered by a reasoned analysis of the present situation in Britain and an objective attempt to assess in the light of current experience and policy the probable course of future action.

It is necessary, therefore, to ask what are the present facts about the limitations on individual freedom in Britain and if there are such limitations, upon how large an area of the fundamental human freedoms they impinge. Secondly, how far do limitations which exist arise solely from current economic difficulties and how far do they spring from permanent trends in Socialist policy? Thirdly, what are the probable consequences upon individual freedom and personal initiatives of the future program of the Labor Government?

Let us begin with the facts. Here is a list of the main limitations upon the freedom of the individual which are in force in Britain today; admittedly, they make what at first sight appears to be a formidable total.

There is control of labor. Any worker changing his job must go to the local office of the Ministry of Labor and can only take a new job approved by the Ministry as in an essential industry.

Managements can only hire workers through the local office of the Ministry of Labor. They are not allowed to take a new worker unless the work for which they want him is approved as essential.

Managements cannot build new factories, extend their plants or raise new capital unless they receive licenses to do so from the Government. The allocation of coal and of essential raw materials to them is administered by Government order. The price manufacturers can charge for many of their products is controlled.

No citizen of Great Britain can obtain foreign exchange to travel abroad except for business purposes approved as necessary by the Government.

No one in Britain can now obtain gasoline to drive an automobile for private purposes unless approval has been given by the Ministry of Fuel and Power.

No new magazine or newspapers for general circulation can be started by any British publisher and the size of existing newspapers and magazines is limited under order of the Board of Trade.

No foreign books can be imported except under license and the importation of foreign films is governed by so heavy an import tax that the importation of American films, formerly the main diet of British movie fans, has come to an end.

The supply of all staple foodstuffs and of clothes is controlled and the consumer's right of purchase restricted to the rations fixed by the Ministry of Food and the Board of Trade.

No houses can be built except under license and the number of licenses issued for private building is small.

Farmers receive directions as to the crops they must grow and their land may be taken over by a Government-sponsored county agricultural committee if they are judged not to be farming their land efficiently.

Now, admittedly, this seems to represent at first sight a considerable inroad upon private freedom—particularly, perhaps, to American eyes, although much less so to those of the inhabitants of most European countries.

But before a true assessment of the long-term significance of these measures is made and their relevance assessed as evidence for or against the argument that British socialism must inevitably lead to the undemocratic control of the individual, two things are necessary:

First, one must see how many of these restrictions spring directly from present economic difficulties and represent a purely pragmatic and administrative attempt to meet current temporary problems and how many spring directly from Socialist philosophy and represent a permanent intervention by the Government in the field of individual enterprise. Second, it is necessary to consider how large an area of the fundamental human freedoms remains untouched by any of these controls.

The controls on workers changing their jobs, on the hiring of labor by managements, on the allocation of essential raw materials to industry, on the import of foreign films and foreign books and the prohibitions on foreign travel and on private motoring, substantial infringements on individual freedom though they are, all arise directly from the current foreign-exchange crisis. They are temporary measures to overcome that crisis.

The order controlling the engagement of labor, for example, legally expires at the end of 1948. Indeed, what is most significant about this order which represents in many ways the most substantial curtailment of the freedom of the ordinary individual so far is not its extent but that it goes much less far than many of the opponents of the Government believe to be necessary in a situation in which many of the export industries essential to British economic recovery are seriously undermanned while labor is being wasted in industries less vital.

Moreover, at a time when the Government was being urged on all sides to drastic action it deliberately delayed action in this field until prolonged negotiations had taken place with both employers and trades unions and agreement reached with both sides on the extent of labor controls.

It is similarly significant that the Government preferred to risk and actually incur considerable political unpopularity and to give an appearance of indecision by delaying the announcement of its major plans for increasing essential production and expanding exports to close the foreign exchange gap until those plans had been discussed and accepted as workable in their main essentials by representatives of both sides of industry.

The second large group of controls which involve a curtailment of the freedom of the individual—rationing, price control, the agricultural directives, the restriction on the size of newspapers and magazines and the prohibition of new publications and the house building controls—although of longer life spring directly from the shortages which have faced Britain since the war.

Many of them are continuations of wartime restrictions. They do not in any sense arise from fundamental Socialist policy but from scarcity and have their counterpart in all other countries governed by scarcity conditions, irrespective of the politics of their Governments.

It is true, of course, that even under scarcity conditions some of these controls would not have been imposed or continued by a non-Socialist Government, although others, like the main rationing and price controls, would have been unavoidable under any Government. The Labor Administration has, because of its general political outlook, used controls as a weapon to meet scarcity and secure efficient distribution to a greater extent than a non-Socialist Government.

There remains, however, a third group of controls which does exist as a direct result of the Socialist conception of a planned society. Unlike the other two groups it provides, therefore, valid evidence as to the extent of the permanent inroad likely to be made by the Labor Government upon the area of individual freedom which commonly exists in a free-enterprise society.

In this group fall the investment controls which prohibit the raising of public capital by bond or share issues for any purpose not approved by the Government, the prohibition upon the building of new factories without approval and the requirement laid upon a wide range of industries to follow general lines of development laid down by the Government. The question arises, therefore, as to how far this group of permanent controls is likely to extend and what additions, if any, there may be to it as a result of future policy.

This can be judged only against the general pattern of the Labor Government's policy. This policy can be described briefly in these terms:

(1) The planned control by the Government of banking and of short and long term capital investment in order to insure that the first charge upon these investment resources is the financing of industrial developments of basic importance to the national economy.

This policy has been largely shaped in the light of experience in the between-war years when large amounts of investment capital were diverted into speculative and luxury enterprises (and millions of small investors lost their savings in the subsequent crashes), while many of the basic industries such as coal, steel and engineering went short of the capital essential for their efficient reorganization.

(2) The nationalization of industries so basic to the national economy that they ought to be subject to a social control and particularly of industries within this group which are either so inefficient or require such large capital investment for their moderni-

zation that it would be impossible to raise the money without state assistance. Also of industries in which monopoly conditions have developed to such a stage as to be socially dangerous.

(3) The planning of the unnationalized sector of industry (which will remain far and away the largest sector) in such a way as to utilize to the full scarce resources of physical power, raw materials and manpower and to prevent a repetition either of mass unemployment or of large pockets of unemployment in depressed areas.

These three principles fit into one pattern partly derived from Socialist philosophy and partly from the current circumstances of the British economic position. Thus it has always been a cardinal tenet of British Socialist thinking that finance and the main basic industries should be socially controlled particularly where there was a danger of a monopoly cartel situation developing as in steel or where, as in coal, relations between owners and workers were so bad as to prevent efficient working.

And it has equally been a tenet of Socialist philosophy that there must be a sufficient planning of the economic life to prevent the recurrence of mass unemployment. But this philosophic approach has been reinforced by the post-war needs of Britain and particularly by the fact that an overall and permanent shortage of manpower makes it economically essential to avoid so far as possible waste of manpower resources through unemployment and to allocate scarce raw materials which have to be paid for by exports in such a way as to avoid waste.

The pattern which has emerged from this marriage of theory and practical necessity involves the supervision of all new investment, the nationalization of the basic sources of industrial power such as coal, electricity and gas and of the secondary basic industries such as steel (which needs an immense new capitalization for its modernization). It involves also control of new factory development and of the planning of new industries in order that new industrial developments shall not compete for manpower in areas where there is already a scarcity of labor but shall go to those districts where there is actual or prospective unemployment.

In addition, those industries that remain unnationalized—and these will be by far the largest number—are required so to reorganize themselves that they will be able to compete effectively in overseas markets and to offer wages and conditions which will attract the necessary number of workers in a society where the old recruiting factor of a permanent army of unemployed no longer exists.

The method followed in these industries is the appointment of working parties consisting of representatives of both sides of the industry under an independent chairman to draw up plans for future development which will in many cases be assisted by financial guarantees from the Government. It is hoped by this system to establish a partnership in which both social planning and the initiative of industrial managements will play a part.

Finally the policy involves nationalization of all railway and road transport. If private managements are to be required under the full-employment policy to site their factories in those areas where labor is available they must be assured both of efficient and cheap supplies of gas and electric power and of transport facilities as good as those existing in all other industrial areas. It is considered in light of past experience that this can only be done under national ownership.

Such restrictions upon individual liberty as British socialism involves flow from this pattern. They are precise and they are restricted in scope to clearly defined economic purposes. They do not impinge upon any of the fundamental human democratic freedoms. Nor is there any reason, judging by experience so far, to believe that they will do so. These basic freedoms are freedom of worship, freedom of association, freedom of political opposition, freedom of expression whether by the spoken or written word and the existence of a judicial system independent of the state and free from political influence.

In no particular have any of these basic human freedoms been curtailed or attacked. On the contrary, the Labor Government has been under heavy attack from some quarters because so far from curtailing the right of association and of expression of opinion it is regarded as too liberal in the rights it has accorded even to anti-democratic groups to hold public meetings and propagate totalitarian doctrines of the right or the left.

So far from limiting the independent power of the judiciary, it abolished in July last by the Crown Proceedings Act a centuries-old privilege of the Crown—which in modern constitutional practice means the Government—which made it impossible for a private citizen to sue the Government. Now for the first time under a Labor Administration any ordinary citizen can bring an action against the Government in a court of law before a judge and jury. So far from curtailing opposition and criticism the Labor Government has been freely subjected to both in Parliament and in the press.

It is true that an inquiry into the press has been instituted following a demand by the professional body, the National Union of Journalists, supported by a majority in Parliament. But the royal commission set up to report primarily on the development of newspaper monopolies was selected on a strictly non-party basis of men and women of high academic, legal and professional status—among them the former editor of one of the best-known Conservative newspapers in the country.

Here clearly is no evidence of any threat to the fundamental democratic rights of the individual. Moreover, it is significant that in carrying out its economic policy the Labor Government has as a safeguard against totalitarian methods developed a machinery for joint consultation with employers and trades unions which promises steadily to increase in importance.

There is a Joint Planning Board on which representatives of the employers' organizations, the trades unions and the Government sit together and which is concerned with the general pattern the national economy is to follow. There is a National Joint Advisory Council on which, again, representatives of both sides of industry sit with the Government and which is consulted on all matters affecting wages, labor conditions or management problems. And there are a series of Regional Boards for Industry under the chairmanship in some cases of an employer, in others of a trades unionist, which are constituted in the same way as the national committee.

These boards handle all matters of regional industrial policy, including such things as the industrial allocation of coal and other materials in short supply and the staggering of factory hours to ease the burden on the heavily strained electrical power system. Thus the long-established British tradition of cooperation between management and workers has been utilized and to it new authority has been given to meet the requirements of a new situation.

It is a Socialist pattern of society which is being developed in Britain but a pattern essentially democratic and essentially British. For the British Labor party has derived its philosophy not from Marx and Continental socialism but from a British liberal tradition and a British belief in practical compromise and cooperation.

It is in that tradition, in the moral and libertarian convictions of the British Labor leaders and of the British people, in the fact that British socialism, like British political philosophy in general, is undogmatic in character and has developed out of British circumstances to meet British needs, that there lies the greatest assurance that democratic values will be safeguarded. There will be many changes in the social and economic life of Britain in the next few years. But I have no fear that a suppression of liberty will ever be among them.

Britain Faces a Decisive Choice

by Barbara Ward

IT IS THE small minority of voters in the center who normally determine British elections. Most voters adhere solidly all their lives to one party—Liberal or Conservative before 1914, Labor or Conservative today. The center voter, however, has no party affiliations and no set political views. When he has seen one set of men in office for a certain period—normally two Parliaments—he begins to feel he would like a change. The result is the remarkable regularity with which, for the last 100 years, British politics have swung on a pendulum from right to left and then back again.

On this showing, the Conservatives stand a good chance of winning this week's election. In the 1950 elections, the pendulum had not completed its swing and the result was a tiny majority for Labor. Now the Conservatives can argue—and the opinion polls have agreed with them—that the middle-of-the-road voter really wants a change.

The pendulum, however, is not the whole truth about British political life. From time to time, a parliamentary cataclysm occurs which is instantly recognized as ushering in a new phase of political life. The Reform Bill of 1832 was the first in the modern manner. The great Liberal victory in 1906 was another. In 1945, the astonishing Labor landslide was palpably the opening of a new epoch. Such upheavals have this in common—they reflect the erupting into active politics of new political thoughts and ideals. As such they are quite distinct from panic landslides—the 1918 "Hang-the-Kaiser" election or the 1931 contest at the bottom of the depression —which mark nothing but the evil influence on voters of intense irrational emotion.

The great creative upheavals have all had a strong content of thought and theory and ideal. They accentuate the swing of the pendulum, and even dislodge some voters from their traditional loyalties. If conditions for upheaval were present in Britain this year, the ordinary law of the pendulum would have to be suspended. But one does not need to be much of a prophet to say that nothing could be less likely.

The Labor Government has changed virtually none of the ideas with which it was swept to power six years ago. In the sphere of ideals, this is not surprising since most of the aims of Labor could not be changed without betraying the humane and generous purposes which underlie most modern democratic thought. A society in which all can work and prosper and live in peace, in which class differences are lessened and equal opportunity genuinely given to all is not an ideal that is likely to be abandoned in democratic Britain. On the contrary, it is now so deeply ingrained that the Conservatives have virtually adopted it.

What has remained rigidly unaltered are some of Labor's ideas on how this ideal society should be helped to birth. The force which gave Labor its victory in 1945 was in part a revulsion against Conservative rule in the Thirties—the age of appeasement and mass unemployment. Inevitably, therefore, in approaching post-war problems, the Labor party had the Thirties in mind quite as much as contemporary difficulties.

It conceived its program more in pre-war than actual post-war terms. Unemployment was first on the agenda and, with it, an attack upon the "stagnation"—economic and social—of the Thirties. Then came the reaction against privilege, against the "old school tie" which had become the pre-war symbol of exclusiveness and exclusion. With this approach was bound up the principle of welfare for all, and of "fair shares." Foreign policy played virtually no part in the election. It was generally believed that the Big Three could be relied on to make world peace. The issues in 1945 were intensely domestic.

The problems then had been fixed by the preceding decade. The proposed solutions had an even longer history. The new ideas which reached the surface in 1945 had been brewing for decades. The old Fabian confidence that the state could be made an instrument of welfare was one. Another was the new and oversimplified confidence in Lord Keynes' theory for controlling the trade cycle and maintaining high employment. Yet a third, a very moderate dose—was the conversion of a very few of the party's theorists to milk-and-water Marxism.

With these concepts to guide them, the Labor party set about maintaining full employment, restoring vigor to the community and attacking privilege. In practice it meant the nationalization of certain key services and industries; it meant a complete set of social services, including heavy subsidies to keep down the cost of living, and rationing to share out scarce foods and commodities; it meant heavy government spending in every desirable direction; it meant taxation practically as high as wartime taxation itself.

The strength of Labor ideas and performance should not be underestimated. Solid wealth has been added to the country's social patrimony in new investment, in capital expansion, in housing, in schools, in the nation's health. For millions of workers and their families there can be no doubt that as fear of unemployment has receded, unions and men alike have begun to consider ways of bettering output and increasing productivity.

Nor is it a "stagnant" community that can almost take in its stride such burdens as the change from world creditor to world debtor, the need for a 75 per cent increase in exports and the acceptance of a whole new range of obligations to a vigorous Commonwealth. The single-mindedness with which Sir Stafford Cripps pursued the aim of expanding exports was one of the chief reasons why it was possible for Britain to develop a real degree of economic strength in 1949 and 1950. Nor can Labor be blamed for the fantastic inflation of world prices at the end of 1950, which increased Britain's import bill by £800 millions sterling in a few months. It can be argued that without the Korean campaign the British economy under Labor direction would have steered into calmer waters by now.

The present stringency must also not be allowed to overshadow Labor's achievements in other fields. Such a feat of statesmanship as the granting of India's freedom will not be forgotten. In another sphere, the artistic revival in Britain which has flowered in this year's festival must be credited in part to the Government's enlightened determination to foster the arts.

Yet the difficulty remains that in looking back to the problems of the Thirties and in adhering rigidly to the ideas and policies developed even before that time, the Labor Government has contrived to give more and more the impression that it overlooks the real issues and has, in any case, no solution for them.

The question of nationalization is disappointing to the independent center voter. He has seen coal remain the problem child of British industry and become a worse problem in 1951 than in 1949. There is no connection between the nationalization of iron and steel and the present decline in British steel output. But the voter may not always make the distinction. Power shortages continue. In fact, the certainty of a fuel crisis next winter is one reason why the Government decided for an autumn election. Yet if nationalization does not improve output nor, apparently, content the worker, where is its justification?

The Labor reply that it is essential to a policy of full employment carried more conviction in 1945 than it does today. The reason is that for the unaffiliated man of the center full employment does not seem to be a very live issue in 1951. Deflation is a remote danger. What stares him in the face and excites his deep concern is the opposite of unemployment—it is inflation and over-full employment. The Keynesian technique of spending—valid, certainly, in the wealthy but depressed economy of the Thirties—is inappropriate in the overspending economy of today.

Huge budgets balanced by huge taxation have covered the universal spending of the last six years. Already in 1950 the desire of the middle-class taxpayer—the man with £1,000 to £1,200 a year—to have a little more money to spend at his own discretion was an electoral factor. Since 1950 the need to finance rearmament and the startling rise in the cost of living—nearly 30 per cent in a year—have made the problem even more urgent.

Yet Labor apparently has no answer. It cannot be blamed for the need for a defense program nor for the rise in world prices.

But inescapably as a Government it has to face their consequences. The trade unions demand higher subsidies and bigger taxation. Yet to abolish all income above £2,000 a year would bring in only £53 million—about an eighth of the annual cost of the health services. What of a rearmament program of nearly £5,000 million to be carried through in the next three years?

There are really only two alternatives—to cut other expenditure or greatly to increase output. Labor refuses to consider the former and has sustained a party split by charging the patient half the price of health-service spectacles and dentures. To pursue the latter policy of expansion demands more capital, more managerial skill and better work. Yet inflation discourages all three and the rise in productivity (after substantial increases during the last three years) is actually slackening. This is the basic deadlock of Labor's economic policy.

It is closely linked with an equal deadlock in social policy. To attack privilege is not unpopular with the center voter—although the bitter spirit of class hatred repels him and Aneurin Bevan's attacks on "Tory vermin" still stick in his throat. But when the attack on privilege becomes a general leveling down, a determination to see as "rich" anyone earning more than £2,000 a year and an apparent indifference to standards of performance and the relative value of work, then the mood of liberal opinion begins to change.

If no rewards may be given—in the name of "fair shares"—to superior performance, how are productivity and enterprise to be rewarded? If full employment means less output, much leisure and the penalization of all who want to earn more, then the hope of expanded output is a pipe dream. Once again Labor policy appears to have reached a deadlock. Just as in attacking unemployment it conjured up the devil of inflation, in abolishing privilege it appears to have abolished incentives as well.

This feeling of general rigidity, of a policy so strictly determined by opposing pressures that no movement is possible in any direction, has, of course, been accentuated by the threatening situation in the world. Before Korea, the outlook was much more promising. The British economy was earning trade surpluses and replenishing its financial reserves. But the hard facts of foreign policy, far from offering an excuse for Labor's difficulty, are proving an added liability. It is in this field that in 1945 it entered on power without a shadow of policy. It is now in this field that its unity and therefore its coherence is most threatened.

The massive good sense of Ernest Bevin prevented the folly of a "Socialist foreign policy" casting longing and loving glances at Moscow. Bevin realized—from his own union experience—that there is no one a Communist hates more than a Socialist and it may be, too, that his long years of negotiating for labor taught him that one can "do business with capitalists."

He, therefore, with the support of the moderate leaders—Attlee and Morrison—built up a working partnership with the United States. The Marshall Plan in its scope and generosity silenced the doctrinaire critics. The greater knowledge of America obtained through the Anglo-American Council on Productivity encouraged the rank and file. But one cannot say that the solidarity of the English-speaking peoples became the emotional center of Labor's foreign policy. On the contrary, official references to America remained coy.

Now in the period of rearmament the alliance must undergo new strains. The moderate Labor leaders, massively backed by the trade unions, have accepted the implications of Korea, fully support the rearmament drive and are willing members of the Atlantic community. Yet it is on these very issues that three Ministers—including the volatile champion of the extreme wing, Aneurin Bevan—have left the Government and sought to rally support among Labor voters for a policy of reducing arms in favor of welfare spending and of "cutting loose from American imperialism." It is not the least of contemporary ironies that the first pamphlet published after Attlee's announcement of new elections was a violent attack upon rearmament and association with America issued by the rebel three.

It cannot be repeated too often that the bulk of the Labor party accept the American connection and the need to withstand Russia. The surprising success of Bevan's followers in the elections to the Labor party's Executive Committee reflects the mood of only a section of the party and has nothing to do with the solid, sane trade union core of the movement. Nevertheless, foreign policy has not helped Labor in its campaign. On the one hand, Attlee and the moderates have been necessarily imprecise and hedging in order to plaster over the split. On the other, the independent elector may have smelled a whiff of communism in the trend of rebel policies, and Soviet Russia has no warm admirers among the center vote.

On balance, one can say that in the campaign Labor has produced no new ideas. And indeed the Labor election manifesto with its emphasis on consolidation bears out this estimate. It is true that both the Chancellor of the Exchequer, Hugh Gaitskell, and Leonard Callaghan, Labor parliamentary secretary, have hinted publicly at an interesting new approach to the central problem of "social control" of industry. They have suggested that, in place of nationalization, an association of workers with profit-sharing should be considered. But this new lead is not an official policy, while the Bevanites are unashamed nationalizers.

The party is likewise unable to give promise of new men. Gaitskell has earned respect, Minister of Materials Richard Stokes' short record is impressive, but the feeling remains that most of the leaders are weary men worn down by eleven years of office—in war and peace.

The traditional pendulum swing—"to give the other chap a chance"—seems likely to be strong. Have the Conservatives turned it from a swing to a landslide? Have they given evidence of new thinking and new energy? Is there a ground swell of thought, comparable to the new ideas of the Webbs or of Keynes, which might carry them forward not only to power but to a new era?

It is not absolutely clear how decisive a part foreign policy has played in the campaign: Labor leaders have tried to follow Bevan in suggesting that Churchill and the Tories are "warmongers." The center voter is unlikely to have been impressed, especially after the British scuttle from Abadan and its repercussions in the Middle East. The average man's sense of national pride is keen enough to ask whether weakness and collapse are the only alternatives to the risks of war.

The real test, however, is over domestic issues. It is here that victorious Conservatives would have to face immediately the deadlocks left behind by Labor—the clash between inflationary spending with over-full employment, high taxation and trade deficits on the one hand, and on the other the measure of deflation necessary for solvency and vigor with the risk of reducing employment and cutting desirable services. They would be equally saddled with the other deadlock—between the desire to avoid favor and privilege and the need to reward efficiency and enterprise.

It can be said at once that if the Conservatives have not produced new theories and solutions to deal with these—the fundamental dilemmas of the welfare state—neither has anybody else. The free world over, these are the test of statesmanship. If the answer were known, the test would already have been passed.

One must also admit that the Conservatives are in many ways as much prisoners of the past as are the Labor men. The "stagnant" Thirties occurred under their direction and leadership, and it is difficult to say whether they have had genuine second thoughts. The essence of their policy then was rigidity and protection—external protection by tariffs, internal protection by price rings and trade associations. Many of the industrial leaders and politicians are still the same. Have they become radically converted to more competition, more efficient management, more investment, more research? It is too soon to say.

The question of privilege is perhaps less damaging. Undoubtedly modern Conservatism accepts the welfare state. But if the welfare state is to be maintained, the economy must conquer inflation and then expand. On their past record, the Conservatives are decidedly not artists in expansion.

There is some evidence of new light to be recorded. One of the ablest younger Conservative back-benchers, David Eccles, in a speech at Sturminster last summer placed "more and fair competition" squarely in the Conservative program, and thus defined his party's policy: "We shall make both ends meet by expanding the national income and taking care to live within it."

More recently, a party organization—the Conservative Political Center—has given its blessing to a pamphlet on employment which strongly advocates expansion, productivity, competition and enterprise. In it one may even read a direct disavowal of the Conservative Thirties: "The state can help by discouraging tendencies * * * to stifle competition. In the Thirties, the record of the state was a long series of restrictive practices."

One of the first official Conservative pamphlets to be produced in the election period was—by chance—concerned with industrial policy and the need for trade unionists to recognize the necessity of higher productivity. This Conservative pamphlet, "The New Approach," written by an active trade unionist and working-class colleague, specifically rejects the Conservatism of the Thirties and proclaims the party's second thoughts on higher output and productivity and the worker's interest in both.

It is doubtful, however, whether these new signs of forward thinking go further yet than a small group of Conservatives. Certainly no body of coherent compelling doctrine has been built up comparable to Liberalism in 1906 or Fabian Socialism in 1945. The Conservatives, too, may be handicapped by the desire to out-trump Labor's promises of full employment and full social services and could in this way produce a brand of Conservatism as rigid as that of the Labor party it seeks to supplant.

This danger is apparent in the Conservative party manifesto. Hopeful hints of greater productivity and expanding production remain hints and nothing more. It cannot be said that either Britain's dangerous economic situation or firm measures to extricate the community from it are given pride of place. On the contrary, the scale of Government spending bids fair to be unaltered—the housing program, for instance, is rather larger than Labor's and there is a suggestion of higher pensions—while the actual means for increasing production are barely discussed.

It may be asking too much to expect any political party to tell the people in time of near peace that the going will be tough and that they will need "blood, sweat and tears" to come through. Yet if election promises contain almost no mention of a cut in Government expenditures and still pledge to continue all existing benefits—"all this and rearmament, too,"—the Conservative party, if it returns to power, may find itself caught in Labor's straitjacket—between expenditures which cannot be cut and production which cannot rise. Yet, one way or another, the British community must learn, as Eccles put it, "to live within the national income," and each day makes it clear that national production cannot rise until national expenditure has been cut.

One should not, however, take too tragically the fact that neither party is producing a great revolution in thought and policy on the scale of the upheavals of 1906 and 1945. New thinking about problems of free industrial society is apparent—on both sides of the Atlantic. It is not yet coherent and self-confident enough to appear as a New Liberalism or New Radicalism. Its tendencies, however, are already clear—toward greater productivity, closer association of the worker with profits and management, a greater understanding of fiscal control for full but not over-full employment. There are promising signs that this new thinking is permeating both parties in Britain. In another decade a new upheaval will be in the making, bringing with it fresh and decisive direction to the democratic policies of Britain—and in the whole free world.

This better prospect leaves, however, the possibility that meanwhile the British ship will have to sail on an uncertain course and with a poor navigation chart. In fact, the outlook is much less grim. The truth is that just beyond the elections, whichever party returns to power, lies a sharp crisis in solvency and trade which will of itself force firm decisions on the British Government. Crises are powerful educators. The dollar crisis of 1947 gave Sir Stafford Cripps his opportunity and in 1948 the measure of deflation he enforced produced a new one throughout the British economy. The certain economic crisis of 1952 can have a comparable effect.

The reason for this confidence is quite simply the quality of the British community. Any government can rely upon the uncanny stability and common sense of the people at large. Strong measures elicit not panic but strong support. Even if Britain—along with the other free nations—must await emergence of a coherent body of economic and social thought fitted to the problems of twentieth-century freedom, the community has ballast enough and to spare for a time of searching ahead. And once the new direction is discovered and set Britain will arise, like Milton's "puissant eagle," reinvigorated and refreshed.

The Labor Party: A Study in Schizophrenia

by Hugh Massingham

LONDON

THERE IS a sense in which Britain's general election at the end of this month has caught the Labor party on the wrong foot. "Never have we been so united," its leaders tell us, and the press is invited to the church to observe the shot-gun wedding between Herbert Morrison, the boss of the party's Right Wing and a blushing Aneurin Bevan, the picturesque and eloquent ex-miner who for the last five years has persistently rebelled against official policy. So, amid showers of confetti, the happy pair emerge to the rousing chords of Mendelssohn.

It is all a little too good to be true. One notices the telltale bruises on Mr. Morrison's face, and Mr. Bevan's shining black eye. One remembers that these two were at one another's throat just before the bell sounded for the opening of the election.

"Ah," said one of the saddened elders of the Labor movement the other day, "if we only hated our enemies half as much as we hate one another, what a triumphant force we should be."

He was thinking of the party meeting that decided to withdraw the Whip from Bevan for persistent bad behavior—a move that stripped him, for a time, of his party standing in Parliament. It was a meeting that will rank among the bitterest in recent years. Imagine for a moment the scene in one of the committee rooms of the House—the trade-union members smoking heavy, black-encrusted pipes, while here and there, like exquisite orchids blooming among weeds, were the whey-faced intellectuals, fanning themselves with their handkerchiefs.

It was a very full house because everybody in the room realized that far more might be at stake than the future of Mr. Bevan. In view of the probability of the Conservatives' call for a general election—which was made shortly afterward for May 26—this was an historic occasion. Although some believed that the party would not suffer in the least if Bevan were banished to the wilderness, others were haunted by the fear that the struggle might eventually end in hopelessly splitting the movement. Labor might then go the way of the Socialist parties in France and Italy, and the Communists, so far a negligible force in Britain, might take over the leadership of the workers.

It was an audience that tells us a great deal about what has happened to the Labor movement since it was born fifty years ago. The Socialist party in Britain mainly came out of the hundreds of ugly little Nonconformist chapels that are to be found in English villages and once had such a profound influence on British society.

To most of the pioneers, socialism was the faith of God unto salvation—hence the pacificism that lingers on in the Labor party, the moral protests against the use of the hydrogen bomb, the persistent idealism that is sometimes genuine and is sometimes watered down to sentimentality. It was a Biblical vision that possessed the mind of the founding fathers. Just as the Jews had been brought out of Egypt, so the workers would be freed from the bondage of capitalism and led into a honey-fat land where the lion would turn vegetarian and man would at long last cease to slay his brother.

It was never Marxist, as socialism was in France and elsewhere; it was a radical party, a latter-day version of Chartism, the Anti-Corn Law League and the other nineteenth-century movements for reform. The pioneers were not even thinking of forming a new party along the lines of the existing ones; they merely wanted to have working-class representatives in the House. Every Labor M. P. was to be a "servant of the movement" and the Parliamentary party—that is, the party members in Parliament—was not to be allowed to have a life of its own but was to take its policy from the annual conference.

Much of this remains, at least in theory; the annual conference —which consists of representatives of the trade unions, the co-operative societies, and the constituency organizations—is still supposed to have the last word on policy. It meets and thunders and passes resolutions, but it is no longer the king-maker it was. The Parliamentary party has grown into an autonomous body, and while the movement outside can influence its actions while it is in opposition, the annual conference has very little power when there is a Labor Government.

The same change has occurred in the position of the leader. Originally he was merely a chairman—a somewhat nebulous person, frustrated and often ignored. But during fifty years of incubation this drab creature has hatched out into the queen of the hive. While Labor is out of office he is the person to whom the ambitious must look for future promotion, and when the party is returned he, and he alone, chooses the members of his Cabinet.

Whatever the theory may be, Clement Attlee is just as much of a force on his side as Sir Anthony Eden is in the Conservative party. In fact, one might go further. The Labor movement is ruled from the top, power being in the hands of a few trade-union officials and the leaders of the Parliamentary party. Its annual conference may be a more lively affair than the yearly meeting of the Conservatives, but its strident tone should not deceive us. The Labor party has gone the way of all flesh; to win power there has to be a machine, and a machine inevitably becomes the instrument of the rulers and not the ruled.

But although the movement has greatly changed, there is a sense in which its problem is eternal. How fascinating it is to go back and study those early days, fifty years ago, when the party was being born. How hauntingly familiar it all seems. Then, as now, there were those who cried forward and those who cried back: there were those who thought that the party should merely represent the narrow economic needs of the workers and there were the theorists who wanted a complete transformation of society.

These differences have bedeviled the party ever since. We have the trade-union M. P.'s who are instinctively suspicious of theoretical ideas and think in terms of bread and butter—of pay and conditions and social status—and opposed to them are the Bevanites who look upon nationalization as a sacred dogma, handed down from Mount Sinai with the Ten Commandments. When Mr. Bevan talks so passionately about socialism his admirers feel that he has run off with the Holy Grail.

With this in mind, let us now come back to the packed meeting that decided to withdraw the Whip from Mr. Bevan. Observe how the representatives of the middle class and the managerial revolution have infiltrated into the ranks of the movement. They are by no means all on the Left. Study Mr. Hugh Gaitskell, who has had such a dazzling ascent that he is often talked of, at least in Right-Wing circles, as the man most likely to succeed Attlee.

To Mr. Gaitskell nationalization has never been a sacred principle that has been handed down to the Labor movement from on high. Cool and detached, deeply suspicious of rhetoric, he sees nationalization purely in empirical terms; it may work in certain cases and not in others.

Harold Wilson, who in five years time will probably fight it out with Mr. Gaitskell for the leadership of the party, is not present at the meeting; discreet as always, he has flown away to France for a day or two. Mr. Wilson is short, snub-nosed, undistinguished in appearance—no one would pick him out in a crowd. Like Mr. Gaitskell, he too has a donnish background.

Though these two men are rivals and greatly dislike one another, they differ intellectually only in degree. Mr. Wilson does not feel with Mr. Bevan that nationalization is one of God's decrees; his attitude is that British industry needs a major operation and nationalization must be the knife. But no tears come to his eyes when he says this and the sufferings of the oppressed can seldom have disturbed his quiet night's sleep.

Turn now to the rest of the people on the platform. Are these the heirs of the pioneers, of the hunger marchers and the passionate agitators who used to cry for blood at the street corners? It seems much more likely that they are members of the local Rotarian Club, meeting to discuss the latest bromide.

Consider Sir Frank Soskice. He is a brilliant lawyer and a man of infinite charm, but he has come to the Labor party from the top, not the bottom. Or examine James Callaghan. Mr. Callaghan was once a trade-union official, but you would not think so to look at him—he might be a typical member of the middle class. In other words, Labor has largely ceased to be a party only for the workers. It has broadened out and become a truly national movement.

When Mr. Bevan temporarily lost his place in the Parliamentary party on that memorable day there were many people who thought that he would be subsequently expelled from the party. After three weeks of fury and alarm, he was saved by about the tenth of a gnat's eyebrow—that is to say, a compromise resolution was passed by only one vote. Thus for the first time in four years his enemies were defeated on a major issue and Mr. Bevan remains within the fold.

But this latest rumpus should not be seen in isolation. It is the newest clash in a prolonged struggle that has cruelly troubled the movement ever since Bevan resigned from the last Labor Government.

When the quarrel first broke out some people argued that Bevan's criticism of official policy would stimulate thought within the party and help it to solve its intellectual difficulties. The mating season in the Labor movement has always, they pointed out, been ushered in to the merry tune of breaking glass and the beloved has never been wholly happy until she was able to display the proud favor of two lovely black eyes.

Unfortunately, the controversy stifled thought instead of encouraging it. The quarrel dragged on so long and became so embittered that people came to think only in terms of personalities. "Nowadays," a Labor M. P. said to me the other day, "I vote the ticket."

That perfectly reveals the intellectual decay that has happened in the last four years. Brother has been so busy smiting brother that the party has had neither the time nor the inclination to work out a new approach to the social and economic problems of the day. As Socialist Commentary remarks, "If socialism is no longer merely 'the common ownership of the means of production,' then what is it?" The sad truth is that no one really knows the answer.

What is even more serious is that the Bevanite quarrel has long ceased to be a struggle at the top. The whole movement has become engaged. Every constituency has been turned into a battlefield, with Bevanite supporters on one side, and anti-Bevanites on the other.

Here, again, the struggle has gone on too long for it to be a stimulant. On the contrary, the evidence is that it has begun to take the heart out of that great army of voluntary workers on whose loyalty the movement must ultimately depend. If they do not turn out to help the party machine with their usual enthusiasm, the Conservatives will almost certainly win.

But the Bevanite quarrel is not the only burden the party has to bear. Just after the war, when the movement was so overwhelmingly returned to power, socialism seemed to offer a new and more exciting world. The homing soldier remembered the bad old days of the Nineteen Thirties when there were two million unemployed and whole towns remained year after year in stagnant idleness. Whatever happened, he did not want that kind of thing again, and he therefore turned out the Conservatives and put the Labor party into power.

But in 1955 socialism does not look quite so romantic. The vast monolithic structure of the welfare state, built so laboriously by the 1945 Labor Government, does not now seem so imposing as it did. Its style is found to be a little old-fashioned, and the cynical claim to see cracks and blemishes in the façade.

Even the workers in the industries nationalized by Labor are not so enthusiastic as they used to be. It was no doubt absurd of them to suppose that a new heaven and earth could be decreed by an act of Parliament—but people *are* unreasonable and absurd. The railwaymen, for instance, have discovered that, far from being the aristocrats of the working class, as they once were, they have steadily gone down the social ladder in both wages and status. As for the general public, it complains that the carriages are dirty, the food in the restaurants mediocre, and the trains often late.

At the same time it would be quite wrong to suggest that Labor has no chance of winning, even though the latest Gallup poll shows that the Conservatives should be returned by an increased majority. Indeed, the importance of the Bevanite controversy can be overstressed. Dispirited as the voluntary workers may have become, one cannot help feeling that they will begin to rally once again to the party as the campaign continues.

There is another point that should not be forgotten. Labor has increased its total poll at every election since the war—it is a remarkable record. If this progress can be maintained—if it is automatic, no matter what the issues happen to be—the party will do much better than many people think. "Don't fuss yourself," said one of the elder statesmen, a man who knows the movement forward and backward and has been in it since he was a boy, "we shall win, little as we may deserve it."

It is difficult to be certain because these are several unknown factors in the equation that might or might not turn out to the party's advantage. The Conservatives have just lost their greatest son—Sir Winston Churchill—and no one can tell how the public is reacting to his successor. There have, too, been whispers of a trade recession—whispers that may have alarmed the electorate and turned them against the Government. Or some utterly unexpected crisis may suddenly blow up and decide the day.

These are the imponderables, and they may, for all we know, influence the result. In the meantime the Labor party is fighting hard, though haunted by the thought that if it is returned, it may find itself grappling with forces beyond its control.

The Hard-Bitten Herr Schumacher

by Flora Lewis

HANOVER

LIKE THE FACE of Germany, Kurt Schumacher's deeply lined face has taken on a new glow of health. As leader of the German Social Democratic party he is fighting to achieve his ambition, which is hardly personal and only partly German, but is largely European. His aim is to see a Socialist and democratic Germany—he is convinced the country must be both or will be neither—take its place as an equal partner in a free European union, secure against dictatorship and the brutalities of communism, fascism, or aggressive nationalism. Schumacher's energies at the moment are directed toward the first general elections of the West German state on Aug. 14.

Both the leading politician and most controversial figure of his country, he has been constantly mentioned by prognosticators as the first President or Chancellor of the Western German Republic, born at Bonn recently. They are almost certainly wrong. Schumacher has indicated that he doesn't want these jobs, at least not now.

His reasons for this attitude sketch a quick picture of the man himself. For one thing, he said recently that he had no wish to lead or share in the leadership of a partial German State. "While Germany is divided, we must have a party which our people in the Soviet Zone can trust, a party which does not have a West German complex. That is not all. The Military Government has been acting lately as though the occupation were four months, instead of four years, old. I do not take well to that."

When he emerged from a concentration camp during the breakdown of the Nazi regime which preceded final victory in early 1945, Schumacher was, as his friends put it, "a brain without a body." He had lost one arm as a German soldier on the Russian front in the first World War. Ten years in a concentration camp had left a heavy film over his eyes so that he could barely see; a mouth jagged with broken and missing teeth; a stomach hardly worthy of the name, and a narrow frame hung thinly with crumpled, sallow skin. He expected to live about two years and confided that he was determined to make up in that short time for the wasted, wasting decade spent behind barbed wire because he opposed the Nazis.

He had been imprisoned in 1933 when he refused to flee the country after Hitler declared the Social Democratic party illegal. Although he was but one of the lesser lights of the party, he had spoken openly and bitterly in the Reichstag, where he was deputy from Wuerttemberg. In 1943 the Nazis released him. Although he was then only 48 years old, they considered him a harmless ghoul. Still, they insisted he must not return to Stuttgart, his old constituency, but find instead a place in Germany where he would be unknown and inconspicuous. He went to Hanover. In 1944, after the unsuccessful attempt to assassinate Hitler on July 20—for which several thousand Germans were executed—Schumacher was reimprisoned. Early in 1945, when the guards had gone, he went again to Hanover, which thus became the party's headquarters.

That April, even before the Allied armies had taken over, he began organizing the party. He found an old air raid warden's post, which became the office. For months there was no furniture, no pencils or paper, but he immediately went to work to establish contact with other Social Democrats all over Germany.

By October he had found enough to call a conference. But the British Military Government refused permission for an all-German conference. So, on successive days, Schumacher met with Social

Democrats from each of the four zones and surreptitiously they formed a new national executive. The fiery and devoted Schumacher was made chairman.

Ill though he was, Schumacher began stumping the country. He would stand on a speaker's platform, pouring his whole life's energy into the dramatic, acid oratory which held huge crowds spellbound for two or three hours.

Some hasty observers compared his speaking style to Hitler's, and superficially there is a resemblance. Schumacher gesticulates fiercely with his one arm, screws and wrinkles his face into wild, frenzied patterns, and sometimes lets his low throaty voice burst out into full roar. But alongside Hitler's rantings, his rhetoric would be dry and sardonic.

His Marxist training shows in his penchant for approaching his point through long historical analyses and comparisons. But he avoids the Marxist tendency to make the point in flat utopian platitudes. He argues for what he believes right with an endless flow of sarcasm mixed with a passionate contempt for what he believes is wrong.

During a 1947 tour of Germany he lived on coffee and cigarettes, bicarbonate of soda and sleeping pills. Once, during a Berlin visit, he accidentally took a handful of sleeping pills in the mistaken belief that they were the soda. Twenty-four hours later he went into a deep coma and his secretary, unable to detect any pulse in him, ran screaming from his room. Her mother, a stout Berliner, went into Schumacher's room, whacked him solidly on the back as if he were a breathless new-born babe, and brought him out of his coma.

Shortly after, he developed a thrombosis. He could not use his leg and doctors advised amputation. For months he fought to save his leg, although colleagues pleaded that his life was at stake. Finally, Gen. Lucius D. Clay, then American Military Governor, sent his doctors to see Schumacher's. Minutes after they left, Schumacher changed his mind. The amputation was performed three days later.

During his convalescence of a year, he never abandoned for a minute his position as party leader. He worked, received visitors, read, and wrote speeches and pamphlets. Two months ago he came forth again, looking better than ever before, with more flesh on his bones.

But once again, at 54, he had to make up for lost time. His year in bed had given his political enemies, of which he always has made many, a chance to renew their vitriolic attacks on him.

About the one thing Schumacher's detractors have in common is their bitterness. Most violent against him are the Communists, who call him a "traitor" and puppet of the West who "has sold German workers out for American dollars." He receives threats of assassination daily. "They are anonymous but some bear marks of Russian camps," he adds with a twinkle in his eye.

His German opponents to the Right call him a tool of the British Labor Government, an authoritarian, politicking opportunist. When he first met General Clay, he received a sharp rebuke for his fierce attacks on the Soviets which ended with: "You must not forget that the Russians are our allies." Schumacher answered, "You must remember, General, that the Communists are our enemies." An important British official in Germany denounced him as a "dogmatic, doctrinaire, distorted old man with a twisted mind." Schumacher laughs at all this.

Schumacher's program for Germany today is a mild one in Marxist terms: A large-scale government housing program; central planning on extension of credits and production; a capital levy combined with grants to equalize the burdens of war; an organized refugee program to resettle Germans who have been expelled from Eastern Europe or have fled the Soviet Zone; socialization of basic industries, especially in the Ruhr, and enough sure authority in the Federal Government's hands to carry out these projects.

These are the points Schumacher recently laid down as the conditions on which his party would enter a coalition government with the right of center Christian Democrats, the other large party in Western Germany.

The strength of the two parties, of course, cannot be determined until after the elections on Aug. 14, but right now they are considered almost equal. Of the eleven Laender of West Germany, five have Social Democrats as Premiers and five Christian Democrats. At Bonn, on the council which wrote the constitution for the West German State, the two large parties were equally represented.

In the forthcoming election the Social Democrats expect to poll about 40 per cent of the vote and the Christian Democrats about 60 per cent. But most political observers in Western Germany think the election will be closer. For one thing, the minor parties, which fall partly between the two big parties but mostly to the Right of the Christian Democrats, may well poll 15 to 20 per cent of the vote, and so hold a balance of power, making coalition inevitable if the new state is to have any political stability.

Schumacher, whose own role probably will be that of party leader in the Bundestag—lower house—of the parliament, insists: "It will be very difficult to arrange coalition." He was speaking of his own terms as well as of the clericalism on which the Christian Democrats will insist.

Schumacher is by no means a dictatorial Fuehrer, as his opponents charge, but he does have a tight grip on his party and more clean-cut authority than any other political leader in Germany, including Communist leaders. The strength of his position is due partly to his own commanding personality, partly to the nature of the Social Democratic party.

Like all Socialist parties, it is more tightly organized than is usually the case in bourgeois politics. It has 800,000 members in Western Germany, compared with about one million in all Germany just before Hitler's rise. The figure is all the more impressive when it is remembered that most Germans today are reluctant to join any party for fear their experience with denazification might be repeated and they might find, at some future date, that they held a dangerously wrong membership card.

Schumacher has no real rivals for leadership. Deputy Chairman Erich Ollenhauer usually presides at meetings because he has a smooth, easy-going temperament. Another member of the executive committee said recently, "I have been trying for twenty years to get Ollenhauer into a rage without success. With Schumacher, I do not have to try."

Yet Ollenhauer and his boss have a perfect working relationship and realize that they complement one another. Ollenhauer spent the Hitler years in England and Schumacher leans on him for advice about a world which was dead to him for over a decade. Ollenhauer gets on far better with the Allied authorities, who say with a little snicker, obviously meant for the party's chief, "It's because he (Ollenhauer) did not stay and develop that dungeon mentality."

When the firm Russian grip on the Soviet Zone relaxes, Schumacher says, Socialists of that region will be reclaimed. Rank-and-file members who were tossed into the Socialist Unity party will flock back to their old party and will be welcomed. As for former leaders of the Social Democrats in the Eastern Zone, including Otto Grotewohl, who helped engineer the merger and has become, Schumacher says, "more Stalinist than Stalin—the Social Democrats might as well take in Nazi Gauleiters as have such men back."

To their mutual satisfaction, Schumacher and the American Military Government have had little direct contact. Because his headquarters is in the British Zone, Schumacher, when he is obliged to deal with occupation authorities, usually deals with the British. It is an advantage, but less than most American Military Government officials imagine it to be.

Still Americans are inclined to blame the British for secretly backing Schumacher. Behind the scenes the British have done this to a slightly lesser extent than the Americans have supported the Christian Democrats. But the Americans distrust Schumacher immediately because he is Socialist.

They deal more regularly with Carlo Schmid, Schumacher's envoy at Bonn and a suaver, more comfortable personality than his boss. Their difference in tone has led the American Military Government people to suppose that when Schmid is troublesome it is due to Schumacher's snappish orders, and when Schmid is conciliatory it is due to his rebellion against Schumacher's snappish orders. They call Schumacher "bumbling" and "awkward," mostly because he upsets their plans and refuses to look through their eyes at the maze of complications in efforts to make Germany safe for democracy.

None of this perturbs Schumacher. In his low, cool voice, he replies calmly that "the Allies have to get over their governess complex."

Schumacher was born in the river town of Kulm in 1895, the son of a merchant. It was a Polish city in Prussia, awarded to Poland under the Treaty of Versailles. Schumacher says the reactionary Polish clergy and Prussian military convinced him as a youngster that he must turn to socialism. He became anti-Communist when he first read Lenin's fighting book, "War and Revolution." "I never believed the Russians wanted world revolution," he says. "They were after national expansion and subordination of other countries to Russian foreign policy."

He studied in Berlin and watched, in the capital, the violence that followed the 1918 German defeat. A mutilated veteran, he was unable to take part in the Socialist government's battle to put down the Communist rebellion, but he remembered how the extreme left first strengthened the militarists and far right by rising against the Socialists, and later made an open alliance which, he says, resulted in Hitler's rise to power.

In 1919, he joined the Socialist party and after a while, became editor of the party's paper in Stuttgart. In 1930, he was elected to the Reichstag, a feat for a young man in a party so well filled with venerable elders. Outspoken and energetic, he shoved his way up. People said, "He has only one arm but at least a dozen elbows." When he got to Berlin again, he joined forces with two other young Socialists—Mierendorff and Haubach—and formed the "Iron Front," a group which tried to force the party into a more belligerent and open stand against Hitler.

In the concentration camp Schumacher worked with Communist prisoners in camp plots and organizations, but he never changed his views about them.

This spring, when the Communists sought West German support for their "unity campaign" to back the Russian stand at the Council of Foreign Ministers' meeting in Paris, Schumacher turned down their invitation to a meeting in Brunswick with a growl. "We cannot confer with people who have put our colleagues to torture," he said.

He is equally determined not to knuckle under to the Western powers. Again and again his cry has been, "We will be happy to join with the rest of Europe on an equal basis."

This stand, together with his insistence that Germany's eastern frontier on the Oder-Neisse must be favorably revised, have earned him the tag of nationalist in some foreign quarters.

Schumacher explains his stand on nationalism as simple common sense. "The magic gleam of the revolutionary idea in Germany is *kaputt,*" he says. "The brutal, bureaucratic way of communism has disillusioned those who were at first attracted. * * * The danger is * * * that the people will not become pro-Russian, but that they may become anti-American, anti-British, and anti-democratic."

On the whole, the Western Allies agree with him and his evaluation of the Social Democrats.

Mollet and the Socialists Make Their Bid in France

by Robert C. Doty

PARIS, JAN. 21—The first attempt to govern France's new and theoretically ungovernable National Assembly probably will be made by Guy Mollet, secretary-general of the Socialist party, sometime next week.

M. Mollet is co-leader and, by the strength of his party, senior partner in the left-of-center Republican Front coalition of which former Premier Pierre Mendès-France, Radical party leader, is the chief architect and co-proprietor. The Jan. 2 elections gave the front only a qualified and still disputed victory and its claims to power rest more on momentum and aggressive tactics than on actual voting strength.

Still, if anyone can turn the trick of finding a majority among the 390 moderate Deputies squeezed between 151 Communists and fifty-one representatives of the Fascist-tinged petty bourgeois movement led by Pierre Poujade, M. Mollet is currently conceded to have the best chance.

Position of the Socialists

This is both a tribute to M. Mollet's reputation for integrity and intelligence and recognition of the pivotal position of the Socialist party in the splintered and disorganized block of democratic, moderate, center parties. With ninety-six seats, the Socialists are in a position to approve or block the formation of any moderate majority.

What would it mean for France and her allies if this nation were to "go Socialist" even to the limited extent that would be possible in a coalition including the more conservative, inaptly named Radicals?

Theoretically, M. Mollet and the Communist parliamentary leader Jacques Duclos seek the same Marxist economic and social objectives and, by tradition, the Socialists are revolutionaries.

Foe of Communism

In fact, M. Mollet is probably the most effective antagonist of communism in France. The Marxist dogma of the Socialists has been much modified by liberal concepts based on economic developments since Marx's time and the party is now reformist rather than revolutionary.

The "French Section of the Workers' International" (the formal label of the Socialist party) was fifty years old last year. Among its founders was "the great tribune" Jean Jaurès, assassinated in 1914, whose shade and sanction still is invoked by both Socialists and Communists.

In 1920, following the pattern set in Russia, the Bolshevist or Communist faction broke off in the "great schism" of the Congress of Tours. They formed the French Communist party and seized many of the assets, including most of the proletarian clientele, Jaurès' newspaper, Humanité, and strong elements of the General Confederation of Labor. Léon Blum, leader of the moderates, kept the old party label and traditions.

"Popular Front" Period

The Socialists rallied from the schism and held their own with the Communists throughout most of the inter-war period. M. Blum led the Popular Front of 1936 in uneasy alliance with the Communists. Both left-wing groups emerged from the Nazi occupation greatly strengthened by their role in the resistance and by the strong, hopeful current of demand for change and renaissance that was running at the time of the liberation. The Socialist strength was more than 300,000 and the Communists had a peak membership of 800,000 in 1947.

Socialist Premiers Blum and Paul Ramadier, leading Socialist-Communist-Popular Republican majorities, put through nationalizations of railroads, coal mines, electricity, gas and banking and established an extensive welfare-state mechanism. Significantly, it was M. Ramadier, in 1947, who ousted the Communists from the Government when they threatened to obstruct French participation in the Marshall Plan and construction of the Atlantic alliance.

In Governments

For the next four years, the Socialists represented the left wing of "Third Force" coalition Governments. In 1951 they went into the opposition over the issue of state aid to Catholic schools, a violation of the Socialist tradition of anti-clericalism.

Isolated from most of the allies with whom they fought the 1951 election campaign, the Socialists were picked in advance by most experts to suffer the heaviest losses this year. Instead, the party won 3,250,000 popular votes, an increase of half a million, and held 96 of the 104 seats it won by the alliance system five years ago.

Party membership today stands at 120,000 in 5,000 locals and 103 departmental and overseas federations topped by a thirty-one-member directing committee which is democratically selected and responsive to rank-and-file opinion.

Party Composition

Although strong key federations in the industrial Nord and Pas de Calais Departments assay as high as 80 per cent manual workers, they do not constitute more than 30 per cent of the party as a whole. Another 25 per cent are Government employes, including many teachers; 12 per cent are pensioners; 10 per cent are farmers, 10 per cent white-collar workers and the rest are in the liberal professions and other miscellaneous categories.

These indices sketch the outlines of a party sufficiently mature and diverse in interests to move toward social reform in many fields and to eliminate any attempt to achieve it by a "dictatorship of the proletariat."

In the international field, the Socialists are solidly in the camp of the European federalists and the defenders of the Atlantic alliance.

M. Mollet, at 50, is one of the most widely respected figures in French politics. The qualities that set him off most markedly from many of his colleagues are an inability to say one thing and mean another, a disinclination to duck the hard questions and clear evidence, confirmed in his recent stand against compromise with forces outside the Republican Front, that he would rather be right according to his lights than be Premier.

A Norman, son of a weaver, M. Mollet was educated at state expense on his outstanding record at the lower levels. As a teacher of English, he was almost continuously at odds with the authorities over his demands for better treatment for the teaching force.

He was a wartime Resistance leader and Léon Blum picked him out of the party rank and file for post-war leadership. A pioneer of the European movement, he is a past president of the Strasbourg Council of Europe and currently is a member of the action committee working to set up a six-nation atomic pool.

M. Mollet lacks the flair for drama that M. Mendès-France displays. He is not remarkable in appearance, speech or manner—a blond man of middle height with a direct blue-eyed glance behind horn-rimmed spectacles, M. Mollet is unlikely to create a mass personal following, as M. Mendès-France has done.

Personal Relationships

On the other hand, he is better at relationships at a personal level than is his political partner. M. Mendès-France has alienated many individuals by an abrupt manner that sometimes appears to smack of intellectual arrogance.

M. Mollet is a rugged, aggressive debater and has many political antagonists but few personal enemies.

According to close associates, M. Mollet has few moments of

full relaxation. Those he can snatch from his duties as a party leader, Deputy and Mayor of Arras he spends with his wife and two daughters. He has little taste or talent for humor, and seldom laughs.

No one about to tackle the job of Premier of France in 1956 has anything to laugh about, anyway.

Part 4

THE 1960's: UNCERTAIN REVIVAL

THE SIX ARTICLES in this section attest to the continuity of Socialist politics, policies, and problems in the half-century beginning in 1918. Sidney Hook is concerned with socialism's "profound retreat from Marxism" in an effort to win social reform, while Gunnar Myrdal demonstrates that the Swedish experience in socialism has hardly been a revolutionary one. Robert Doty and David Binder conclude that the Italian and German Socialist parties have abandoned ideology and soft-pedaled socialism itself in their climb toward power, while Sydney Gruson and Anthony Lewis show that the British Labor party has internal divisions, does not speak of socialism, and has difficulty in maintaining its credibility when it is in power.

In his general overview of the state of socialism in 1960, Professor Hook detected a tendency of Socialists to surrender their old ideology in return for an opportunity to win social reforms—as evidenced by the German Social Democratic abandonment of Marxism and the Labor party's downgrading of nationalization in favor of social welfare programs. Hook believed that socialism had a future, though he was uncertain about the role of Socialist parties. His strange prediction that political life would become "more responsible, less sloganized, more literate" should be taken as an example of misplaced confidence rather than as a total misreading of the future. In general, Hook's predictions about Socialist behavior have proved to be quite accurate, as demonstrated by Myrdal's article, written in 1966. Myrdal was pleased with the record of Swedish socialism, in power for more than a third of a century, noting that it had provided welfare and social security and had eschewed extreme measures, such as nationalization of industry. He did confess that socialism produced both a decline in popular self-rule as well as boredom; both factors might account for the apparent indifference of many Swedish youth to the official socialism of today.

The articles by Doty and Binder need little further explanation. Doty traces the transformation of the aging Pietro Nenni into a willing partner in Italian politics, aligning himself with the forces of reform against his old comrades for revolution. Binder discusses the career of Willy Brandt, West German Chancellor since 1969, and argues that his commitment is to reform, hardly to revolutionary change.

The two articles on the Labor party were written six years apart, the first on the eve of Labor's victory in the election of 1964 and the second shortly before its defeat in 1970. Gruson shows how, despite a certain ideological tension within its fold, the Labor party continued as a party of reform, directing its appeal to a broad social spectrum, and he writes with irony of the fact that Harold Wilson was elected party leader by the party's left, but immediately surrounded himself with men from its right. Despite the unfortunate choice of title, given the fact of defeat, Lewis offers a good general account of six years of Labor rule. Lewis' obvious antipathy to Harold Wilson seems justified by his catalog of Wilson's astonishing reversals of policy—many times against the grain of Labor's promises and humanitarian commitment. The inconsistencies of Wilson's policies, his refusal to speak the word "socialism," and his political unscrupulousness nonetheless indicated to Lewis that Labor just might win the election. Perhaps these very characteristics sealed Labor's defeat.

A New Ism for Socialism

by Sidney Hook

SOCIALIST PARTIES in Europe and in some countries of Asia are undergoing important transformations under the whiplash of recent electoral defeats. More and more they are surrendering their traditional ideology and becoming broad movements of social reform.

Their familiar programs and slogans have proved unable to win them public support in the face of the relatively high levels of prosperity and employment achieved under conservative governments. Despite increased industrialization and urbanization (processes which, according to Socialist theory, were expected to prepare the way for Socialist triumph) the appeal of their message—even to the workers whose interests they were organized to further—has declined. This appears to be as true in the Scandinavian countries as in Israel, in England as in central Europe. The rise of a new Social Democratic party in Japan under Nishio Suchero is also in line with this tendency.

The momentous change in the orientation of socialism has been dramatized by these three events: the abandonment of the traditional Marxist program by the West German Social Democratic party; the post-election discussion of the British Labor party at Blackpool and in the English Labor press, and last summer's meeting of the Sixth Congress of the Socialist International at Hamburg.

The German Social Democratic party, launched with the blessings of Marx and Engels, has always been a classic example of Socialist orthodoxy. Last fall the party adopted a new "program of principles." Not only did that program avoid the usual Marxist clichés—even terms like "class" and "class struggle" were replaced by euphemisms—but it openly acknowledged the value of private enterprise in major sectors of the economy. For "common or public ownership" it substituted the more flexible notion of "public control." The adoption of such a program (summed up in the pronouncement "as much competition as possible, as much planning as necessary") can be compared to the abandonment of basic doctrines by a religion.

In England the Labor party, under the leadership of Hugh Gaitskell, faces the possibility of a similar turn. British Labor has always placed its greatest emphasis upon the nationalization of industry. But at the Blackpool conference following the general elections, Gaitskell cautiously suggested that the emphasis be shifted from nationalization to social welfare aspects of the program.

Aroused by the Gaitskell proposal, the war horses of Socialist orthodoxy are calling for a return to "Socialist first principles," which to them means more nationalization. Since they still muster the support of an old and eloquent rank and file, who distrust the dulcet tones and uncalloused hands of the younger intellectual leaders, it will probably take some time before any change is officially adopted.

The deliberations last summer of the Sixth Congress of the Socialist International emphasized the view that Socialists must now speak not only for a class but for the public welfare. Hardly anyone at the congress identified public welfare with nationalization. The dominant mood was expressed in a remark of the Dutch Socialist Voogd: "The most important question for Socialists is no longer who owns the means of production in society but how people live in society."

The ideological revolution signaled by these three events can be summarized as a recognition by Socialists that today, when democracy is threatened by totalitarianism and war, the political rather than the economic structure of a country is more important in achieving Socialist goals.

The importance of this change from doctrinaire to liberal socialism can be understood only against the background of the traditional Socialist credo and the four chief reasons offered for its acceptance.

First among the cardinal articles of Socialist belief was public ownership or nationalization of the means of production. This was justified on two main grounds: economic, and ethical or political. Nationalization, it was felt, merely continued a process of economic expansion and monopoly already observable in capitalist society. But there was this important difference: since industry would be operated for public service rather than for private profit, its wheels could always be kept turning and the evils of the business cycle avoided.

Nationalization would also put an end to unemployment, for there would be no curb on production so long as there was a social need for what was produced. Just as important was the ethical or political justification. Since property is a form of power, those who own the means of production exert a very great control over those who must live by them. Socialists hoped that nationalization would free workers from the arbitrary exercise of power by those who owned industry.

The second main feature of socialism was planning. It was regarded as the only means by which waste of natural and human resources could be avoided. Viewing the economic plant of society as a whole, Socialists argued that planning would eliminate duplication and the unnecessary costs of competition. It would also strengthen those public services, from conservation of natural resources to education, with which government must be increasingly concerned.

Third was socialism's emphasis upon human welfare and social justice. Socialists believed that, just as all who consumed the wealth produced by society owed it some service, so society was obligated to provide adequate vocational opportunities for all who were able and willing to work. Private industry could do this only fitfully, depending upon market conditions. In its drive toward efficiency and profitable labor-saving machinery, it could not concern itself with the human and social costs of technological innovation.

Further, Socialists believed society—in order to provide equality of opportunity—must reward according to need as well as capacity. Depending upon the level of the productive forces, it must provide a constantly rising floor of compensation for all who do useful work, and a steadily declining ceiling of income for those who live on inherited wealth.

The fourth element in socialism was humanistic—the desire to bring about a society in which every individual would mature into an independent harmonious personality, developing as far as his abilities permitted. He would be either a creator or, more likely, someone capable of making creative and meaningful use of leisure. Socialists were always fond of saying, "Nothing of genuine value or culture is too good for the workers."

It was hoped that under socialism there would be a revulsion against monetary values, that human beings would learn that life's real wealth can be found only where one finds its joys—in human beings and ideas, in art, religion and science.

What happened to all these brave aspirations? To the surprise of Socialists, some of them were realized through gradual changes in the existing economic system. The capitalism of "the robber barons" gave way to a mixed economy, which was no longer a strictly free-enterprise system either in law or in fact.

Even more striking was the discovery that public ownership was not a cure-all, that human beings could be exploited and feel themselves exploited just as much by publicly owned industries as by private ones. Of this, the Communist countries furnished frightening proof. It was clear that in the absence of democratic processes, bureaucrats have far greater power over human beings—including the power of life and death—than do private owners, subject as they are to law and the countervailing force of strong and free labor unions.

Furthermore, the principles of social welfare and responsibility for the unemployed, the aged, the sick and disabled—traditional staples of the Socialist program—were adopted by those who were not Socialists. This was a universal phenomenon. The Democratic party platform of 1932 reads very much like the Republican party platform; but the record of New Deal achievements reads like the Socialist party platform of 1932—nationalization excepted.

Similarly, when the Tory party came to power in England, although it opposed further nationalization, it did not scrap the social services introduced by the Labor party. Indeed, at one time it even boasted that it had constructed more public housing than had Labor.

Rising standards of living after the war, coupled with almost full employment and the allure of modern gadgetry, took some of the fighting spirit out of the Socialist rank and file—just as the previous period of tight wartime controls had left many of them with mixed feelings about the desirability of socialism. Socialism became a movement associated with middle age, respectability and moral earnestness. It seemed to bore the young, who were looking for a good time rather than a good cause.

Finally and most important, one must list the revitalization of the ethical and democratic aspects of socialism. Socialists began to realize that large-scale industrialization and mass culture, whether under capitalism or socialism, often imperil the individual's sense of independence, of integrity, of counting for something. They returned to their original insight that the organization of production was only a means to an end—to a free, secure and significant life.

To a cog in a vast machine it matters little who sits at the levers of power—individual owner, government bureaucrat or corporate manager. What does matter, to a human being who seeks to find some meaning in his work and life, is whether he can share or influence power, whatever the legal forms of ownership. (The German Socialists have concluded that one of the ways they can best further the interest of working people is by a policy of "co-determination" which would give workers the right to elect representatives to the managerial boards of industry.)

All this represents, if not a complete abandonment of Marxism, at least a profound retreat from or revision of Marxism. Socialists are still pledged to continue the class struggle, despite their new vocabulary. But it is obvious to European Socialists that they have much more in common with their democratic non-Socialist brethren than with the Communists, whose shadow lies athwart the Continent. When threatened, the freedoms to speak and agitate, to organize and strike become better understood and more precious than before.

Does all this mean that Socialists consider their great battles have been won? It is difficult to answer unequivocally yes or no. Considerable pockets of poverty still exist. The legal forms of ownership are in the main unaltered. Nonetheless, in the area of social welfare—especially recognition of both state and industry responsibility for raising the living standards and humanizing the lives of the working population—some of the major battles have been substantially won. The opponents of socialism have accepted the welfare state in practice if not in theory—though they have sometimes done this to prevent Socialists from carrying out a more extreme program.

If this is so, does socialism have a future as a separate movement and as a separate political party? That it will have some role is indisputable. Whether it will be successful, in terms of winning elections, is less certain. Let us consider the two points independently.

Once the monolithic, chock-a-block conception of socialism is discarded, Socialist parties can no longer speak in prophetic or apocalyptic tones. They can no longer offer total solutions, only piecemeal proposals to improve this or that. They once believed that a basic economic change was sufficient for the solution of all capitalist society's major problems.

Today they know better. The evils of society, in their present view, do not all flow from free enterprise as such. Therefore Socialist party platforms of the future will not call for across-the-board nationalization, but will admit the desirability of combining competition and free enterprise in some sectors of the economy with public service corporations of various kinds in others.

With this new orientation, Socialist parties will become the parties of continuous social reform, spokesmen for all forgotten or oppressed groups, the tribunes for more social welfare. They not only will fight for measures that will increase production and insure maximum employment, but will seek to equalize opportunities, to raise the standards of health, housing, education and culture.

The reforms they advocate may be similar to those drawn up by conservative parties, but Socialists will demand more public funds for social welfare and more guarantees that the rise in standards of living will not be accompanied by erosion of personal freedoms. Socialist parties will therefore present themselves not as class parties but as the protagonists of all worthy causes that further the democratic way of life.

Will this role win elections? The answer is much more uncertain, even though the emphasis on reform rather than doctrinaire socialism recently enabled the German Socialists to win their first election over Adenauer's Christian Democratic Union in predominantly Catholic Bavaria.

Except when a country is aroused by grave political abuses, elections are won by the patient and continuous work of political organization. There is reason to believe that what Socialists may gain in popular appeal they may lose in organizational cohesiveness, once the fervor of Messianism is lost. The transformation of the Socialist parties into opposition reform parties may cost them the devotion and day-in-day-out support of the "Jimmy Higginses," the humble rank and file whose faith rests on a shining vision rather than on the slow unexciting evidence of progress. And it may well become more difficult to attract young men and women out to transform the world.

At any rate, political life in England, Germany and other countries in which the Socialist parties complete this evolution will not be as dramatic in the near future as in the past. It will be more responsible, less sloganized, more literate. (The Russian and Chinese Communists and the repercussions of their foreign policy on the domestic scene can be counted on to keep it from becoming boring.)

Outside the arena of party politics, socialism will become an ethical movement, applying the methods of scientific intelligence to the problems of national and international life. The stronger such a movement grows, the closer we in the free world will come to a society without ideologies or permanent political factions in which men will temporarily divide over specific issues independently of their overarching religious or philosophical commitments.

The rise of Fascist and Communist totalitarianism in the twentieth century should be the most powerful argument in persuading the genuinely democratic parties of the free world that what they have in common is more important than what divides them. Differences there will always be; but however grave, they need not be divisive to a point of violent conflict if common needs and aspirations and a faith in intelligence are taken as a basis for settling them.

What Is Wrong with the Welfare State?

by Gunnar Myrdal

STOCKHOLM

THERE IS A popular theory that the Swedes have been mentally and morally damaged by having too much welfare and security. In a society organized to eliminate the risks in life there must be such a lack of adventure and drama that people become frustrated and unhappy. So runs the theory of the malaise in the welfare state. Frankly, I believe it is bunk.

The reasoning is obviously too often in the nature of sour grapes, a compensating rationalization of envy. Sweden is now the richest country in Europe. The United States has a somewhat higher national income per capita, but this statistic disregards the wastage in a less well-organized society—in particular, the disutilities caused by America's slums. If we omit from the comparison a numerically small class of the very rich, ordinary Swedes are now as well off as ordinary Americans—perhaps a little better off. Americans, themselves bearing the odium of being rich, should be the first to appreciate that, quite aside from her advanced social policies, Sweden's opulence gives an emotional motive to fault-finding.

It is noteworthy that the theory of the welfare state is broadly shared by both radicals and conservatives outside Sweden. To the radicals, it is scandalous and ominous that Sweden has had a Social-Democratic (labor) Government for a third of a century that has not nationalized anything. To them, the advanced social-security legislation seems a cheap substitute for Socialism, and one that might even raise obstacles for more revolutionary changes by obliterating the misery of the poor while leaving the commanding heights securely held by the capitalists. The conservatives, on their side, dislike that type of legislation almost as much as Socialism. About the malaise of the Swedes they both cordially agree.

The popular theory about the frustrated and sad Swedes has sought support in some specific points which are all erroneous. One is the assertion of a high suicide rate in Sweden. Poor General Eisenhower—at that juncture incompetently advised by his public-relations people—some years ago made a statement to the effect that "a friendly Socialist country" was punished for its welfare state by the prevalence of suicides, among other misfortunes. Even taking the statistics at their face value, this is a plain mistake. Many countries—for instance, Finland, Denmark, Hungary, Western Germany and Austria—emerge with higher suicide rates in the official statistics. Moreover, the trend is not rising with the perfection of the welfare state.

Finally, this statistic is affected by a heavy bias which raised the apparent Swedish rate in comparison with all, or almost all, other countries. In England, for example, suicide is still a crime. In most countries, particularly the Catholic ones, it is a grave sin against the Creator. In secularized Sweden, it is not a crime and not a sin, though a regrettable deviation from normal behavior. When committed with a sane mind it is gradually becoming viewed, however, as almost a human right and a civil liberty. In any case, it is a strictly personal and family matter. Among the absolute taboos in Swedish journalism, which no newspaperman would think of transgressing, is the rule never to give publicity to suicides or divorces—they are assumed to belong to an intimate sphere from which outsiders should keep away. Thus, there is much less temptation in Sweden than in other countries for relatives to press for a verdict of accidental death when a man falls from a window or a woman takes too large a dose of sleeping pills.

Another popular idea abroad concerns the prevalence of "sin" in Sweden, meaning sexual freedom. One moot point, to begin with, is how this type of "sin" could demonstrate frustration and sadness. Moreover, the studies of sexual behavior in the wake of the Kinsey Report show a remarkable conformity in all Western countries; also, the increasing openness in discussion of sexual matters seems to be common. Finally, it should be noted that, on the whole, sexual freedom in behavior and speech in Sweden centers upon premarital relations.

Leaving aside such spurious ideas as the prevalence of suicide and sin, more fundamental questions must be raised: How is the causal relation thought to run *from* the welfare state *to* frustration and sadness? If there is continually full employment, so that mass unemployment disappears; if there is an increasingly effective public service for aiding those individuals in danger of becoming unemployed in a lagging industry, so that even the exceptional unemployment risk is reduced; if all citizens in case of illness have medical facilities at their disposal for only a nominal fee; if they can look forward to a pension in old age that, in stable value, will amount to two-thirds of their income in their best 15 years; if decent living standards are guaranteed by the state for children, widows, invalids and the handicapped; if by law it is forbidden to dismiss a woman for family reasons; if women in public service before and after childbirth are given paid leave from employment and all women are compensated for various costs relating to the event; if all schools are free and students (and their families) also are gradually relieved of the necessity of paying their living costs; if strenuous efforts are made to help families in modest circumstances find decent homes, and so on—how can all that make people feel unhappy and less free and relaxed?

There are growing pains while the welfare state is being established. There is queueing at hospitals and schools, and there are not enough nurses and teachers. There is inflationary pressure. Sweden also has its share of maladjusted youths. Generally, it is recognized that—now that the material needs of children and youths, the invalids and aged are being met—the time has come for society to organize itself to meet their needs for diversified personal attention and care as well. Thus there is a craving for the further perfection of the welfare state. But in that there is no malaise.

The real trouble with the welfare state is not what it gives the people in terms of opportunity and security. Neither is it what it costs them in taxes. They get full compensation, and generally considerably more, for great economies result from the social organization of the satisfaction of many needs, as well as from maintaining full employment and avoiding labor conflicts. This is, in fact, the explanation of why the welfare state can be so economically progressive.

A minority of the well-to-do have to pay more for such services than they get from them, it is true. And those few might indeed for a time feel frustrated and sad—until they get accustomed to the system as they do to the weather. In the end, they mostly realize that welfare and social security of this type is so highly conducive to economic growth that even they come out of it better off. The real trouble—if it is a trouble—is that a society is emerging with much less dissatisfaction, fewer burning social problems and less incitement to political struggle.

Public discussion becomes ever more technical and concerns less and less sharply dividing issues. Neither radicals nor reactionaries can find much following and have to tone down their positions if they do not want to live as mavericks—which, of course, is fully permitted in a free society. But the political parties, which must seek mass appeal, are forced to compete with one another in pressing for ever more reforms to perfect the welfare state. This is what I have called "created harmony"—in contrast to the natural harmony falsely assumed to come by itself in old liberal economic theory—and what, from his point of view, a Swedish political scientist has characterized as the "service state." Sweden has come far in this direction.

A few of us intellectuals may regret the lack of drama in which we have enjoyed playing leading roles. Sweden's welfare society does not need rebels and ardent reformers, and neither is there any place for die-hard philosophers of reaction. Instead, Sweden has use for large cadres of practical tacticians, organizers and bureaucrats.

Most potential intellectuals are now early in life being drawn into these cadres; their adventurousness is calmed and they seem happy to be engaged in practical matters. But, of course, not all react in this way. I will honestly confess that to me personally

Sweden has become somewhat boring, while I feel excited about America, the underdeveloped regions and most other countries where there are staggering problems and spectacular struggles to wage.

That foreign intellectuals, not invited to join the cadres of well-adjusted collaborators in running the welfare state, should feel bored is only natural. I suggest that the hundreds of articles about the malaise in the welfare state are written by such visiting intellectuals—though not those of the highest caliber, who have better control over their thinking. They make, of course, a cardinal mistake if they project their boredom, when viewing a happy society which has not much use for their type of special talent, into a judgment of what goes on in the minds of ordinary people in Sweden.

Intellectuals have also another reason for their grudge. Undoubtedly, the rise in material welfare and security for the masses has not been accompanied by the sharp increase in cultural participation which we believed would result from the social reforms at the time when we had to fight for them. We certainly believed, for instance, that four weeks of paid vacation would be put to somewhat other uses than those for which we now see them commonly used. But that was a mistake in our analysis of things to come. Least of all should it be taken as showing malaise among the people. Apparently, they are not so keen on higher culture as we romantically believed, but are quite happy with a small—though rising—share in it.

The culture popularly appreciated is a material culture. In all things surrounding the body—textiles, glassware, furniture, houses—Swedish consumption has reached unsurpassed levels of beauty and quality. Indeed, in this field Sweden has even become an exporter of ideas.

In literature, the effective demand has been rising more slowly. The national language, unintelligible to foreigners, acts as a protective barrier, beyond which our authors would have to meet the international competition, as harsh as ever. In the last generation few Swedish writers have ventured a flight out of the secure and gradually widening home market. The learned professions have also in recent decades mainly kept on the receiving side, except in medicine and natural science.

Undoubtedly, Swedish standards suffer from this provincialism. But why should not the cultural workers feel happy in their relative isolation? They are great at home; they can form contesting cliques or cultivate prestigious loneliness; they can discuss, criticize or praise each other. In a word, they can live as full-fledged intellectuals, and to them their small world is rich and meaningful enough. They, too, like their national audience, show few signs of malaise.

There are a number of specific elements in the situation and history of Sweden that explain why it is some years, or decades, ahead of the development of other Western countries and now provides such happiness to its own people—albeit reflected as boredom to the foreign intellectuals. For one thing, the nation is homogeneous, with no awareness of any important racial, religious or other splits. It was early in instituting popular education, and the whole nation was literate well before the onset of industrialization. Perhaps uniquely in Europe, the peasants had remained free from bondage through the centuries for they always succeeded, with the help of the kings, in crushing feudalism in its bud.

Also uniquely, Sweden has never been invaded by a foreign army. The nearest the Russians came in the many old wars, always started by the Swedes, was to burn some small towns on the eastern coast. Sweden now has enjoyed peace for 150 years.

The country is not overcrowded, and has plenty of the material resources that became important with the industrial revolution. The traditional policy of no—or very low—tariff protection has maintained an aggressive competitiveness in industry at home and abroad. Taking all these things into account, my feeling is that the Swedes ought to have been able to come much further ahead than they actually have in creating the good society.

Local self-government is the tradition from pagan times. A little more than one generation ago—and even further back, except that then the larger part of the people had no vote—Sweden was probably nearer the realization of those ideals that in America are associated with Thomas Jefferson than any other society anywhere. A large portion of the people served as active members of all sorts of local boards and committees.

In this milieu of broad-based popular participation in government, the modern civic movements grew naturally into organizations through which people fought for improvement of their living conditions; they were built and served by unpaid individuals with a zeal for the cause. This was the political basis upon which the modern democratic welfare state was erected.

In recent times, the organizations have multiplied and grown and Sweden has become the organizational state. Even very specific common interests—for instance, those of old-age pensioners and invalids, or of those suffering from diabetes or even less frequent illnesses, such as rheumatism—have now their own nationwide organizations with district branches.

Meanwhile, however, technological and administrative advance is diluting the basis of popular participation, and this development may become a real worry for the welfare state. In local administration, the active share in direct responsibility and activity of the many thousands of board members of an earlier time has, in effect, been taken over by salaried professionals. This is the trend, even when local self-government is retained.

But centralization is, at the same time, proceeding. Local units are enlarged, or local responsibility is taken over by the state. Maintenance of the roads can no longer be left to the farmers. We now drive our cars on the highways without many of us being able to recall even the name of the central authority that decides on these matters. The village cooperative is disappearing and, thereby, so is the people's fairly direct responsibility of cooperative management. The cooperatives have grown immensely and become consolidated into huge, progressive business concerns, operating industries, department stores and supermarkets—not essentially different from other big and successful private corporations except that there are no shareholders. But, of course, shareholders are of less importance in corporations, too, than they used to be.

The trade-union system is coming to embrace the workers 100 per cent—not by any legislated or contracted "closed shops," but because it is becoming the accepted mores—and the employers' unions are becoming equally inclusive.

Together they come to function as organs for what in reality is public policy. The state can abstain from interference in the labor market, because these organizations regularly reach agreement after their bargainings, and in Sweden there are virtually no longer any working days lost because of labor conflicts.

Generally, more and more of public policy is, in fact, delegated to such powerful organizations, releasing the Swedes from much state interference that in the United States, for instance, is necessary.

For the rest, the state itself creates the central administrative machinery it needs for carrying out its policies, not least in the welfare field. These state organs work closely with the organizations; the members of the Government and Parliament are often recruited from the hierarchies of these organizations.

This development toward professionalism and centralization means, however, a gradual decrease of the intense popular participation that once was the basis for the erection of the welfare state. The power is more and more expropriated by the hierarchies in the organizations, the various branches of administration and the political parties. In our type of society these different hierarchies—or establishments, to use a British term—have much in common. Many years ago, a group of American journalists were bewildered by being invited to a dinner given jointly by the central organizations of trade unions and employers. But this was, I explained to them, perfectly natural from a Swedish point of view. These people were one other's closest colleagues and had common business daily. Why should they not do their entertaining together—particularly as it would cut the costs in half?

This situation implies, of course, less control from below. The hierarchies operate efficiently in defending the interests of workers, employers, consumers, and so on. It is true that in no other country do they work harder to keep up contact with their clientele and to promote educational activity. But no establishment can be expected to turn against itself. It must tend to give guidance, rather than foster criticism. And so the public-relations activity directed toward the membership naturally increases the satisfaction of the members with their organizations. In this situation, it is but natural that the top echelons tend to perpetuate themselves in power, selecting their own recruits. The same is true of the political parties and, of course, the Administration.

Particularly with the extraordinary power of the several hierarchies, and the close relations among them, the question must be raised whether there is not danger of collusion and corruption. As far as I can judge, this danger has not materialized. There is little moral decay in the organizations, the administrations or politics. With watchful publicity and the force of tradition, it may be possible to prevent it, at least for the foreseeable future.

What remains, then, is that as a result of technological and organizational advance the ordinary citizen is becoming more and more distant from the actual pursuance of government in its wide meaning. Things are taken care of for him by a "topside" that is certainly more democratic than the British prototype—based as it is more on merit and advance within the several hierarchies and less on caste, family and personal wealth—but, nevertheless, fairly independent of the constituencies.

The question is whether or not this release from immediate responsibility is to the liking of ordinary people. The Communists assert that when class differences are obliterated, there is no need for party strife. Adolf Hitler wrote in *"Mein Kampf"* that it was not natural for people to be deeply interested in politics. Our dislike for Communism and Nazism should not close our eyes to the possibility that they might have a point here. If, in a society, opportunities are equalized to a reasonable extent, and if people feel—and are brought to feel—that things are well taken care of, they might be happy to be released of the immediate responsibility for managing their society.

A very few of us intellectuals, who are not swallowed up in the establishments (or, as foreigners, are given no chance to be), may not be equally happy. But we are not the regular ones. Our feelings of malaise in a society too quietly progressing by bargaining and cooperation among the hierarchies in the political parties, the Administration and the organizations—more and more above the heads of the people, without much glory of struggle—should not be taken to represent how people in general feel. Swedes in general are now the freer to enjoy their private pleasures in life—which are what really interests them.

There are only two more observations that must be made, but they are important. All rich countries have for a long time been on the same road to the democratic and capitalistic welfare state. When Sweden has been picked out for special attention abroad, it is only because it is some distance ahead of the others. In regard to affluence, which is such an essential precondition for an advanced welfare state, Sweden is only some years, or at most a decade or two ahead of other European countries, and is on a par with the United States.

In regard to the redistributional reforms aimed at building a floor of security and opportunity for all the citizens, the other Scandinavian countries are not far behind. And, in all the rich countries, these reforms are being pushed, although with varying force. In the United States, President Johnson's Great Society is the final recognition of the welfare state as a national goal. With its huge slum sectors—implying, among other things, the need to rebuild completely its big cities—a generation might have to pass before the country reaches a more complete realization of that goal. Many countries, especially the United States, will for various reasons meet greater difficulties in building such organizational infrastructures as Sweden has, with the result that more things will have to be managed, in the meantime, by state intervention, legislation and administration. But whatever the differences and difficulties are, all rich countries are now set on the road to the welfare state. Do they really feel that what they are striving toward is tainted by popular malaise?

The second observation is that outside our little minority of affluent countries, gradually perfecting the welfare state, there is the huge world slum. Nobody has found the means by which the development toward an ever-widening gap between incomes of the colored majority of very poor people and the rich white nations can be turned. And no one can predict what the outcome of that development will be for them and for us.

Now Nenni Calls Ideology a Fetish

by Robert C. Doty

ROME, NOV. 5—Italian Socialism appeared to have completed last week its long evolution from doctrinaire revolutionary Marxism to the common European Socialist pattern of reform and serious candidacy for power within the democratic system.

This objective of the newly unified Socialist-Democratic Socialist party was put succinctly by the man who led the Socialists first in their post-war alliance with Communism, then the break 10 years ago, and finally into a share of power in the center-left coalition, 75-year-old Deputy Premier Pietro Nenni:

"[We want] a party not the slave of ideological fetishes, but based on a policy and a program, without dogmas, without an internal or external 'Church'; a party able to give to intellectuals, to women, to the young, something that neither the Christian Democrats nor the Communists have been able to offer."

Commitment to Reform

Statements in that vein, echoed by most other speakers—Socialist and Democratic Socialist—at their unification congress last Sunday seemed to indicate that the last old line Marxist Socialist party in Western Europe had made its commitment to the reformist course followed by the other European Socialist parties.

In the first few post-war years, the alliance of Catholic, Communist and Socialist forces forged in the various resistance movements governed in much of Western Europe, notably in France and Italy.

This "tripartism" was one of the earliest victims of the Cold War that followed the split between Russia and the Western Allies, and the Socialists were the principal losers. The Catholic parties, moving to the right, seized the bulk of the middle-class electorate terrified by the threat of a Communist takeover, and the Communists won the lion's share of the discontented worker left.

The Socialists, caught in the middle, too Marxist for the middle classes, not militant enough for the workers in the then depressed economic conditions of Europe, came off a bad third, again, particularly in France and Italy.

On most of the continent, Socialists rallied quickly by aligning themselves with democratic center forces, endorsing the Atlantic Alliance against Soviet military threats, supporting European economic integration and boycotting the authoritarian pro-Soviet Communist Left. This process of participation in Center coalitions involved progressive dilution of such traditional Socialist aims as nationalizations—though some were carried out in most countries —and total abandonment of revolutionary tactics.

This moved most European Socialist parties closer to the position of those of the Scandinavian countries, gradualists in power much of the time since the Nineteen-thirties, and of Great Britain's Labor party, a pragmatic, nondoctrinaire force emerging from war on more or less equal terms with the Conservatives.

However, in Italy, the Socialists under Mr. Nenni with their strong roots of conventional class warfare Marxism and anticlericalism, clung to "unity of the working class" with the Communists. Giuseppe Saragat, today Italy's President, dissented and, in 1947, led an anti-Communist minority out of the Socialist party, formed the Democratic Socialist party. He followed the European pattern of socialist gradualism, participation with Christian Democrats and liberals in Center governments and support for the Atlantic Alliance and European integration.

Hungary, Stalinism, and the arrogance and lack of internal party democracy of their Communist partners gradually disillusioned the

Nenni Socialists. By 1962, they were ready to support, by 1963, to enter, a center-left coalition government with Christian Democrats and Saragat Democratic Socialists. With the Communist bone of contention removed, reunification of the two Socialist parties followed naturally.

It is now the objective of the reunified Socialists to attract votes from among disillusioned Communists and leftwing Christian Democrats, increase their strength in Parliament in the 1968 elections and be in position to bid for national leadership instead of junior partnership in power five years later.

Elsewhere in Europe, Socialist fortunes defy attempts to trace a common pattern. Three decades of Socialist dominance have been overturned in Norway and shaken in Sweden and Denmark, suggesting that Socialist parties, like bourgeois parties, are subject to the erosion, fatigue and decay brought about by exercise of power.

In Britain, the Labor party exercises power with a comfortable majority, but an uncomfortable economic situation forcing adoption of unpopular, un-Socialist austerity measures that outrage the party's left wing.

Potential in Germany

In West Germany, the Socialists, heirs to the entire left with Communism outlawed, virtually abandoned the traditional Socialist aim of nationalization of industry in 1959. Under the dynamic leadership of Berlin Mayor Willy Brandt, the German Socialists may emerge from the present crisis of the Christian Democratic Government either as equal partners with the Christian Democrats or as leaders of a coalition with the small Free Democratic party.

Their "Socialism" is of such a bland variety that it frightens German free enterprisers about as much as the United States Democratic party frightens the National Association of Manufacturers.

Socialists in Belgium, in opposition after participation in most post-war Governments, and in the Netherlands, still in coalition with the Catholics, are floundering in a welter of purely local issues and both have lost strength in recent elections. Like Socialist parties everywhere, they still have heavy backing from organized labor.

In France, the Socialists, like the other traditional parties, are overshadowed by the dominant figure of President Charles de

Gaulle. Their leader, former Premier Guy Mollet, has led them through an ideological maze. This has included leadership of the 1956 British-French invasion of Egypt, efforts to "integrate" Algeria by force of arms, a bit of 1958-59 Gaullism and a stern anti-Communism summed up in the epigram: "The Communists are not of the Left they are of the East." Mr. Mollet, swinging full circle, is now dickering for alliances with the Communists against Gaullism.

Willy Brandt's *Wanderjahre* Are Finished

by David Binder

BONN

AT 11 A.M., Central European Time, on Tuesday, Sept. 23, Foreign Minister Willy Brandt started looking like the Chancellor of the German Federal Republic.

It was still 117 hours before the polls were to open, 132 hours before his decision that his Social Democratic party (S.P.D.) had won enough votes for him to bid for the Chancellorship, and 28 full days before his actual election as Chancellor in the Rhineside Bundestag. In addition, he had just interrupted three grueling weeks of campaigning to make a blitz visit to the United Nations in New York, taking advantage of the opportunity that the opening of the General Assembly offers to confer in one day with no fewer than eight fellow foreign ministers—especially Secretary of State William Rogers, Andrei Gromyko of the Soviet Union and Corneliu Manescu of Communist Rumania—and Assembly President Angie Brooks. Yet, here he was in the modern, rosewood-paneled press conference room at Bonn's Tulpenfeld Plaza looking as fresh as if he had just come from a holiday, grinning broadly and cracking jokes with the 150 assembled newsmen.

For those who had watched him on the campaign trail a few

days before in Baden-Württemberg, it seemed as if an exhausted Foreign Minister Willy Brandt had suddenly been transformed into a vigorous man who was about to win the highest governmental post in the land. He even allowed himself a few modest replies to questions on how he would run the Chancellery.

Brandt's election Oct. 21 by his "minicoalition" of Social and Free Democrats is the culmination of one of the most extraordinary political odysseys of modern times and an achievement that seems to defy nearly every convention of what is generally assumed to be "German." By traditional German standards he had nearly everything against him. He was born out of wedlock in a country which, until a reform last spring, retained a legal code that discriminated against not only illegitimate children but also their mothers, by denying inheritance rights to the children and legal guardianship to the mothers. He was from 1933 until 1945 an expatriate in Scandinavia while most of his contemporaries were swearing oaths to live and die for Adolf Hitler and the German Fatherland. He was even interned briefly in a German prisoner-of-war camp as a "Norwegian soldier" in a Norwegian uniform, and he had gone to Berlin in December, 1946, in the uniform of a Norwegian officer as a member of Oslo's military mission in the occupied city. Finally, he was a member of that same Social Democratic party of Germany which Chancellor Otto von Bismarck had once denounced as "an enemy of the Reich."

In this context, his elevation to the Chancellorship as the first Social Democrat to hold this office in Germany since Hermann Müller stepped down in 1930 marks not only a turning point in national politics but also in national mores. It underscores the vast changes that have taken place in the minds of the Germans of the Federal Republic—away from a narrow concept of nationalism and patriotism, and away from absolute and prejudiced views of what constitutes a "good family." Today's Germans, or at least a thin political majority of them, neither fear nor resent "foreign" influences as they were told to in Hitler's day. They relish foreign delicacies in a thousand foreign restaurants. They live easily with 1.4 million Italians, Turks, Spaniards, Greeks and Yugoslavs who have come here to work. They travel abroad in ever-growing numbers—10 million this year. They are reveling in their own "sex revolution" and, following vicious smear campaigns against his origins in 1961 and 1965, they now are welcoming Willy Brandt as a politician who is intelligent, hardworking and effective. Brandt himself recently took note of this enormous change of mind, observing: "He who has a sense of history will not lightly overlook that a man of my origin and convictions has become the German Minister of Foreign Affairs."

Relaxing on the sunny terrace of a country house in the Eifel hills 11 days after the election and his arduous coalition talks with the leaders of the small Free Democratic party, Chancellor Brandt recalled that September press conference and why he had suddenly come into such a good mood that morning: "I had been a bit down, you know. My vocal chords had gone several times, and I had become depressed by that disgusting routine of campaigning around like a gypsy without being able to do any reasonable work. I had behaved in New York and gone to bed early—10:30—and really slept for the first time in weeks. Then I caught some more sleep on the flight back. When I got here, I knew it was just a little bit more to go to the end of the week and the campaign." He sipped a gin and tonic and concluded: "All at once I felt good."

On this day, he was still feeling good, bubbling with dry wit. Lighting one of his current brand of cigarillos called "Attaché" he observed with a broad grin: "I will have to change brands—as Chancellor I can't smoke Attachés. A Chancellor has to be beyond good and evil."

He then dilated on the theme of his coming Chancellorship. "You notice I said I would be a Chancellor of domestic reforms. There will be a lot of domestic policy making. Heck [Bruno Heck, the conservative party manager of the Christian Democratic Union] said democracy is good for the state but not for society. But our position is to overcome the distinction between *Untertanen* [subjects] and *Obrigkeit* [authority], to create co-responsibility in society. We have a potent economy, but we still have terrible discrepancies. There is not enough free flow from one profession to another. People must become less biased."

Specifically, the Brandt Administration hopes to eliminate some of the more shocking discrepancies between income groups here, whereby a farmhand gets $125 a month, an industrial worker about $400 a month and industrial managers anywhere from

$2,500 to $5,000. He and his Free Democratic partners want to do this by redistributing tax burdens as well as introducing legislation to stimulate the acquisition of private capital by workers.

"As for Germany's position in the world," Brandt continued, "we must connect all we do with a full affirmation to the Federal Republic—less a foreign policy than a Germany policy. After all, the national existence of the Federal Republic is not provisory. This means caring about what comes in the future in the national sense—that is, moving toward the other part of Germany and not away from it."

Brandt sees this task in the same way as does his party's deputy leader, Herbert Wehner, who defined West Germany's postwar situation two years ago as that of a country with a "critical size—too big to play no role in the balance of power and too small to keep the powers around it balanced." It is their attempt to recognize the "reality" of a country with an area of 95,900 square miles—or less than half the area of the German Reich created by Bismarck in the 19th century.

What they and Walter Scheel, the urbane leader of the Free Democrats, want is a policy which is measured according to that "critical size," seeking good relations with West Germany's neighbors and thereby contributing to "peaceful solutions" of all the problems remaining as vestiges of World War II.

"The Poles," said Brandt, "the Soviets, the Hungarians have their own interests in differentiating their policies toward us. I do not think the D.D.R. [German Democratic Republic] can escape this. But we will avoid everything that seems like Social Democratic infiltration of the East. Why break our heads over their problems? We have to do what we think is right and see what comes of it."

The Brandt administration will offer East Germany a treaty to renounce the use of force between the two German states and to recognize the inviolability of each other's borders as well as the territorial integrity of the two states.

Brandt, relaxed in his wicker chair, looked up to the sky and paused for a minute. "What's that bird circling there?" he inquired. "I've got a pair of binoculars upstairs. Just a minute." But Brandt, as notorious for his lack of knowledge of birds, beasts and machines as he is noted for his sagacity in political affairs, could not identify the large-winged creature. His host, Werner von Schnitzler, said: "It is indubitably a buzzard." "That is one problem solved," said Brandt, and sat down again.

A man who looks bigger than his 5 feet 10½ inches and his 198 pounds, he was wearing the kind of loafing clothes he likes on his vacations in Norway—brown corduroy trousers, and light blue, open-necked shirt under a dark blue lounging jacket. He retained a deep tan from the sunny September days of his outdoor campaigning, and the fatigue wrinkles seemed to have given way to the worry and laugh wrinkles that permanently line his large face. He looked a bit like the seaman he once wanted to be, and one was reminded that one of his few treasures is an old sailor's chest from his native Lübeck, a Hanseatic town that grew great on shipping in the Middle Ages. Brandt keeps his private papers in it—among them the notes he sketched out earlier this year when contemplating whom he would put into his Cabinet if he gained the Chancellorship.

Picking up the thread of his remarks on the Chancellorship, Brandt resumed in that husky voice which has often been described as "gravelly"—and which is certainly closer to that of Louis Armstrong than to that of Mel Torme. "I said during the campaign that we would have a hundred days of action, but perhaps it would be better to talk of half a year."

He explained that he had become uncomfortable about his "hundred days" usage after it occurred to him that, in the German postelection calendar, Christmas, New Year's and the Rhineland *Karneval* (Mardi Gras) vacations cut heavily into the working time of a new Government. However, in the next "hundred days," he can be expected to make a concrete bid to the Soviet Union for completing an exchange of multilateral declarations to renounce the use of force between West Germany and all the Soviet-bloc states. He can also be expected to initiate legislation in numerous domestic fields—beginning with education and scientific development. Tax-reform legislation will follow in the spring of 1970, along with bills on expanding the Federal transport budget and regional industrialization programs.

The "hundred days" remark was, of course, an allusion to the swift actions undertaken in 1933 by Franklin D. Roosevelt, and proclaimed again by the Administration of John F. Kennedy in 1961. Brandt, a constant student of politics, knows a lot about Roosevelt and admires, with European reservations, the style of Kennedy.

West Germany is in a period of economic boom and continuing social stability, so that razzle-dazzle is not an order of the day. Brandt knows this. But he also knows that his administration, with its narrow, 12-vote majority in the Bundestag, must produce popular results fast if his coalition with the Free Democrats is to hold on to power. Failure could bring defections—not from among his well-disciplined Social Democrats, but among the fair-weatherers in the Free Democratic party who have wobbled like barometers in tempestuous times before. The Free Democrats got only 5.8 per cent of the vote this time, and therefore have only 30 members in Parliament—but at least three of them are considered waverers. If another three should become defectors, the small coalition would be finished.

Brandt has high admiration for the Free Democrats' Scheel as the man who swung his still-conservative members into line to vote last March 5 for Gustav Heinemann as the first Social Democratic President of the Federal Republic, giving him a tiny majority. He has also publicly stated his respect for Scheel's ability in foreign affairs. It seems to be one of Brandt's most effective qualities as a politician that he never fails to acknowledge the contributions and capabilities of his associates. This is an element of his profound belief in what he calls, in English, "teamwork." Perhaps it derives also from not having a mean bone in his body. During the war, in 1941, when he was in political exile, he wrote a Swedish friend: "If it were the way some say, that the entire German people consisted of Nazis, then Hitler would certainly not need to rule with the help of terror, Gestapo and concentration camps." Of his four-week term in the P.O.W. camp in the Norwegian town of Dovre, he observed: "In the German Army there were Nazis—and Germans."

Winding up his talk on the sunny terrace, Brandt answered a question on how he decided to make his bid for the Chancellorship, which he presented on national television at 11:45 P.M., before the votes were all tallied, on Election Day. Alluding to the contradiction between the television-sponsored computer projections which had put the Christian Democratic Union parties at a dominant 47.6 per cent of the returns, instead of their final 46.1 per cent, Brandt grinned. "One has to be able to count," he said.

Asked whether that applied also to President Nixon, who swallowed the erroneous computer projections and prematurely telephoned Chancellor Kurt Georg Kiesinger of the Christian Democrats during the election night to congratulate him, Brandt, the experienced diplomat, merely chuckled. Some of his Social Democratic associates had reported earlier that Brandt was so irritated by that call he almost called in the American Ambassador to protest against interference in Germany's internal affairs.

Shortly after Brandt's chuckle ended, his personal assistant, the jurist Claus Sönksen, came out to tell him that lunch was ready and that his potato pancakes were getting cold. Beyond Moselle wine, beer, whisky and gin, Brandt likes the heavier dishes from the German kitchen—kale and smoked pork, mutton and cabbage and lentil soup.

The career of Willy Brandt had the least auspicious beginnings imaginable. He was born Herbert Ernst Karl Frahm on Dec. 18, 1913. His mother, Martha Frahm, was only 19 and supported herself as a shopgirl in Lübeck. The father, whom Brandt never saw, had already moved on. He recalls having heard the man's name when he was about 14, and thought it sounded Scandinavian. The father was not mentioned in the household—a flat with one room and a kitchen. But Herbert remained devoted to his mother until her death last summer.

He was often alone as a child, and it was not until 1918, when his grandfather returned from the war, that a semblance of family life began for the Frahms. The boy doted on his grandfather, a farmhand from neighboring Mecklenburg who had seen his own father whipped by his master. Grandfather Frahm, whom Herbert called "Papa," had become the first member of the Social Democratic party in his village, and he resumed party activity in Lübeck, where he got a job as a truck driver at the Draeger works. "I was born into Socialism," said Willy Brandt in his 1960 "autobiography," "My Road to Berlin," "as told to" Leo Lania.

One of his earliest memories from the inflation period of the early nineteen-twenties was of a strike in which "Papa" was active. One day, an official of the Draeger works gave young Herbert money to buy rolls at a bakery. "Take the bread back," ordered Grandfather. "A striker accepts no gifts. We ask for our rights—not for gifts." The boy obeyed.

A bright boy, he was admitted to the Johanneum High School at 13 on a scholarship. That same year, his mother married a bricklayer, Emil Kuhlmann, whom Herbert immediately liked. He was already busy in Social Democratic youth groups—the *Kinderfreunde* (Children's Friends), then the Workers Mandolin Club and, afterward, the S.P.D.'s scout organization, *Die Falken* (The Falcons). His first acquaintance with Scandinavia came in 1927 on a summer outing to Denmark.

At the Johanneum, he began writing articles for the Lübeck S.P.D. paper, Der Volksbote (The People's Messenger). The editor of Der Volksbote was Julius Leber, an Alsatian German war veteran who was the most prominent Social Democrat of the area. He took a liking to the gifted youth, and it was mutual. "There was an emptiness in my life," Brandt recalled three decades later. "Leber filled it."

"I had many friends," Brandt went on in his recollections, "but not one who was really close to me. I felt it difficult to confide in other people. From my early years, I maintained this reserve. Accustomed to live within myself, I found it not easy to share my sentiments and inner thoughts with others." People who know Brandt today say this is still true. One of his rare intimates, a Swedish diplomat, said: "Sometimes we hardly spoke for hours on end, and yet I feel these were moments of deep friendship."

In 1930, Leber sponsored Herbert Frahm's membership in the Social Democratic party. He was, at 16, two years too young, but the party made an exception at Leber's behest. The brown clouds of Hitler's Nazi party were already hovering on Germany's political horizon, and through Leber the boy learned to recognize the peril. But he had the impetuosity of youth and it seemed to him the Social Democratic party was too lax and formal to meet the danger.

Soon, he was marching in radical Socialist street demonstrations with the slogan: "Republic—that's too tame. Socialism is the aim." His grandfather admonished him: "How could you be so ungrateful?"

These were months when Socialists and Nazis were clashing on the streets of a hundred German cities. Herbert Frahm, grown tall and sturdy, mixed it up more than once with the Nazi toughs. It seemed to him and his friends that the radical situation called for radical policies. Against Leber's pleas—"You are quite normal; you don't belong with that gang of sectarians"—he quit the S.P.D. in 1931 and joined an extremist splinter group called the Socialist Workers party. Five years ago he explained this switch in an interview as "going out to be confronted in another way." He went on: "It was Bebel's social democracy [August Bebel, the great 19th-century S.P.D. leader] that was alive in the young left Socialists, and it was dissatisfaction with the Weimar state, whereby we believed then—and that was the real mistake—that it was due to too little socialism. But it was really due to too little fighting democracy. As a young man then, I attributed more significance to dogmatic programs than I would today. But I don't regret the experience in the splinter group. I was put to the test more than as a member of a mass party."

In 1932, he earned his high-school *Abitur,* the equivalent of a junior-college diploma in the United States, and, to support himself, got a job as a clerk in a ship brokerage firm. It was the closest he ever got to being a "worker" in the proletarian sense handed down by three generations of German Socialists from Karl Marx, Friedrich Engels and Ferdinand Lassalle. This explains partly why Willy Brandt's early dogmatism never froze into a permanent mold, as was the case with so many Socialists who grew up in the trade-union movement.

Meanwhile, he was beginning to earn a few marks with his newspaper articles under the pen name "Willy Brandt." In July, 1932, he and his Workers party friends came together again with the Social Democratic regulars in Lübeck for an anti-Nazi rally at which Leber was the principal speaker. Storm Troopers broke up the meeting and Leber had to fight his way free with a chair. Brandt saw Leber once more—at a large rally on Feb. 19, 1933, three weeks after Hitler had seized power. The dauntless Social Democrat had been released from a prison hospital where he was recovering from injuries suffered in an assault by Nazis. Brandt heard him speak one word: "Liberty." He never saw him again.

Soon after, Brandt was instructed by his splinter group to make his way to Oslo to set up an exile office. Through friends he had acquired in the ship brokerage and from a previous visit to Norway, he got a ride on a fishing boat to the Danish island of Lolland.

While he was to return to Berlin briefly in 1936 as an undercover observer for his splinter party, the voyage from Germany was the beginning of a 12-year exile and much more. He shed his given name and became Willy Brandt. As he later explained: "Everything I was, since I grew up—everything I did for the good, and sometimes not-so-well-thought-out, things, with all the mistakes included—was concerned with this name. That was the name under which I was sent to the Norwegians, under which I wrote and spoke. In the real sense of the word, I made my name, this name since I was 19."

Denmark, Norway, Sweden, the principal stations of his exile, were also stopping places in the *Wanderjahre* of a political journeyman who, following his Lübeck apprenticeship, exile and return to Germany, has surely earned his master's diploma in politics, if nothing else. For politics is to Brandt what painting is to Picasso—the beginning and end of his day. His wife of 21 years, Rut, says: "Sometimes I think he dreams politics."

Had Brandt stayed in Germany, he might conceivably have been drawn to the Communist party, as was his Socialist Worker friend Jacob Walcher, who joined up with Walter Ulbricht in East Germany after World War II. But his Scandinavian experience, which he freely calls "very decisive," became for him a liberation from his youthful commitment to dogmatism.

Brandt was immediately adopted by the Norwegian Labor party, then considered radical in the European Socialist movement. He was given space in the party paper, Arbeiderbladet, a monthly allowance, and a job as head of the Refugee Federation. He got a scholarship to study history at Oslo University in 1934, and money to meet some of his German party friends in Holland that same year. He quickly learned Norwegian and, within a few months, was making public speeches in the language. His linguistic talent later expanded to include Swedish, English and French.

In February, 1937, with the sponsorship of several Scandinavian papers, he went to Republican Spain to cover the Civil War for five months. There, where George Orwell, Ernest Hemingway and so many others were getting a taste of the war to come, Brandt witnessed firsthand the brutality of the Fascists and their allies—as well as of the Stalinists, who were subverting the Republic. One of his friends, Mark Rein, the son of a prominent Russian Socialist, was executed by the Communists during his stay. Some of his experiences found their way into the first of his six books, "War Aims of the Great Powers and the New Europe," published in Oslo in 1940. Throughout these years, he was frequently on the road—to Copenhagen in 1935 to meet his mother, to Brno, Czechoslovakia, in 1936 to confer with party colleagues, to Paris in 1938 for a conference attempting to erect a Popular Front movement against Hitler.

Back in Oslo, Brandt fell in love with a Norwegian girl named Carlota, and in 1940 they married. She became pregnant shortly before the Wehrmacht invaded the country, April 9, 1940. As a political exile and a stateless person, Brandt was in double jeopardy. His wife agreed he should flee northward. On May 1, in the fjord town of Andalsnes, the Germans caught up with him. He threw away his papers, donned a Norwegian uniform, and entered internment as a Norwegian. (Only later did he acquire Norwegian citizenship papers, having been "denaturalized" by Hitler's Nuremberg Laws in 1936.) After release from the P.O.W. camp, he returned to Oslo and, in July, went on to neutral Sweden, crossing the guarded border on foot. His wife and infant daughter, Ninja, followed a year later. Brandt returned several times to Oslo on underground missions.

In Stockholm, he continued writing books and newspaper articles and was active in Social Democratic exile circles. His next two books, "Guerrilla Warfare" and "After Victory," were published in Sweden. In the second, he wrote: "I have lost my fatherland twice during these years. I am working to regain two fatherlands—a free Norway and a democratic Germany. The day will come when hatred, which is unavoidable in war, is overcome. One day, Europe must become a reality in which Europeans can live."

Reading Brandt's exile writings 25 years later, one has the impression of a lucid mind, clear exposition and an almost instinctive grasp of the political realities of the day. In some cases, he was clearly prescient, and in no case did he bore his readers with platitudes. But his métier was always the politics of a situation, rather than its sound, sight or smell. Summing up his Scandinavian years recently, Brandt said it had been a time of "deideologization."

Evidently the viscissitudes of exile wore hard on his marriage. He and Carlota parted in 1944 "without hard feelings," as he described it, adding, "Politics is a stern master. I would always find it difficult to lead a normal family life." Their daughter, now an Oslo school teacher, continues to visit her father.

Brandt met his second wife, Rut, a few months before the war ended. She was also married, to an ailing Norwegian refugee in Stockholm, who died soon after. The two exiles were drawn to each other and kept close together until they married in Berlin in early 1948.

Brandt returned to defeated, occupied Germany in October, 1945, to cover the first of the Nuremberg war crimes trials. He also scouted the devastated political landscape, resuming contact with the Social Democratic leaders who had survived the war in concentration camps or exile. But, as he notes, Brandt was not a "man of the first hour" in the re-establishment of the party in occupied Germany. Though he met with Kurt Schumacher, the crippled party leader, and Ernst Reuter, later Mayor of Berlin, he resisted their offers of jobs in Germany for almost two years. He was, after all, a Norwegian citizen and, although he had rejoined the Social Democratic movement in Scandinavia, he had quit the German party in 1931.

Brandt returned to Germany in stages. He became the Norwegian press attaché in Berlin in 1946. He resumed German citizenship in his native Lübeck at the end of 1947. At this time, he rejoined the S.P.D. and, at the request of Schumacher, took the job of representative of the party executive in Berlin. Writing his Norwegian friends and sponsors of his decision, he expressed "deepest thanks for all that the Norwegian workers' movement has given me for the further journey."

His *Wanderjahre* were finished and his career as a practicing politician began. But it was not until Nov. 5, 1956, that he was accepted by Berliners as one of their own. On that day, he twice stopped mobs angered over the crushing of the Hungarian rebellion by Red Army tanks from rushing into East Berlin and precipitating certain bloodshed. With Rut at his side, he calmed the demonstrators by leading them in singing "I Had a Comrade" and the German national anthem. After that, he seemed a natural choice to succeed the governing Mayor, Otto Suhr, when he died the following year.

Like his predecessors, Brandt conceived his role of West Berlin's Mayor as primarily one of keeping the problem of the isolated city before the eyes of the West. With this in mind, he traveled the world and cultivated its leaders, keeping them up to date on what was happening in his city, 110 miles inside Communist East Germany. His critics in the city charge that in the process he neglected some key aspects of West Berlin's domestic problems, including mounting frustration and radicalization of the university students over their archaic educational system. Brandt's successors, Heinrich Albertz and Klaus Schütz, paid the price for that neglect in a series of violent riots in 1967 and 1968. Therefore it is with keen interest that his critics heard Brandt promise to be a "Chancellor of domestic reforms" in West Germany.

But nobody in Berlin or elsewhere in this country doubted that Brandt was the man to have around on Aug. 13, 1961, when the East Germans of Walter Ulbricht began raising the barriers that soon became today's thick concrete wall across Berlin. He interrupted election campaigning in Lower Saxony and took the first plane to the beleagured city. Chancellor Adenauer waited nine days. Facing the three Allied commandants that afternoon, Brandt told them coldly: "You let yourselves be kicked in the behind by Ulbricht last night." The embarrassed generals remained silent. They had no orders to do anything against the barriers.

Brandt's gravest problem was the morale of the 2.2 million West Berliners, which had been undermined by the complete lack of Western response to their predicament. His principal aide, Egon Bahr, said to him: "We are sold out but not yet delivered." Brandt replied: "Kennedy cooked our goose."

Two days later, he wrote to John F. Kennedy, who had gone sailing: "I estimate the situation to be serious enough to write you, Mr. President, with complete frankness, as is possible only among friends who trust each other completely." "Trust," snorted Kennedy to Pierre Salinger, his press spokesman, "I don't trust this man at all." But after hearing more pleas from Americans who had served in Berlin, he dispatched an infantry battalion and Vice President Johnson to West Berlin.

Two years later, Kennedy visited the city and, overwhelmed by a huge ovation, declared: *"Ich bin ein Berliner* [I am a Berliner]." Since then, Brandt has spoken warmly of Kennedy, and, in his latest book, "Peace Policy for Europe," published here in 1968, he wrote: "I stick by the strategy of peace conceived by John F. Kennedy."

By the time he came to Bonn in December, 1966, as Vice Chancellor and Foreign Minister in the grand-coalition Government with Chancellor Kiesinger, he had already suffered two bitter election defeats. The first, in 1961, was envenomed by Adenauer at the height of the wall crisis when he tried to smear the Social Democratic standard-bearer by recalling his illegitimate birth with the phrase "Herr Brandt—alias Frahm." The second, in 1965, was bitter because Brandt, by this time chairman of the party, had been led by the polls to believe he would win with his modern, Kennedy-style campaigning. A year later, he joined the coalition with Kiesinger's Christian Democrats with reluctance. But he swiftly took to the Foreign Ministry and became, in the words of Golo Mann, the son of Thomas Mann, "the best Foreign Minister Germany has ever had."

Together with Wehner, his sagacious deputy party leader, he drafted the coalition's "Eastern policy" of trying to normalize West Germany's soured—or nonexistent—relations with Communist Europe, as well as its "Germany policy" of seeking a "regulated juxtaposition" with East Germany. While they succeeded only in breaking with some conservative terminological taboos toward East Germany, their approach to the other Communist countries bore fruit in the form of diplomatic relations with Rumania and Yugoslavia, and the beginning of a thaw with Poland, Czechoslovakia and even the Soviet Union.

As Foreign Minister, Brandt lived up to his maxim of having "no illusions," saying, for example, on the subject of reunification: "Our current Germany policy starts from the assumption that the dissolution of the division of Germany is a process whose duration no one can predict." He added: "The world—whether we like it or not—does not have the feeling it owes us something." As for the rest of his concept of Germany policy, Brandt has become fond of quoting Bismarck, the enemy of the S.P.D., observing: "The word 'dogma' was alien to his policy."

A reading of any of Brandt's recent speeches and his book on peace policy repeatedly shows his respect and friendship for the United States and some of its leading citizens, like Hubert Humphrey. As he puts it: "Friendship for the United States is vitally important for us and remains so. It is that much more important if one is steering toward a Europe that plays its own role and serves peace with its own means. We found in it, and find in it, a reliable representative of our own vital interests. In West Berlin this is clearly visible for everyone today." Brandt says that his political idol is Abraham Lincoln. He likes to quote the 16th American President, and he keeps a bust of Lincoln in his office.

Though he was annoyed by Nixon's election-night phone call to Kiesinger, Brandt observes now: "To err is human, and the more so at that distance. I also recall that, on his last visit, Nixon said it sometimes takes three tries before you win." He takes a generous view of the fact that the United States Government has tended to regard his Social Democratic party as suspiciously pink for the last 20 years and has treated diplomatic contacts with leading party members accordingly. For example, only one member of the American Embassy staff in Bad Godesberg ever took the trouble in all that time to get close to Wehner, a former Communist. The diplomat died this autumn. Nor has any one of the Americans here bothered to read Brandt's books. "We know Willy," said one senior political officer, "and that's enough. I read a couple of passages of his peace book."

In his new post, Brandt is relying on a number of bright young colleagues. His chief trouble-shooter is Horst Ehmke, the 42-year-old former Justice Minister who is now Cabinet Minister without Portfolio. Ehmke is a bouncy Danziger whom Brandt calls "our Horst for everything." Working with Ehmke is Egon Bahr, 47, a shy idealist who has long served in Brandt's braintrust. But for long-range policy planning, Wehner, 63, who plotted the S.P.D.'s victory strategy 10 years ago, will be called over from his new post as the party's parliamentary whip for consultation. On Berlin matters, Brandt is already in close touch with his hard-working protégé, Klaus Schütz, 43. His Government spokesman, Conrad

Ahlers, 47, will also be in on some backroom talks, although he is only an S.P.D. sympathizer and not a party member.

According to present plans, Brandt intends to continue making his home in the Foreign Minister's residence at 12 Kiefernweg on Bonn's wooded Venusberg Hill, and use the "Chancellor Bungalow" next to Schaumburg Palace for conferences. His coalition partner, Walter Scheel, who also lives on the Venusberg, will presumably stay there.

There are three Brandt sons: Peter, 21, Lars, 18, and Matthias, 8. But Peter, who has become a Radical Socialist in the footsteps of the young Willy Brandt, is living in Berlin, where he is studying politics at the Free University.

He has caused his parents some concern by getting arrested for participation in student riots, and by giving interviews denouncing his father's political views. But Brandt takes this in his stride. With a smile, he told his party congress in 1968: "The self-glorification of the young is just as silly as the know-it-all attitude of the adults. A father should say that to himself daily—and I hope the sons say it to themselves, too."

At home, Brandt remains a night owl, sitting up late talking to other politicos or reading or writing. He enjoys a drink—Campari and soda in the daytime, whisky at night. He gets to his office sometime after 9 A.M. and, according to an associate in the foreign office, "isn't much use until 11 A.M. He improves from there on, and by afternoon he's in full swing." Sometimes in private—and in public, too—he seems to turn off his attention, and his gaze wanders into what one might imagine as Nordic mists. But if there is an urgent matter at hand, he remains almost electrically alert.

He is fully in command of himself and, one feels, at peace with himself and his job. Just before he was elected Chancellor, he said to some foreign correspondents with a confident grin: "We will be a loyal ally, but not a comfortable Government. I will not be the Chancellor of a conquered Germany, but of a liberated Germany."

Anatomy of Britain's Labor Party

by Sydney Gruson

LONDON

IT DOES NOT take eavesdropping to know what is being discussed in any cluster of half-a-dozen Labor politicians gathered anywhere in London these days. One will be arguing the latest opinion-poll figures and the Labor party's chances of winning Britain's general election, which has now been set for this fall by Prime Minister Sir Alec Douglas-Home. The other five, scarcely listening, will be Cabinet-building, deciding who will and who will not be likely to do a good job in the ministerial appointments expected if Labor wins—so convinced is Labor of returning to power.

The fortunes of the Labor party after nearly 13 years on the Opposition benches vary in month-to-month nose-counting by pollsters and in by-elections, but for the past two years Labor has had enough of a lead to scent victory. It is gaining ground again now, after a reduction of a few points in its lead during Sir Alec's introductory honeymoon of leadership. It is hard to pin down the reasons, but the renewed spurt seems to be due more to the flustered Conservatives' visible disarray than to Labor's positive appeal.

The intense campaign is under way and it will be an unusually long one, which some Englishmen resent as rather Americanized with its emphasis on television and its tendency to drag out arguments. It will culminate in a feverish short stretch of three to five weeks before polling. Stretching out the course puts a strain on all the politicians involved, particularly the challengers, the party outside the limelight of government seeking to push back in.

The Conservatives are known. They evolve and change leaders, but the experience of power is also a daily opportunity to demonstrate the kind of party and the kind of people they are. But who and what is the Labor party? What kind of government would it give Britain?

Labor is not quite what it used to be. That was the first strong impression on the Prime Minister when he came back to the House of Commons after 12 years in the Lords. In the lobbies of Parliament, it is no longer so obvious on which side a man will take his seat in the House. Clothes, demeanor, accent are not the clear dividers. "They don't look so burly any more," Home said in surprise after his first few weeks of staring at the Opposition from the Government's front bench.

Labor is a party with a strong sense of its origins and history; the strains and loyalties of a long uphill fight pull heavily. The appetites and the aspirations, the freedom from constraint and the stubbornness of life as a political underdog are fused in the alloy. The party leans on the trade unions, on constituency associations, on intellectual societies like the Fabians. But it is the parliamentary party, the men and women who sit in the House of Commons and accept a collective discipline, who give Labor its effective flavor.

The 260 Labor M.P.'s who, except for seven Liberals, fill the Opposition benches, run a wide scale of views and personalities. The new candidates chosen to contest the election assure that if Labor does win enough seats to move across the aisle to the majority side, the flavor will be the same.

Starting from the left, there is a small fringe group which more influential party members call among themselves "the Moscow boys." There is little hesitation at the core of the party in voicing the suspicion that a couple of those far out in left field may even be secretly card-carrying Communists. With others marked down by Labor officials as more or less fellow-travelers, there are about a dozen on the fringe.

Although domestic affairs are Labor's prime concern nowadays and the issue it wants to make central in the campaign, the test of party position remains foreign policy. The far left upholds orthodox radical economic and social theories, but it is more noticed for arguments which tend to be anti-American, anti-German, pro-Soviet. The dozen are lumped together but do not necessarily pull together nor speak for one another. They have no visible influence on the bulk of the party, no compelling personality who can draw waverers away from the moderates. They exist as gadflys who still have their energy but have lost their sting.

The real left of the party is weightier and sometimes less predictable, numbering about 80 if everyone up to dead center is included. The suave and polished Anthony Greenwood, as chairman of the party's national executive, is its most prominent though not its most conspicuous or best-heard member. The red-haired, sharp-tongued Barbara Castle, the unbudgeable, politically fiery and personally gentle, warmly loved Michael Foot, the waspish, brilliant, gleefully irrepressible Richard Crossman have the more resounding voices from the left, although Crossman is such a maverick that he is as likely to stick out his tongue at any label as to let one stick to him.

Frank Cousins, head of the powerful Transport and General Workers' Union, is one of the strongest Labor figures outside Parliament and might well be persuaded to join the Government if Labor wins. He would, of course, have to enter Parliament, but there are always safe seats that can be made available. Cousins is leftist, but with far less visible militancy than a few years ago. Labor's economic program would urgently need union support. There could be an unpredictable tug-of-war with Cousins in a Labor Cabinet, though his inclusion could also work to cut off the rest of the left from its union underpinnings.

A recent incident, which provided one profitable, delightful day for the Conservatives showed how far the left can push, and where it has to stop. Labor's leader, Harold Wilson, was off in Washington conferring with President Johnson. The House of Commons was debating the defense estimates. Suddenly Defense Minister Peter Thorneycroft poked an imperious finger across the despatch box and demanded that Labor answer immediately whether it would keep the U.S. Polaris submarine base at Holy Loch.

George Brown, Labor's Deputy Leader, only scrunched further

down his spine on the straight green leather bench. He gave no answer—and it made ominous headlines. Front-benchers said later that Labor knew the question was coming, and Greenwood had threatened to intervene with an attack on the base if Brown stood up and said yes, it would stay. A quarrel within the party on the floor of the House is as embarrassing and as much to be avoided as a family row in a restaurant.

But the next day, Brown said flatly in a televised speech that of course a Labor Government would keep the base, though it might like the idea of transferring it to NATO. Everybody knew there was no real question about Holy Loch: it is an essential element of Labor's policy to rely on America's strategic deterrent, for the strength of the center and the right is so overwhelming that the intimate nuclear alliance with America cannot be challenged. The left could force a brief equivocation, no more.

The dominance of the center-right is not a matter of personalities, nor even numbers. It is the fruit of the late Hugh Gaitskell's most important triumph over a bickering, faction-ridden, self-engrossed party that was on the verge of flying apart only three years ago. The personal scars, the suspicions, the sore spots easily inflamed in new clashes, are still there. But the issue has been resolved. Gaitskell's immediate victory was over the advocates of unilateral disarmament. His real achievement was to give the party the will to win, to persuade it to become an alternative Government.

It was only three years ago that Crossman argued in a Fabian pamphlet for a very different Labor role. He saw the party's proper purpose as being an almost permanent Opposition, keeping Socialist principles alive and pure without the compromising burdens of power until, in another generation perhaps, it might have educated the public to its views, instead of the other way around. Gaitskell killed this notion, though its ghost still flickers nostalgically at the edges of party gatherings. Gaitskell proclaimed that the people would turn away from any party not interested in power, and his view won.

Labor requires a good deal of support from voters who are basically opposed to Socialist doctrine, if it is to gain power. Its hard-core strongholds remain among industrial workers, although many of these rejected Labor in 1959. Its hopes for victory lie with the white-collar, professional, technical groups—the "meritocrats"—as opposed to the aristocrats. Labor is opposed by business, small as well as large, and it has never made more than small marginal inroads on the true-blue Tory agricultural community.

Basically, the British consider themselves conservative and Labor at best as the relief team. Its chance comes when voters want a change from what is still looked upon as the normal governing party. The natural bias against Labor is increased by the constituency map—Labor's votes are so bunched that it has to have two to three per cent more of the national total to have a number of Parliament seats equal to the Conservatives'. This showed dramatically in 1951 when Labor scored the highest total number of votes given any party in British history, but lost control of Parliament to a narrow Conservative majority.

The party's key figures have recognized that it is only the uncommitted voters who can give them power. And now they want power, none more perhaps than their coolly energetic leader Harold Wilson. Wilson was elected leader primarily by the left, but immediately chose to surround himself with the prominent figures of the right—the trade unions' George Brown, the intellectuals' Patrick Gordon Walker and Denis Healey. Wilson's own position must be placed somewhere near the center. He is above all a practical politician whose ideological litmus reaction would probably show neither pink nor blue, but executive gray.

James Callaghan, a genial, round-faced Irishman, represents perhaps the true center of the party. He is interested in new formulas for applying a tax on capital, but not wedded to ideas for their own sake if they are shown to be an economic or political liability.

The position of Labor's right is the hardest to define, just because it has the least regard for doctrine. Its highly visible figures are mostly university-trained intellectuals, but its bulk comes from the unions whose long traditions in politics, with certain glaring exceptions, have been to recoil from radicalism. A few Communists hold high office in some unions, but they remain without influence in party affairs.

Because the line between right and center is blurred and because this body of the party is no longer doctrinaire, Labor's whole position adds up to words which define an approach rather than a clear-cut program. The words are "modernization," "planning," "technology," "growth."

The party is committed to renationalize the steel and road-haulage industries, which the Conservatives turned back to private ownership, and to see whether new industries should be wholly, partly or not at all under the Government's wing. It is committed to reform education, to buy up urban land for public housing, to enlarge social-welfare services, to raise society's stragglers to a higher minimum. It is committed to economic expansion, with some undefined form of persuasion or control to prevent wages, profits and prices chasing each other up the inflationary ladder.

In foreign policy, Labor is committed to NATO and to Britain's retirement from the production or independent control of nuclear weapons. Wilson has never made it completely clear whether he would cancel the agreement to buy Polaris missiles from the U.S., but he is pledged to turn any atomic weapons Britain has over to NATO and abandon the existing right of withdrawal. Labor is also committed to the Commonwealth, to easing the cold war and to increasing Britain's prestige and influence in the world.

It is no accident that scarcely any of this is concrete enough to provide a framework for legislative or diplomatic decision. There are three reasons. One is that the leadership of a party in opposition does not have the power of a party in authority, so intramural squabbles are easier to avoid with vagueness than to settle. The second is that Wilson and his colleagues really do hope to govern, and do not want to pin themselves to policies which may seem neither wise nor feasible when the time comes. The third, and most important, is that the electorate is obviously more interested in the tone, the attitude, the image of the parties than in specific pledges which have become hard to distinguish and which the voters hardly trust any longer anyway.

At the grass-roots level, Labor campaigners are talking about housing, education, the cost of living, because they are convinced that these are the things which really interest the electors now. Wilson, who sets the tone of the appeal, is offering prosperity and the good life through the energetic use of modern science. The main attack against the Tories is that they are stale, stagnant, tired, without the cohesive vigor or vision to "get Britain rolling again on all wheels," as Wilson put it.

The Labor party never was really Marxist, though it has been acutely class-conscious. Now, its ideal is further than ever from conquest of society by the poorer classes. The idea is, rather, classlessness, of which Wilson is the epitome. When Labor politicians speak of reforming or abolishing the famous public schools, which are very private, this is not to wipe out the bastions of the privileged but to dilute them so the barriers lose meaning.

Therefore, though it clings to the name, it is not a Socialist party in the old sense—the idea of class struggle and single-minded advancement by a general campaign against the barricades of class. Public ownership of the means of production remains inscribed in the party's theoretical program, but in fact nationalization for its own sake has been dropped; the idea of a primarily state-owned economy has been replaced by the idea of a state-directed economy, with public planning to be enforced by a complex and assertedly flexible system of inducements, money management, some controls and the state's entry into production on a competitive rather than monopoly basis where circumstances seem appropriate.

The election campaign has served so far to haze rather than define the differences between programs of a new Labor or Conservative Government. Both use the same catch-all lure words—planning, modernization, world influence. But, though fuzzy, the lines of division do exist. The main ones are:

Planning: The Conservatives' planning would be primarily voluntary and advisory. Labor would give the planners much more Government authority.

Incomes: Both agree that expansion must be guided to prevent inflation. The Conservatives stress the need for restraint in the growing bill for wages.

Labor stresses the need to restrain profits and prices. Techniques have not been defined. But there is an emotional difference in Labor's revulsion against high speculative profits and its concept of excessive profits; the Conservatives are readier for managerial enterprise to seek maximum rewards.

Housing: Both agree a big spurt is needed in construction. The Conservatives want to encourage the lagging free market supply to meet demand. Labor would use controls and public projects to direct supply toward filling social needs, on the ground that the free market wastes limited resources on building to produce profits.

Foreign affairs and defense: The Conservatives say that Britain must keep an independent nuclear arm. Labor says that Britain must give it up, improving conventional strength and relying on America for atomic cover. Labor has more sympathy for the

United Nations than the Conservatives and is more eager to turn to it in crises. Labor is hostile to any British integration with Europe and stresses, in emotional rather than specific terms, the need for strengthening Commonwealth ties. The Conservatives, though divided, remain officially committed to joining the Common Market and see less practical scope for basing policy on the heterogeneous Commonwealth.

There is no easy parallel to describe Labor in American political terms. In content, its position is perhaps closest to that of Northern Democrats. The whole scale of British politics is further left than the American scale, however, and Labor's views are more radical than those of any major U.S. group.

Harold Wilson, as Prime Minister, will have a decisive role in what kind of Government Labor provides if it reaches power. In a year as leader, he has demonstrated an unsuspectedly firm ability to dominate his colleagues, ride above feuds and cliques, win the respectful support if not the affection of reluctant and distrustful co-partisans.

But not even his closest associates pretend to foresee what kind of Government head he would be, apart from being cold and competent. He is a calculator, unmoved by sentiment, unruffled by excitement, unconcerned with gesture. Statistics, dates, details stud his conversation. He is concerned more with being effective than with inspiring people, and he has a penchant for organization that would doubtless change the look of Downing Street.

There has been talk of his assembling a Prime Ministerial brain trust along the lines of President Kennedy's White House staff. But while some experts would be recruited, insiders do not make much of this idea. The British Cabinet system simply could not be made to run that way, they say, since no senior minister would tolerate that kind of outside involvement in his department and no Prime Minister could afford to infuriate several senior ministers at the same time.

Wilson is, said one of his main but uncowed supporters, "a professional politician, and for him 'professional' means the ability to distinguish which side of a question the majority is on. I'll know what kind of a leader he is when I see how he faces his first unpopular decision—conscription, or the multilateral force, or carrying the war to North Vietnam."

It was a deliberately harsh comment, reflecting doubt on the element of courage that could bolster the shrewdness of Wilson's leadership. And—though no one knows yet—it may be unfair, for political courage can sometimes work to most effect by hiding behind a facade of accommodation, as Labor's last Prime Minister, Clement Attlee, showed. In any case, Wilson's is far too strong a will and too tough a personality to be content with mere committee-chairmanship rule. No one doubts that he would run his Government. Whether he could infuse his uncertain nation with the sense of purpose he declares essential is an open question.

The election, as elections are meant to do, will fix the future posture of the Labor party as well as its position on the national landscape. An overwhelming victory, which is unlikely, would loosen the ties which hold its wings together and could set them flapping again in opposite directions. A workable but not huge majority would probably tighten them and strengthen Wilson's rule with the visible need to maintain unity.

His party's victory, Wilson has insisted, would improve Britain's relations with the U.S. and the rest of the world. On United Nations questions, and possibly defense policy, though that remains cloudy and difficult, this may turn out to be true. On other issues where there is friction now between London and Washington—Cuba, East-West trade, attitudes toward Peking and Moscow—relations may be more abrasive with a Labor Government although the party's spokesmen make an unfailing point of stressing their desire to get along well with their essential American allies.

A Labor defeat would not demolish the party as some have predicted: its foundations are too solid for that. But it would undoubtedly provoke such a deep and bitter fratricidal upheaval that Labor could willy-nilly become an almost permanent opposition.

Its greatest appeal to the voters now, and the leadership knows this, is not Labor's views or promises but the argument that it is time for a change. Its chances depend on Wilson's convincing the electorate that he can bring about the kind of change that is wanted —crisp, energetic but not too painful or extreme.

All's Right with the World of Harold Wilson

by Anthony Lewis

LONDON

IN OCTOBER, 1968, Harold Wilson flew down to Gibraltar to parley with Ian Smith, the Prime Minister of rebel Rhodesia, aboard the British warship Fearless. It was an unpromising journey.

Mr. Wilson's Rhodesian policy, on which he had staked much, was an embarrassing failure: sanctions had *not* crushed the white minority's rebellion in weeks, as Mr. Wilson had promised, or months or years. Informed people thought there was no realistic chance of Ian Smith's agreeing to anything with the British Labor Government, and they proved right.

And beyond Rhodesia it was a bad time for Harold Wilson. For a year, since devaluing the pound, he had been in a visibly depressed state—seeing few people outside his immediate entourage, reluctant to appear on television, suspecting party plots against his leadership, almost paranoiac about the press. The polls indicated that, in a general election, Labor would be reduced to a rump in the House of Commons.

But in Gibraltar, astonishingly, the Prime Minister bounced with good cheer. He invited the press aboard Fearless, called for drinks, introduced reporters to the captain, made little jokes and posed for tropical photos.

What was going on, a bewildered observer asked one of Mr. Wilson's political intimates. "Oh, its very simple," this person replied. "Harold's just worked it out that he's going to win the election."

Did he really see his way out of the political despond at that low point? Or was it just some psychological turn that enabled him to shake off the depression? We cannot know, and it does not make all that much difference. For in Harold Wilson, illusion and reality are intertwined. When he thinks things are going wrong, he retreats into a conspiratorial gloom—and his political grip weakens. When he feels good, whether objective events justify that feeling or not, he positively radiates self-confidence—and that is politically effective.

Right now his confidence has a basis. He has called a snap election for June 18, next Thursday, and Labor is the favorite to win. After years of bad showings in the opinion polls and local elections, Labor suddenly shot ahead in those indicators last month, to the general amazement of most pundits. The Wilsonian bravado —quite unbelievable in the autumn of 1968 and most of the time since—suddenly seemed justified. He called the election. In the weeks of campaigning since, the polls and the odds have fluctuated. But the Prime Minister still looks serene.

The brass of Harold Wilson in the end is his most appealing characteristic. For anyone who enjoys politics, there is something delightful in the way he bobs up after some awful defeat, like a heavy-bottomed rubber doll, still smiling, pretending nothing has happened. A labor-union man applied an old joke to him: "If Harold had been captain of the Titanic, he'd have convinced the passengers he'd just stopped to take on ice."

Naturally, not everyone loves the brazen quality. It drives some of his Conservative opponents wild, and there are many serious men in the Labor movement who despise Mr. Wilson for his bland abandonment of party doctrine and personal commitments when he finds them inconvenient. He is probably the most hated party leader this country has had for a long time.

Not that he is a mean person. He is kind in his personal relations, he is brave, and he has the liberal instincts of an ex-Oxford don of lower-middle-class origin, which he is. The complaint against him is that he will stop at nothing to win. The most acute British political analyst, David Watt of The Financial Times, wrote last year:

"He has no properly defined political principles to speak of, he is acutely suspicious, he is a poor judge of subordinates and he has a persistent if not incurable tendency to avert his gaze from unpleasant facts until they are thrust beneath his nose—at which point he usually overreacts."

In his nearly six years as Prime Minister there have been three particularly distasteful episodes. Or at least I found them so.

One was the Government's decision, in the winter of 1968, to deprive British citizens of Asian origin in East Africa of their right to enter Britain. When Kenya, Uganda and Tanzania were given their independence, the British Government offered the Asian residents a choice of local or British citizenship. Now, suddenly, those who had taken up British passports were told that they were barred from their country of nationality. Since Kenya and Uganda were gradually forcing out noncitizens, they found themselves men without a country.

The Labor Government's sordid betrayal of a promise was the worse because it was unnecessary. Mr. Wilson and his Home Secretary, James Callaghan, panicked when a dissident right-wing Conservative, Enoch Powell, began making scary speeches about floods of Kenya Asians entering Britain. Fearful of a racist backlash hurting Labor, they rushed the anti-Asian bill through Parliament in a few days, without time for decent consideration and to the shame of many members. If they had stood up to Mr. Powell, the scare would probably have subsided in a few weeks. The pell-mell legislation in fact aggravated racist feelings in Britain, as was indeed inevitable from its premise—that British citizens with brown skin are worse than others.

That episode was especially instructive because race had often been said to be the one subject on which Harold Wilson did have fixed liberal principles. Later, when a proposed visit to England by a white South African cricket team was a great issue, the Prime Minister exercised his moral outrage; to introduce race into sport as the South Africans did, he said, was beyond the pale. Some wondered how they should characterize the introduction of race into citizenship.

The second matter raising sharp moral doubts was a piece of gerrymandering—a practice familiar enough in political history, American or British, but this time especially crude. For the whole question of political boundaries was supposed to have been settled in a nonpartisan way, and the Labor Government just decided to ignore the rules when they might have hurt.

After World War II, the parties agreed to deal with the whole question of equality in voting districts in a nonpolitical way. The job of periodically redrawing the lines to keep districts more or less equal in population was turned over to impartial boundary commissions. Their recommendations were due to be carried out in 1969.

But when the time came, Home Secretary Callaghan refused to act. He, and the Prime Minister, offered as an excuse the fact that local governments might soon be reformed in Britain—but they did not even believe that themselves. Their real reason was that the unequal populations of the old districts gave Labor an advantage; reform would have given more seats to the Tory suburbs and probably lost Labor 20 places in the Commons. And the end, they reckoned, justified the means.

That piece of cold-blooded jobbery could be got away with because Britain has no written Constitution and no Supreme Court to make political leaders live up to standards of fairness. But Labor will pay a price. That agreed minimum of political decency has been violated, and some day there will be retribution.

Then there was the great D-notice dispute. D-notices are warnings given to the press that stories on certain subjects may violate security. They are issued, under an informal system of press-Government cooperation quite unimaginable in the United States, by a joint committee of editors and officials.

In February, 1967, The Daily Express carried a story saying that cables going out of Britain were being screened by the security authorities. The story, by The Express defense correspondent, Chapman Pincher, did not add up to much new or interesting and seemed just a passing piece of pop sensationalism—until Mr. Wilson intervened. In the House of Commons one day he denounced the story as a "clear breach of two D-notices."

So much heat developed over the Prime Minister's charge that he appointed a distinguished committee under a noted judge, Lord Radcliffe, to investigate. The Radcliffe Committee found the Wilson charge erroneous: the Pincher story had *not* violated any outstanding D-notices.

The House of Commons then debated the issue. Mr. Wilson, closing the debate, rejected his own committee's report and insisted that there had been a security violation. At 9:57 P.M., three minutes before the time for the debate ran out, he raised a new charge against the secretary of the D-notice committee, a retired colonel, Leslie Lohan. Colonel Lohan, he said, had been suspect because of overclose association with Chapman Pincher and had never had "full clearance" for security.

Americans watching that scene from the gallery found it chillingly reminiscent of Senator Joe McCarthy. The Sunday Times of London said Mr. Wilson had chosen "to compound his arrogance with character assassination" and had been "shabby, irresponsible and careless of truth." It added: "The smear was daubed as to the manner born: a partial reading from an unidentified dossier carrying imprecise accusations of security risk and timed to prevent further inquiry."

Mr. Wilson's relationship with the press is a curiosity altogether. He came into office in October, 1964, with a reputation as a great friend of the press. It was said that he had broken with the old British political tradition of regarding reporters as among the lower orders, and would share a drink or a story.

But as things went wrong for the Prime Minister, and the papers were more critical, he showed an extreme sensitivity. He complained that British Broadcasting Corporation interviewers were biased against him. He kept files on individual political reporters and called their editors in to accuse them of what amounted to conspiracies.

Combined with this unpleasantness, from the press point of view, was something a little subtler. Mr. Wilson, even when he was being friendly, made a point of letting reporters know that they were not to think of themselves as his equal, intellectually or politically. He lectured; he played cheap tricks with his trick memory for dates: "You will find the answer to that question in my speech of Nov. 14, 1955. . . ." Often he refused to take serious questions seriously; he gave answers that treated the questioners as children.

As a complete outsider, with no historical reason to be for or against Mr. Wilson or his party but a natural respect for a Prime Minister, I must confess to finding myself upset on more than one occasion by his tone of contempt for the audience. Another American correspondent, seeing him up close for the first time in 1967, wrote: "He was supercilious, arrogant; he toyed with the questions."

But the truth is that such personal press reactions in all likelihood matter not at all in politics. Nor are those three moral failures of the Wilson Government—on gerrymandering, the Kenya Asians and the D-notice affair—significant in terms of votes.There are some Labor party intellectuals deeply and permanently offended by the craven racist appeal of the Asian exclusion legislation; one said to me recently that as long as Harold Wilson was leader of the party, he would spoil his ballot by writing an anti-Wilson obscenity across it. But that must be the view of a tiny minority.

In politics, and statecraft, the real tests of the Wilson years have to be foreign policy and economics. They have been crucial years of transition for Britain, with the painful loss of empire, and Mr. Wilson applied his special mixture of fantasy and pragmatism.

In foreign policy, Wilson the illusionist kept alive for years the myth of Britain as a great power. He loved the idea of a world role, and would talk of his influence at the "top tables" of international discussion with an embarrassingly simple boastfulness: "They are listening to Britain now. We are right there at the top table" (1965).

He flew off to Washington or Moscow with notions of how to end the Vietnam war, annoying Lyndon Johnson and making no great mark on the Russians. (He might actually have got somewhere with Premier Kosygin of the U.S.S.R. on one occasion—the Kosygin visit to London in 1967—if President Johnson had not made a last-minute change in a plan for ending the bombing of North Vietnam and beginning talks.) He flew to Nigeria for an empty gesture at ending that civil war. He flew to Rhodesia. When short of political news, he suddenly promised a "Commonwealth initiative" against famine in India, of which almost nothing was ever heard again.

"We are in Europe," he said in 1966, "but our power and influence are not and must never be confined to Europe." That illusion of the world role died hard. It was killed by necessity after devaluation of the pound at the end of 1967. The new Chancellor of the Exchequer, Roy Jenkins, who had long argued that the attempt to remain a power in Asia and the Middle East was beyond Britain's resources, now prevailed. On Jan. 16, 1968, a pained Harold Wilson had to tell the House of Commons:

"Our security lies fundamentally in Europe. . . . [After 1971] we shall not be maintaining military bases outside Europe and the Mediterranean."

But the even more profound Wilsonian reversal of position came on the European question itself—British membership in the Common Market. Mr. Wilson was a long-time opponent of the idea. As late as March, 1966, during that election campaign, he ridiculed the Conservative pro-Market leadership as a "spaniel" rolling on its back to get in and said Britain should not enter unless given the right to go on buying Commonwealth food and raw materials without change—an impossible condition.

Then, in the autumn of 1966, he became a convert. He toured the Continent preaching the gospel of Europeanism. Unless Britain and the Market got together to resist American domination, he said, they would fall victims to a new "industrial helotry." He even persuaded himself that he could brush aside Charles de Gaulle's opposition to Britain joining the Six; but only now, after de Gaulle, are the negotiations about to begin.

From the moment of taking office, Mr. Wilson made the continuance of close relations with the United States his number one priority in foreign affairs. That would be the instinct of any Prime Minister. In his case the instinct was sharpened by the fact that American support—and money—were essential in the fight for the pound.

Vietnam was the difficulty. The left of the Labor party was deeply opposed to President Johnson's escalation of the war, and over the years that discontent spread right through the party. Mr. Wilson dealt with it, at first, by arguing that he could be a restraining influence on Mr. Johnson if he were not pushed to an open break. Since such influence was hard to detect, the argument gradually lost plausibility. For a period many informed Englishmen had a sense that their Prime Minister was fawning on the President, and accepting Vietnam horrors, for financial reasons. Robert Kennedy, on a visit to London in 1967, told British friends:

"Your politics are losing interest because you don't stand for anything. Agree or disagree with America's position in Vietnam, but do it because you believe it, not to save the pound."

Public discontent about Vietnam subsided in Britain, as in the United States, until President Nixon's decision to strike into Cambodia. Mr. Wilson dealt with his political problem then by expressing concern and saying he hoped the Cambodian adventure would not interfere with the Nixon troop-withdrawal program. This seemed to calm the left, perhaps partly because everyone realizes now that Britain has little or no influence over American policy. If strong British criticism could ever have moderated the U.S. course in Vietnam, the time is past. Accordingly, there are few votes to be won or lost here now on Vietnam.

Mr. Wilson's foreign-policy record is full of airs and inconsistencies, even absurdities. But still, it has come out about right in the essentials—or right as the conventional liberal wisdom sees it. Britain has dropped her pretensions to world power and is seeking her place in Europe. Harold Wilson was certainly slow to see the necessities, but so was his country. And some might think that his bumbling journey to reality enabled Britain to adjust to a diminished role relatively painlessly.

The economic record of the Wilson Government is even more dramatic in its inconsistencies. Within a few days of winning office by a handful of seats in 1964, the Cabinet decided firmly not to devalue. It was a decision out of pride and weakness, a wrong decision for which Britain paid dearly over the next three years in resources drained to pay the trading deficits and keep the pound at $2.80.

A severe crunch came in the summer of 1966. A seven-week seamen's strike hit at exports and hurt foreign confidence in sterling, already fragile. Mr. Wilson, frantic, denounced the strike leaders as Communists; eventually the strike was settled anyway.

In July, 1966, the Prime Minister made a remarkable speech in which he blamed the country's financial troubles on "the defeatist fringe . . . , the sell-Britain-short-brigade . . . , the moaning ninnies and wet editorials." Within a few days he announced drastic new deflationary measures and a six-month wage freeze to save the pound. The Cabinet had again, repeating its mistake, rejected professional economic advice to devalue.

As late as October, 1967, Mr. Wilson was privately giving assurance that the balance of payments was fundamentally sound and sterling safe. A month later the continuing decline of foreign confidence forced devaluation.

Mr. Wilson's public comments on that crushing defeat of his central policy were masterpieces of self-pity and evasion of responsibility. The night of devaluation he went on television and said it had been done to avoid the "irresponsible" course of borrowing more abroad instead, and to avoid "rigid limitations on the ability of our people and Government to solve our problems." Some time later, asked by a television panel whether he had made any mistakes, he said yes, he had to admit one: he had underestimated the determination of the speculators against the pound!

The credibility of the Prime Minister and his Government suffered blows in the devaluation from which it seemed unlikely ever to recover. A long, dark period followed in which respect for Mr. Wilson fell so low that he was portrayed in a stage satire—in London's West End, not some college theater—as a paranoiac bungler dressed in a baggy batman suit.

In the middle of 1969 there was a further blow. Mr. Wilson decided to stake his Government on a bold new program to curb that perennial British plague, the wildcat strike. He proposed legislation. The unions, which supply most of the Labor party's money and much of its manpower, said nay. Mr. Wilson insisted. But by June his parliamentary party and finally his Cabinet were against him, and there was talk of forcing him from the party leadership and 10 Downing Street. He surrendered.

Now it is just a year later, and the ignominy of that episode is dim and distant. The pound is strong, Harold Wilson is bubbling and Labor is the favorite in an election campaign. What happened?

First, it has to be said that Mr. Wilson took his defeat on the union-reform legislation with a chipper grace, without recrimination. He showed none of the bitterness that, for example, President

Nixon displayed over the Senate's rejection of his Supreme Court nominees. He even kept in his Cabinet the man who had publicly opposed the union bill and had been considered a challenger for his job, James Callaghan. He adjusted to political realities with the suppleness of Byron's Julia, who, whispering she would ne'er consent—consented. Party unity was restored.

More important, much more, the Prime Minister had a shrewd and determined colleague who at last made a success of Britain's finances: Roy Jenkins, the Chancellor of the Exchequer. He took the job after devaluation and promised only "two years' hard slog." As that time ran out, many still doubted that the prescription would work. But then, staggeringly, spectacularly, the balance of payments went into the black. The fight that successive political leaders had made Britain's test of manhood had apparently been won.

Just how the economic miracle has occurred is not certain, but then it never is. What is clear is that British exports were given a powerful boost by devaluation, as intended. At the same time Mr. Jenkins held down imports by tough suppression of domestic demand—high interest rates, tight controls on Government spending, sharply increased taxes. In short, orthodox measures.

There may still be doubts about the British performance in the long run. Wage rates are going up; they are in all countries, but productivity still tends to rise less briskly in Britain than in Germany or the United States or Japan. That is a long-run concern, but for now the balance of payments certainly can be claimed as a triumph for Mr. Jenkins and Labor.

Mr. Jenkins became a symbol of nonpolitical rectitude. This spring he produced a budget that, despite the favorable payments picture, gave few tax concessions. The Conservatives thought he had hurt Labor's chances, only to discover that the public (according to polls) enjoyed being treated in an adult way.

With the pound, other aspects of government have begun to look right. The crucial change has been a growing sense of public confidence in the ability of Labor to govern. Others aside from Mr. Jenkins have a reputation for competence, among them Denis Healey, the defense minister, and Anthony Crosland, the first environmental overlord. Mr. Wilson's fundamental objective all along has been to make Labor seem the natural governing party. He is certainly on the way to achieving that—hard as it would have been to imagine a year ago.

One word that does not appear in this impressionistic survey of Harold Wilson's record and aims—and does not much appear on his lips either—is socialism. Mr. Wilson does still talk about social justice; his Government has somewhat enlarged the share of Britain's resources going to public needs, though not enough to please those who fight poverty. But in general, these days, the Wilson posture is that of a defender of the *status quo*. He is appealing to satisfied voters. It is the Conservatives who want sharp changes—in the tax system, unions, farm-price supports, defense, business management.

Mr. Wilson has been lucky in his opponents. That must be true of most successful politicians. But it surely takes exceptional incompetence for an opposition to let a government recover from mistakes of Mr. Wilson's order.

Edward Heath, the leader of the Opposition, was chosen by the Conservatives in the hope that he would be able to match Harold Wilson as a cutthroat politician. He was a grammar-school boy, the son of a carpenter, self-made, a long way from the Tory tradition of inherited ease. Alas, Mr. Heath has turned out simply uneasy. He has neither the rough edge of Harold Wilson's tongue nor the deep natural confidence of an old-fashioned Tory.

Mr. Heath is mincemeat for the Prime Minister in the House of Commons. Again and again he is unable to resist getting up and trying to down Mr. Wilson with some question, only to find himself awash in mockery. The other week the Prime Minister took so long over some answer to Mr. Heath that Conservative backbenchers carped. Mr. Wilson, hardly breaking his stride, remarked: "I've at last got him up. I must be allowed to enjoy it."

Perhaps it is lack of confidence that has let Mr. Heath allow himself to be pushed steadily to the right in his own party, as many believe he has. On such issues as attitudes toward Rhodesia and South Africa, and now in emphasizing the need for more "law and order" in this still remarkably law-abiding country, he presents an increasingly right-wing image.

A radical-minded former Conservative M.P., Humphry Berkeley, has said that the rightward trend in the party may make him vote Labor: "The Conservative party appears to me to be going out of its way to affront intellectual and enlightened opinion. . . ."

Mr. Berkeley and others who would call themselves civil libertarians are concerned especially about race relations in Britain, where there is now a significant minority of West Indian, Indian and Pakistani immigrants. They care also about some of the social-reform measures that a Labor majority in the Commons has made possible, though the bills were not officially sponsored by the Government: the end of capital punishment and theater censorship, easier abortion and divorce.

Those bothered by some of Mr. Wilson's callous changes of view will not draw much comfort from the Heath line. He and most of his party voted for the legislation abandoning a promise made to the Kenya Asians by a Conservative Government. He was lukewarm, at best, on urgently-needed legislation against racial discrimination—a wise attempt to avoid America's follies in this area. Mr. Wilson may have come late to the dropping of world power fantasies; Mr. Heath wants to send British troops back to bases east of Suez.

In economic matters, Mr. Heath has been treated a little unjustly by fate. In the 1966 election campaign he spoke the truth about Britain's desperate situation but made few friends by doing so. Now he is rightly pointing to the dangers of runaway wage inflation—union settlements are zooming out of sight in Britain as in the United States—but bigger pay packets in the pocket are likely to bring Labor voters out. He may be right also in saying that Britain could meet housing and other social needs better by being more selective with public funds, but this arouses old emotions about means tests.

There is a further irony here. Mr. Heath, as a Tory leader in the efficient new managerial image, has produced a whole set of Conservative policies to deal with such matters as strikes. They need dealing with. But an opposition may make a mistake in producing a firm program that can be a target, instead of just denouncing the Government's failures. Mr. Wilson has taken the Heath plan for strikes and labor reform and built from this and other straws an image of a cold party, a heartless group of men who would let the social gains of recent years slip away.

The Conservatives want a more competitive society. Britain undoubtedly could be more productive, more economically efficient. But looking these days at the most productive country on earth, the United States, Britons may feel that their own society—less efficient but more comfortable, more relaxed—may have a lot to say for it. And Harold Wilson, who once advertised himself as the knife edge of the new technology, is now above all the comfortable man.

And here Mr. Heath has a personal image problem. He is a shy man, essentially insecure, and this often translates into seeming brusqueness. He can be charming and sensitive, especially when involved in the loves of his life—music and sailboats—but he can also seem cold, even sneering. And the fact that he has never married has undoubtedly hurt him deeply with the public.

One more difficulty, perhaps again an unfair one: Edward Heath hates Harold Wilson. Long ago he made clear that he considered the Prime Minister a bounder; he has used such words as "maniac." The British political tradition is not congenial to such stark views; and besides, hate is not a way to good judgment in any aspect of life.

Such drastic emotions do not enter into politics for Harold Wilson. It is all fun and games. A few weeks ago, when he was answering questions in the House, he seized on some question to begin quoting at length a recent television appearance of his. When a Tory angrily asked, "Have you got the text of it there, then?", Mr. Wilson snapped cheerfully back: "Yes—I knew someone would be daft enough to ask."

In this easy-going posture he is now, effectively, the conservative candidate in an election that for Britain is unusually focused on the two major party leaders. It is Mr. Heath who wants to change things, Mr. Wilson who says the country is doing fine. That all of this has very little to do with socialism or Labor party principle does not bother him; nor does the fact that he is really running on Roy Jenkins's success at financial orthodoxy.

The campaign has been marked by large amounts of apathy. With Mr. Heath railing at high prices but not saying what he would do about them, and Mr. Wilson puffing his pipe into the cameras, public indifference is not too surprising. Labor strategists figure that should help them, in light of Mr. Wilson's personal hold on the voters: if unaroused by issues, they should vote for him. The risk is of "Dewey complacency."

Mr. Wilson knows that, if it were not for him, Labor would not even be in the picture. He had the nerve to hold the party together for 18 months, govern with a majority of three in the House and then win big in 1966. One of his colleagues, definitely not a personal friend or admirer, said in his darkest days: "Don't underestimate the real steel that lies under the surface—the guts, the stamina, the character of Harold Wilson—even though he might not strike you so well."

When one thinks of that, some of the embarrassing turns in policy seem less horrifying than they did at the time. And for the lover of politics, sheer amazement at Harold Wilson's survival may give sneaking pleasure. He is a bit like camp décor—so funny, so transparent that one succumbs in spite of oneself.

In a particularly candid moment in the Commons this spring, Mr. Wilson said: "However tired people may be of me, I think most people will regard me as the lesser of two evils." He may very well be right.

Suggested Reading

Carl F. Brand, *The British Labour Party: A Short History,* Stanford, Stanford University Press, 1964.

G. D. H. Cole, *History of Socialist Thought,* Vol. 4: *Communism and Social Democracy, 1914–1931,* 2 vols., New York, St. Martin's, 1958, and Vol. 5: *Socialism and Fascism, 1931–1939,* New York, St. Martin's, 1960.

Michael R. Gordon, *Conflict and Consensus in Labour's Foreign Policy, 1914–1965,* Stanford, Stanford University Press, 1969.

Nathanael Greene, *Crisis and Decline: The French Socialist Party in the Popular Front Era,* Ithaca, Cornell University Press, 1969.

Richard N. Hunt, *German Social Democracy, 1918–1933,* New Haven, Yale University Press, 1964 (Quadrangle paperback).

Gabriel Jackson, *The Spanish Republic and the Civil War, 1931–1939,* Princeton, Princeton University Press, 1965 (Princeton paperback).

James Joll, *The Second International, 1889–1914,* New York, Harper & Row, 1966 (Harper paperback).

George Lichtheim, *Marxism: An Historical and Critical Study,* New York, Praeger, 1961 (Praeger paperback).

George Lichtheim, *Marxism in Modern France,* New York, Columbia University Press, 1966 (Columbia paperback).

Joseph La Palombara, *The Italian Labor Movement,* Ithaca, Cornell University Press, 1957.

Stanley G. Payne, *The Spanish Revolution,* New York, Norton, 1969 (Norton paperback).

Henry Pelling, *A Short History of the Labour Party,* New York, St. Martin's, 1968 (St. Martin's paperback).

Carl E. Schorske, *German Social Democracy, 1905–1917,* Cambridge, Mass., Harvard University Press, 1955 (Wiley paperback).

Harvey G. Simmons, *French Socialists in Search of a Role, 1956–1967,* Ithaca, Cornell University Press, 1970.

Adolf Sturmthal, *The Tragedy of European Labor, 1918–1939,* London, Gollancz, 1944.

Robert Wohl, *French Communism in the Making, 1914–1924,* Stanford, Stanford University Press, 1966.

Index

A Note on the Editor

Nathanael Greene is Associate Professor of History at Wesleyan University. Born in Providence, Rhode Island, he studied at Brown University and at Harvard and was a Fulbright Fellow in France. Mr. Greene is the author of *Crisis and Decline: The French Socialist Party in the Popular Front Era* and *From Versailles to Vichy: The Third French Republic, 1919–1940.*

NEW YORK TIMES BOOKS published by QUADRANGLE BOOKS